CM

The Marshall Plan

EUROPE IN TRANSITION: THE NYU EUROPEAN STUDIES SERIES

The Marshall Plan: Fifty Years After
Edited by Martin Schain

The Marshall Plan:
Fifty Years After

Edited by

Martin Schain

palgrave

THE MARSHALL PLAN
© Martin Schain, 2001

First published 2001 by
PALGRAVE
175 Fifth Avenue, New York, N.Y. 10010 and
Houndmills, Basingstoke, Hampshire RG21 6XS.
Companies and representatives throughout the world

PALGRAVE is the new global publishing imprint of St. Martin's Press LLC Scholarly and Reference Division and Palgrave Publishers Ltd (formerly Macmillan Press Ltd).

ISBN 0-312-22962-3 hardback

Library of Congress Cataloging-in-Publication Data

The Marshall plan fifty years after/edited by Martin A. Schain.
    p. cm.—(Europe in transition, the NYU European studies series)
    Includes bibliographical references.
    ISBN 0-312-22962-3.
    1. Marshall Plan. 2. Reconstruction (1939–1951). 3. Europe—Foreign economic relations—United States. 4. United States—Foreign economic relations—Europe. I. Schain, Martin, 1940-II. Series.

HC240.M27317 2001
338.91'7304'09044–dc21

                                           00-045808

A catalogue record for this book is available from the British Library.

Design by Newgen Imaging Systems (P) Ltd, Chennai, India.

First edition: August, 2001
10 9 8 7 6 5 4 3 2 1

Printed in the United States of America.

Contents

Acknowledgments

I would like to thank the staff and students of the Center for European Studies at New York University for the long hours and hard work that they have devoted to this project. In particular, Patrick Lehman, Monique Hofkin and Carolyn Bella Kim, graduate assistants at CES/NYU, have helped to organize and edit this volume. I would also like to thank Michael Flamini and Toby Wahl at Palgrave for their support in launching the *Europe in Transition* series. Finally, I owe a debt of thanks to the reviewers of the Board of Advisors of this series for their comments and reviews of the manuscript.

Martin A. Schain

Preface

Fifty years after the establishment of the Marshall Plan, this collection of articles demonstrates that there is still a great deal of discussion about its value and impact. This volume brings together an impressive group of historians, economists and political scientists from the United States and Europe. As Tony Judt notes in the introduction, the key question that is addressed by these scholars is not the success or failure of the Marshall Plan, but its relevance for post-war European recovery, and its impact on the shape of post-war Europe. Impact is not easy to evaluate, particularly political impact. Nevertheless, from the perspective of fifty years, the debate about impact has grown more, not less complicated. This complicated debate is the focus of this volume, together with the links between the European Recovery Program and the process through which Europe of the 1990s was constructed.

One theme that appears in many of these chapters is the use made of Marshall Plan support by key political leaders in Western Europe to pursue their own political agendas. Beyond any direct impact on economic recovery, the Marshall Plan became an effective political tool in the initiation of European integration and the development of the European welfare state.

The Marshall Plan: Fifty Years After is the first volume of a new series sponsored by the Center for Europe Studies of New York University, published by Palgrave: Europe in Transition. In this series we will explore the core questions facing the new Europe. A decade ago, the collapse of the Soviet empire promised a new era of stability and prosperity in Europe. While part of this promise has been fulfilled, the new era has also been defined by unanticipated conflict and war linked to older conflicts that had been held in abeyance during the long Cold War that began with the implementation of the Marshall Plan. We are now beginning to understand that the involvement of the United States in the economic recovery of Western Europe has also meant its involvement in the politics of Europe, and that this process continues even after the end of the Cold War.

These articles on the Marshall Plan provide us with a prism through which we can understand relations between the United States and Europe after 1947. American involvement in Europe meant intensified economic interaction, but also American influence on the definition of divisions between right and left (as well as divisions within each camp), and anti-American reactions among political elites and voters in Western Europe. These articles demonstrate that the involvement of the United States in Western Europe was deep and pervasive during the period of the Marshall Plan, but also they also demonstrate the sometimes unanticipated ways for which this aid was used.

Thus, this examination of the Marshall Plan from the perspective of the post–Cold War period provides us with useful tools for understanding our own time, and serves as an important first volume for our series on Europe in transition. Many of the issues that are analyzed in this volume will be further elaborated in future books in this series. However, this integrated collection of articles stands on its own both as historical re-examination, and analysis of economic and political development.

Martin A. Schain

Contributors

ABRAMS, BRAD is Assistant Professor of History at Columbia University. He has written widely on early postwar Czechoslovakia, and is completing a manuscript entitled " 'The Struggle for the Soul of the Nation': Czech Culture and Socialism 1945–1948."

CAYROL, ROLAND is a Research Director at the French National Foundation for Political Sciences (Center for the Study of French Political Life). He also acts as the director of the opinion polling company CSA. He is a professor at the Institute of Political Studies in Paris. His most recent books include "Sondages, mode d'emploi" (2000), "Médias et démocratie, la dérive" (1997), both published by Presses de la Fondation Nationale des Sciences Politiques, and "Le grand malentendu, les Français et la politique" (1994), Editions du Seuil.

CINI, MICHELLE is a Jean Monnet Senior Lecturer in European Community Studies in the Department of Politics, University of Bristol, U.K.

CRONIN, JAMES is professor of history at Boston College and an affiliate of the Center for European Studies at Harvard University. He is the author, most recently, of *The World the Cold War Made* (1996).

EICHENGREEN, BARRY is George C. Pardee and Helen N. Pardee Professor of Economics and Political Science at the University of California, Berkeley, Research Associate of the National Bureau of Research, and Research Fellow of the Centre for Economic Policy Research.

GARDNER, ROY is Chancellor's Professor of Economics and West European Studies at Indiana University, as well as Senior Research Fellow at the Center for European Integration Studies, Bonn, Germany. His research applies the theory of games and economic behavior to issues in business, economics, and politics. He is the author of 50 articles and 2 books, most recently *Games for Business and Economics* (Wiley, 1995).

HOWORTH, JOLYON is Jean Monnet Professor of European Politics at the University of Bath. He has been a Visiting Fellow at Harvard University, the *Institut Français des Relations Internationales*, the Western European Union's *Institute for Security Studies*, the *Institut d'Etudes Politiques* (Paris) and the Universities of Wisconsin and Washington. Recent books include: *The European Union and National Defence Policy*, London, Routledge 1997 (edited with Anand Menon) and *European Integration and Defence: the Ultimate Challenge*, Paris, WEU-ISS, 2000 (*Chaillot* Paper No. 43)

JUDT, TONY is Erich Maria Remarque Professor of European Studies at New York University and Director of the Remarque Institute. Among his books are *A Grand Illusion: An Essay on Europe*, and *Past Imperfect: French Intellectuals 1944–1956*. He is currently at work on a History of Europe since World War Two.

LATHAM, ROBERT serves as Director of the SSRC Program on Information Technology, International Cooperation, and Global Security. He currently teaches at Columbia University, School of International and Public Affairs, courses on human rights and foreign policy. His recent book, *The Liberal Moment: Modernity, Security, and the Making of Postwar International Order*, was published by Columbia University Press. He has just co-edited a volume, *Intervention and Transnationalism in Africa: Global/Local Networks of Power*, (forthcoming, Cambridge University Press) and has written numerous articles on topics such as international security, liberalism, human rights, and sovereignty for journals and edited volumes.

MCGLADE, JACQUELINE is an Assistant Professor of History and Chair of the Department of Interdisciplinary Studies at Monmouth University in West Long Branch, New Jersey. She is the author of several articles and essays on the impact of U.S. aid on the postwar development of European business.

PATRICK, STEWART is a Research Associate at the Center on International Cooperation at New York University, where he coordinates the program on Multilateralism and US Foreign Policy. Dr. Patrick is co-editor of the book *Good Intentions: Pledges of Aid for Post-Conflict Recovery.*

SHAPIRO, ROBERT is a professor in the Department of Political Science at Columbia University. He specialized in the study of public opinion, policymaking, and American politics. He is the coauthor of *The Rational Public* (with Benjamin Page, University of Chicago Press,

1992) and, most recently, *Politicians Don't Pander* (with Lawrence Jacobs, University of Chicago, 1992).

WALL, IRWIN is a Professor of History at the University of California, Riverside, and Visiting Scholar at New York University, 2000–2001. His received his Ph.D. from Columbia University, and he is the author of *The United States and the Making of Postwar France, 1945–1954* (Cambridge University Press, 1991) and *France, The United States, and the Algerian War, 1954–1962* (University of California Press, 2001).

WEXLER, IMANUEL is Emeritus Professor of Economics, University of Connecticut. He received a B.A. in Economics (L.S.U.); and M.A. and Ph.D. (Harvard). He is the author of *Fundmental of International Economics* (1968, 1972); *The Marshall Plan Revisited* (1983); and many articles, most recently "Marshall Plan," in *Encyclopedia of U.S. Foreign Relations* (1997).

ZACHARIOU, STELIOS is a research consultant at the Historical Archives of the Greek Ministry of Foreign Affairs. He has written extensively on Greek–U.S. relations during the Cold War. Most recently, he has served as the head of a team that is responsible for the declassification process of the NATO archives.

Introduction

Tony Judt

For an undertaking whose image in the popular mind is that of an unmitigated success, the Marshall Plan has been curiously controversial. At the time of its inception, Republican critics in the United States charged that the plan represented an uncontrolled subsidy for the socializing planners of postwar Europe. For its opponents in Europe itself, the Plan represented U.S. imperialism in its most naked, material incarnation. Even those critics not predisposed to accept the communist interpretation of Marshall's motives were hesitant to welcome the European Recovery Program (ERP) for fear of the strings that might be attached.

Among scholars in more recent years, the Marshall Plan has been charged not so much with malevolence or self-interest as irrelevance. Europe would have recovered in any event, they claim; at best the injection of Marshall credits and cash smoothed over a temporary dollar shortfall. More ambitious claims that were once made on behalf of the Marshall planners—notably that they engineered the subsequent cooperation of the West European economies and thus bear some credit for the making of the European Union—have been dismissed as hyperbole. The Marshall Plan, in this view, represented not much more than a moment (albeit important) in the story of Western Europe's postwar reconstruction; a story whose origins and complexities far transcend the occasion of Marshall aid in the late 1940s.

At a distance of half a century from the decision of the Truman administration to offer substantial aid to postwar Europe, many of these criticisms and controversies seem somehow muted, even moot. After all, Western Europe *did* recover, and no one questions that Marshall aid played a role in that process. The Soviet critique of the Marshall Plan is now regarded not only as mistaken, but also the source of a significant strategic error on Stalin's part: since Marshall aid was offered to any European country interested in taking it up (the USSR included), Stalin's refusal, and his insistence that all the "friendly" countries of Central and Eastern Europe refuse in their turn, deprived Europe's eastern half of crucial external assistance at an important moment. Whether or not Stalin's rejection was inevitable given his suspicions of the West and his tactics in Eastern Europe, it remains an error.

In the meantime we can now see more clearly the unambiguous originality of the Marshall proposals. What was being suggested, after all? That the United States should make available to any interested European partner sums of money that would eventually total $12.6 billion in order to assist in their economic recovery. This was more than all previous U.S. overseas aid combined, and it is not surprising that isolationists and other critics in Congress were genuinely taken aback. In today's (1999) dollars the Marshall Plan would cost at least $100 billion, and as a comparable proportion of U.S. gross domestic product (GDP) rather more. Whatever its motives and however unclear its precise achievements, the European Recovery Plan proposed by Secretary of State Marshall in June 1947 was a major foreign policy departure for the U.S., and a genuine surprise to most Europeans.

Nonetheless the Marshall Plan did not come out of nowhere. It has a number of distinct contexts, which help explain both its origin and its objectives. By 1945 the collapse of Europe—first into depression, then war—had led many commentators to the conclusion that something quite new and different would be required if Europe (and therefore the world) were to break out of the cycle of economic stagnation and political frustration that had characterized the continent for the previous two decades. If another unsuccessful postwar era was to be avoided, and political extremists of all kind prevented from coming to power once again, democratic governments would need to take a quite different and more activist view of their capacities and responsibilities.

The experience of war contributed its own lessons. As in World War I, wartime governments had taken responsibility for economic mobilization, planning, controls, and the national direction of people and resources in ways that would hitherto have been unthinkable in time of peace. As a result, by 1945 there were many in Europe, by no means only on the Left, who took the view that the advantages of wartime planning and government intervention could translate into sustained peacetime administration. In Britain and France, as in Germany and the Benelux countries (though to a rather lesser extent in Italy) a new political and administrative elite was thus much more receptive to the sort of planning and cooperation that would be required of them by the Marshall Plan than would have been the case for their predecessors in an earlier generation.

But even if the old orthodoxies had not taken such a beating at the hands of history, the postwar circumstances would in any case have paved the way for significant American involvement in European affairs. Like it or not, the West Europeans after 1945 needed the United States. Indeed, between the end of the War and the inception of the Marshall Plan, U.S. aid to Europe in various forms already totalled $9 billion. Some of this took the form of direct assistance in refugee and resettlement programs; some of it represented a de facto continuation of wartime Lend-Lease plans, renegotiated in 1946. But none of this aid was dispatched as part of any broader strategic design. From the end of the war through 1947 the United States was simultaneously withdrawing itself from Europe on the military front while helping shore up the still uncertain and fragile political arrangements put in place following the Liberation.

The peculiarity of the Marshall Plan was rooted in the distinctive circumstances of its emergence. 1947 was a year of crisis throughout Europe. The steady onward march of Communism appeared to many to be inexorable. In Eastern Europe, Communist parties had begun to absorb or destroy their non-Communist opponents, while in Western Europe Communists in government (in Italy, France, and Belgium) seemed well-placed to influence if not actively undermine the unstable coalitions of which they were a powerful member. The influence of the Communists in Western Europe was underscored by their ability to take advantage, even while in office, of popular frustration and discontent at the slow pace of postwar economic recovery.

Despite American assistance, the economies of Europe in 1947 seemed hardly to have moved on from their disastrous condition at the termination of hostilities. Production had nowhere recovered even to the Depression-era levels of 1938. Rationing of daily necessities was universal, the black market ubiquitous. Attempts at the imposition of austerity by democratic governments in Western Europe faced hostility from communist-backed trade unions, while long term domestic planning (not to mention international economic cooperation) was stymied by the continuing failure of the great powers to resolve the problems of Germany. In the absence of German recovery, the other countries of Western Europe were doomed to stagnation—either because they depended on Germany as a trading partner or else because they required German coal or steel for their own industries.

This combination of political uncertainty and economic stagnation boded ill for Europe; a situation made worse in 1947 by an unusually severe winter that placed great strain on coal supplies and the still-damaged transportation networks while threatening the harvest later in the year. To many at the time it seemed as though the sputtering post-war recovery of Europe had come to a halt and that democracy and stability in Western Europe were once again under siege. It was to these immediate circumstances, as well as the history of the previous fifteen years, that Marshall was referring when, in his commencement speech at Harvard on June 5, 1947, he spoke of the need to "break the vicious circle."

The essays in this collection discuss in various ways Marshall's success in breaking that circle and the consequences of that success. In the short term the achievement of the Marshall Plan is clear. The guarantees of aid from America, and American encouragement for the establishment of domestic and international agencies capable of putting that aid to good use, transformed first the expectations and then the institutions of Western Europe. Production increased, the financial stability of America's West European partners improved, and before the end of the Plan all the major West European recipients of Marshall aid had exceeded their 1938 output levels and were already embarked upon the first stages of what we have come to see as the post–World War II era of sustained prosperity. The long descent of the European economies into self-defeating policies of deflation and autarky was reversed, and a pattern of intra-European trade, cooperation, and initiative was set in place.

It is a little harder to be quite so confident about the long-term effects of the Marshall Plan, at least upon the economy. Without any question the Plan brought the United States back into Europe in a quite unanticipated manner, and there it has remained ever since. How far this close interweaving of European and American concerns can be attributed to the Marshall Plan alone is a matter for legitimate debate. After all, Marshall aid had by 1951 begun to metamorphose into military aid of various kinds under the auspices of NATO and in the nervous atmosphere of the Korean War. But at the very least one can say that the European Recovery Program was a fundamental building block in the forging of this transatlantic relationship.

Similarly, the process whereby the continental states of Western Europe came together first to form a Coal and Steel Community (in 1951) and then, after 1955, to forge the European Economic Community and its successor institutions in Brussels is not directly attributable to anything undertaken or intended by planners in Washington. The origins of the European Coal and Steel Community lie as much in the domestic needs of France and the unusual circumstances of Germany as they do in American strategy. Nonetheless it remains true that the Americans were enthusiastic early proponents of European cooperation, and the Organization for European Economic Cooperation (OEEC) was manifestly influential in forging habits of cross border discussion and information exchange that would have been altogether unthinkable before 1939.

Finally, the Marshall Plan helped divide Europe. This, of course, was far from being its intention (though there are grounds for believing that in offering Marshall aid to the Eastern half of Europe as well the Americans at least half-anticipated and perhaps hoped that it would be rejected). But because the Eastern half of Europe was constrained to reject the Marshall Plan, the tremendous injection of confidence and dollars that it represented was confined to Europe's Western half, which thereby took a great leap ahead of the rest of the continent. It is not altogether coincidental that the Marshall Plan was finally approved in Congress just weeks after the Communist coup in Czechoslovakia and in anticipation of vital and bitterly fought Italian elections the following month. The Plan itself did not contribute by its design to the definitive drawing of Cold War lines in Europe, but its timing and implementation served to accentuate the significance of these divisions at a crucial moment.

Was the Marshall Plan necessary? This question may appear redundant. If it had all the qualities and characteristics I have just noted, and was so vital an intervention at so crucial a moment, than how could it in any sense have been "unnecessary"? And yet there is a case for this view. The West Europeans themselves, after all, were not wholly passive. From Ernest Bevin's 1945 vision of West European cooperation built around an Anglo-French alliance through the Brussels Treaty of 1948, the Monnet Plan for French reconstruction and the related strategy of European cooperation in the production of coal and steel, postwar European statesmen and planners had their own new ideas about how to break clear of the vicious historical cycle. The American Marshall planners may have had strongly held opinions about how European trade and productivity should be expanded and sustained, but they were not preaching in a wilderness.

Moreover, the Cold War in Europe at least did not begin in 1947 or 1948, and thus the Marshall Plan cannot really be credited with having drawn the line that defined it. Ever since Lenin's revolution of 1917

European political and cultural life had been increasingly polarized between defenders and opponents of Bolshevism. Indeed within the socialist and trade union movements of Europe, from Scotland to Czechoslovakia, a "cold war" can be said to have been going strong from 1919 at least, as some contributors to this collection rightly note. What was a novel and disturbing situation for Americans was more familiar to Europeans—though the apparently more immediate threat of a communist takeover in West Europe itself in 1947 was of course quite new.

The strongest argument against the need for a Marshall Plan has been made by Professor Alan Milward, and his thesis is referred to on many occasions in the essays that follow. It is, to put it briefly, that the European economic crisis of the spring and summer of 1947 was a crisis of expansion and growth. It was precisely because the European economies had begun to recover and were now sucking in goods and materials from the United States in order to fuel that recovery, that they were so dependant on dollars (with which to buy these goods) and thus saw the shortage of dollars facing them in 1947 as a major impediment to a sustained economic recovery. In its own terms this line of reasoning seems hard to refute; the relative ease and speed with which the West European economies began to pick up again in the years of the Marshall Plan suggest that the underlying postwar recovery was already underway by 1947. In purely technical terms, then, the Marshall Plan was not redundant but it was not the most vital single element in Europe's post-war reconstruction.

But what does this mean? At most that in strictly limited economic terms, the Marshall Plan was only one in a number of factors which would come together to produce the 'miracle' of West European prosperity in the coming decades. But the Marshall Plan was never just about economics and any attempt to reduce it thus misses its most important characteristic. The Marshall Plan was important not so much for its substance as for its timing (as its designers understood). The problem in Western Europe was that many planners and at least some politicians knew perfectly well that they could sustain economic recovery and growth quite successfully if they were allowed to restrain consumption and impose measures of austerity for an extended period. But to defer consumption, restrain demand, and force people and resources into the primary productive sectors would have required the sort of powers and control that democratic governments were reluctant to appropriate—and that might well have provoked popular uprising. In short, the political costs of implementing the required economic programs without overseas aid would have been dangerously high. The Marshall Plan made stabilization possible without requiring the sorts of economic policies that might have had destabilizing social consequences.

Moreover, if we forego the privilege of hindsight we can appreciate that much of what now seems inevitable, inscribed as it were in the postwar trajectory of Western Europe, did not seem so at the time. Cooperation between France and Western Germany, for example, was far from sure seen from the perspective of 1947; indeed the prospects for such cooperation looked decidedly dim. No one in June 1947 could be sure that the Communist threat to Western Europe was illusory. As it happens we can now say with some confidence that the Communist parties of France and Italy had probably passed their peak by the time Marshall aid was offered and would never again achieve the levels of popularity or credibility that they had reached in the immediate post-war months. But well into 1948 the fear of a Communist coup in Western Europe—or else a Soviet invasion designed to trigger such a coup—was widespread and genuine. Indeed, developments in Prague during February 1948 only accentuated this fear.

The Marshall Plan, in short, was not just economic and political; it was also and perhaps above all psychological. It offered to the peoples of Western Europe the promise of North American aid and the prospect of stability and eventual improvement at a time when many Europeans (including many non-Communist politicians) were quite pessimistic about the prospects for their continent. Overcoming this widespread sense of gloom and incipient disaster and restoring public confidence was the first order of business. Without this, the economic programs and plans being discussed in postwar Europe could never hope to work.

To that extent, the psychological boost provided by the Marshall Plan was much more important than the dollars themselves and was without a doubt absolutely necessary. The fear of Communism, the widespread sense of frustration and disappointment and the belief that Europe's postwar problems had not even been addressed, much less resolved, are today frequently dismissed as merely a matter of mistaken contemporary perception. But in a democracy, perception counts for much. And insofar as it changed people's perceptions, the Marshall Plan probably *was* the most important single factor in Western Europe's transition out of the immediate post-war era.

We are now 50 years on from the Marshall Plan and the circumstances of its emergence can seem very distant indeed. But as more than one of the contributor to this book has noted, the Marshall Plan has reappeared on the agenda of scholars and public policy makers because of the revolutionary transformations in Eastern Europe. In the aftermath of forty-plus years of repression and stagnation, the societies and economies of Europe's eastern half—liberated since 1989 from Communism but still far from integrated into the West—seem urgently to be in need of an injection of confidence and assistance of the kind provided to Western Europe by the ERP. As many have argued, Eastern Europe (and especially the Balkans) needs a Marshall Plan.

The difficulty of course is that, as I have suggested, the Marshall Plan can only be understood as a product of its time. Whatever its achievements, they were secured because of the moment and manner of its implementation. At the time of the Marshall Plan there was widespread consensus in Europe that it was the duty of governments and the state to undertake to design and administer large-scale projects, even if the long term objective was to liberate the market to do its own work (a view far from universal at the time). But in the aftermath of half a century of state socialism, few East Europeans have much faith in the capacity of their own states to generate freedom or wellbeing.

And things have changed in the West as well. We too no longer share the post–World War II faith of Marshall, Monnet, and their contemporaries in the power of planning and prescription. Moreover, as many have noted, Western Europe in the 1940s had inherited a long tradition of efficient and reasonably uncorrupt government, functioning markets and a productive, profit-oriented private sector. But post-1989 Eastern Europe is lacking in all these respects. Even if there were a western country or group of countries willing and able to spend the equivalent of the Marshall Plan to help reconstruct the states and societies of Eastern Europe, it is not clear that the money could be efficiently, productively, or even honestly spent.

In any event, the point is moot. The United States most certainly has no intention of coming up with a new Marshall Plan for post-Communist Eastern Europe. The European Union, whose responsibility it surely is to address the problem of the East—if only to prepare the countries of Eastern Europe for membership in the Union—clearly does not and will not envisage expenditure on a scale comparable to the ERP. In order for Brussels to match the Marshall Plan at today's prices, it would need to be spending approximately ten times more than it currently does on its plans for expansion.

Some commentators have suggested that a Marshall Plan for Eastern Europe would in any event be redundant today, since (unlike 1947) the private sector can generate sufficient resources on its own account. This is perhaps formally correct but misses the point. If the Marshall Plan in 1947 was as much about politics, perception, and psychology as it was about dollars and institutions, then the same would be true today. The problem facing planners and politicians in post-Communist Eastern Europe is not that their economies may not grow and prosper in due course; the dramatic transformations in Hungary or Poland since 1989 are evidence to the contrary. The question is whether it will prove possible to convince the skeptical electors of Central and Eastern Europe to be patient until the good times come. As in 1947, so in 1999: if people believe that a large scale Plan represents a crucial stepping stone to a better future, and if that Plan helps cushion the transition to that future, then on these grounds alone it will play a major part in that process whatever its economic function. And this is something that private capital alone can never achieve: not just because it lacks the clout and impetus of a one-time international undertaking, but because it can so easily be withdrawn if the short-term rewards prove disappointing.

Eastern Europe, then, would undoubtedly benefit from a Marshall Plan. But it is not about to get one. The hesitancy and relatively parsimonious degree of engagement exhibited by the Western governments in the face of the challenge of rebuilding Eastern Europe cannot help but cast into flattering relief the qualities and achievement of the men of 1947. In Washington as in Western Europe the unprecedented circumstances following upon the defeat of Hitler gave rise to a quite remarkable sequence of decisions and institutions. Just as these were unprecedented in their scale and impact, so they have had no successors. Debate will continue no doubt for a very long time over the particular motives, circumstances, and results of Secretary of State Marshall's decision to recommend a European Recovery Plan; but in the light of the European continent's rather uncertain trajectory since 1989, one thing is clear. Western Europe in 1947 had a stroke of extraordinary good fortune.

PART ONE

The Marshall Plan and European Construction

CHAPTER 1

From the Marshall Plan to EEC: Direct and Indirect Influences

Michelle Cini

The casual relationship between the initiation of the Marshall Plan and the establishment of the European Economic Community (EEC) is often taken for granted. The assumption is that the institutionalization of the Organisation for European Economic Recovery (OEEC) forces the West Europeans to cooperate in a manner they would not otherwise have chosen, and that this provided the foundation upon which the European integration process was constructed. In exploring this assumption, the chapter unpacks the relationship between the Marshall Plan and the EEC to focus on some of the more indirect influences: namely, the role of the Plan in altering Allied perceptions towards Germany, and the part it played in inspiring among West European elites a sense of optimism and self-confidence with regard to the reconstruction not only of Western Europe's economy, but also of its political systems.

"The point of the Marshall Plan was not to rebuild Europe at all, but to build an entirely new Europe. Its most enduring legacy is visible not so much in the steel mills and railways and farmlands of nations like Germany and France. It is visible in the institutions that ended centuries of European conflict, transcended old ways of thinking, and formed the basis for West European and Trans-Atlantic unity."[1]

The causal relationship between the Marshall Plan and the European Economic Community (EEC) is often taken for granted. It is characterized, even in the most respectable of studies, by unsubstantiated assertions of the Plan's role in initiating the European integration process of the 1950s. Urwin, for example, claims that the Marshall Plan "is part of the story of European integration,"[2] and many other accounts of the Plan pay lip-service, without evidence, to its European legacy. Yet a direct relationship between the Marshall Plan and the EEC should not be assumed, and must be detached from the retrospective myth-making that surrounds at least some historical overviews of postwar Europe. At the very least, the relationship is more complicated and subtle than it might at first appear. This chapter argues that while there is little evidence to suggest any direct Marshall Plan impact on the European integration process, more indirect influences are manifold. To make this case, the chapter looks both at U.S. policy toward Western Europe in the last years of the 1940s, and at West European responses to that policy.

The American Perspective

Understanding the Marshall Plan from a European integration perspective involves uncovering American elite attitudes to Western Europe's postwar economic recovery and to its political future. Thus, this section of the chapter deals with U.S. motives in promoting European integration; the emergence and reassessment of American policy toward Western Europe; and the strategies that were developed within the Marshall Plan to achieve U.S. policy goals.

U.S. Motives

The motives behind American support for European integration were varied. The U.S. Administration wanted to ensure political stability in Western Europe and judged economic reconstruction to be a means to that end. It also saw the reintegration of (West) Germany as an essential condition for Western Europe's economic recovery. The U.S. Administration was keen to see the establishment of a large, open, and integrated West European market for American exports, a market that would itself help to revitalize the U.S. economy. Moreover, U.S. thinking at this time was driven by humanitarian concerns, although this was as much a justification for U.S. financial support (when a political consensus on aid to Western Europe was still absent) as it was a motive in its own right.

The Truman Doctrine that pledged American support for "free peoples who are resisting subjugation by armed minorities or outside pressures" reflected a sea-change in American foreign policy after World War II. It "marked the opening of a more aggressive phase ... giving it a new purpose and crusade. Its immediate target and beneficiary was Western Europe where hitherto, despite its words, the United States had been somewhat reluctant to intervene."[3]

For some, the Marshall Plan did little more than add an economic dimension to an already well-established security policy vis-à-vis Western Europe, a policy that would be complemented militarily once the North Atlantic Treaty was signed. An internal struggle between those in the U.S. leadership who wanted to see a return to the more isolationist policies of the interwar years and those who advocated a more interventionist strategy, was thus played out in the West European policy arena. However, the argument that a Western Europe placed on a sound economic footing would best be able to defend itself against possible Soviet aggression was one that was hard to counter.

Europe's economic condition in 1947 was dire. Claims were made at the time that it would take 20 to 25 years to get the European economy back on its feet.[4] In France, inflation had been increasing since 1946 and there was little prospect of any imminent recovery.[5] The harsh winter of 1947–48 had exacerbated the situation. Industrial and agricultural production remained below prewar levels and on the ground starvation and destitution were rife. For the national exchequers, balance of payments problems were perhaps the biggest challenge. The West Europeans simply did not have any way of earning the dollars required to purchase the American goods they so desperately needed. This situation was further exacerbated by America's own low import requirements. So even though Urwin claims that the underlying economic situation was not quite as bad as the West Europeans were making out,[6] it was blatantly clear that America's pre-1947 aid policy, which had pumped $9 billion into Western Europe, had not shown the results anticipated. This was of grave concern to the United States, given that economic instability was thought to imply political vulnerability. The assumption was that improved economic conditions would reduce popular sympathy for communism and mobilize support for U.S.-sponsored democratic and liberal solutions to Western Europe's problems.[7] However, it was felt that while West Europeans would not rally round an anti-Communist banner, some other ideological hook could achieve the same ends. It was European integration that was intended to provide this emotional attachment to liberal-democracy that was otherwise missing.[8]

A second if related strand in American thinking at the time revolved around Germany's reintegration into the West European fold. By mid-1947, the close relationship between West German rehabilitation and European integration had become explicit.[9] Germany was believed to provide the key to the revival of the West European economy, while European integration was the key to resolving legitimate French security concerns about German recovery. By linking together German reintegration and European integration, the mistakes of the interwar period might be avoided. The ultimate objective was to extract Western Europe from economic and political crisis and to ensure that the history of the first half of the twentieth century did not repeat itself.

Third, American interest in providing aid to Western Europe was not driven by political and security ends alone. The vision of Western Europe as a vital market for American exports was also an important motivating force behind U.S. policy in 1947. In promoting Western Europe as a large, unified, and open economic space, the United States sought to create (or at least to encourage the creation of) a European market in its own image. This involved not only proliberalization inducements but also the introduction of new management techniques, the promotion of mass production along U.S. lines, and "the fostering of new modes of thinking" about industrial organization.[10] The United States would thus encourage (by example) "the development ... of new ways for neighbors to work together and think of each other, based essentially on the American experience of organizing a continental economy and judging performance by results."[11] This fertilization process would only be possible, however, if industry was organized on a Europe-wide regional basis, rather than along traditional national lines. The Americans thus foresaw the future of Western Europe in much the same way as it assessed its own past: as one based on economic prosperity and social harmony driven by the operation of a large, effective, and free internal market.[12]

The humanitarian motive behind American involvement in the Marshall Plan is perhaps hardest to demonstrate, as this involves distinguishing the Marshall Plan rhetoric from the underlying motives of actors involved in the making of policy. Regardless of whether those motives existed, the language of altruism was clearly helpful in rallying support for the aid program. The Marshall Plan's "fleeced factor" which was important in ensuring the support of U.S. public opinion and Congress was a necessary if not a sufficient element in the promotion of a political consensus on Marshall Aid.[13] It is not surprising, then, that the European Recovery Program should be couched in the language of humanitarianism.[14]

What is much less clear is the extent to which these arguments applied only to Western Europe, rather than to the European continent as a whole. Indeed, it is not always obvious where motives toward "Europe" ended and those toward "Western Europe" began. Even for Marshall himself it seems that this was not a simple matter. It is said that on the trip to Harvard in June 1947 to give his famous Commencement Day speech, he scored out "Western Europe" in his speech notes, and wrote "Europe" in its place.[15] Whether Marshall really believed that the Soviet Union would allow East European states to accept Marshall aid remains contested, as does whether Stalin and Molotov ever seriously considered their participation in the program.

The conclusions to be drawn from this brief overview of U.S. motives are that by Spring 1947 it was acknowledged that some form of European integration was necessary for the achievement of American policy objectives in Western Europe. Hogan confirms this and takes the point further in stating that

> their ambitions stopped at nothing less than a major reorganization of the European state system into a more viable framework for controlling the Germans, containing the Soviets and putting the continental countries on the road to economic recovery and multilateral trade. This they would do by merging separate economic sovereignties into an integrated economic order superintended by supranational institutions of coordination and control. The political assumptions behind this strategy held that an integrated and supranational system would enable France and other participating countries to make full use of Germany's resources without fear of becoming her dependents. This would resolve the tension between economic and security imperatives that had earlier stalled progress, clear a path to Germany's economic recovery and political reintegration, and lead to a final peace settlement between the states of western Europe.[16]

For the Americans, then, European integration became the avenue down which all of their other policy objectives toward Western Europe would be channeled.[17] It thus became a means to a set of ends, as well as an end in its own right.

Assessing and Reassessing Integration

These assessments of U.S. motives beg a number of questions about the sort of European integration that the U.S. foresaw. Indeed, while it is all too easy to generalize about the U.S. "vision," deciphering the American line on European integration in the period after World War II is not an easy task. For a start, there were several discrete U.S. positions on European interstate relations and not a small amount of blurring at the margins. Espousing a commitment to European integration could mean anything from recommending political integration in the form of a federal United States of Europe to promoting a West European free trade area.

U.S. positions changed and to some extent merged as efforts were made to define an official American line on Western Europe. These different positions carried more or less weight at different times in the first five postwar years. There was in fact little evidence of official support for European integration within the U.S. Administration before 1947. The approach to European economic reconstruction had been largely ad hoc and was organized bilaterally. There was an underlying hostility to those in Western Europe who advocated supranational or federal approaches to European reconstruction, with many in the U.S. Administration seeing this as much more of a threat than a potential opportunity.[18] Yet the idea of establishing an integrated Europe had been floated in government circles even during the war. For example, Count Coudenhove Kalergi, the founder of the Pan-Europa Movement, had spent the war years in the United States, based at New York University, actively lobbying for a united Europe, and Jean Monnet, one of the founders of the European Community, was well known and well connected in Washington.[19] After the war, the idea of European integration had found favor with junior officials like Paul Porter at the American Economic Mission in London, who was at the time recommending the internationalization of the Ruhr as a first step toward European unification.[20] Although such ideas may not have been taken on board officially, and did not come from within the Administration, they were familiar to many in the U.S. political elite well before 1947.[21]

However, from early 1947, things began to change. The debate moved from public commentary to policy deliberation.[22] Numerous reports both private and official, public and unofficial, on European integration began to circulate more widely.[23] There was also some discussion about the use of aid as a tool of European integration at this time. Over the course of 1947 both the media (with Walter Lippmann's prointegration journalism) and Congress (with two resolutions in March 1947 supporting the creation of a United States of Europe) tapped into this new approach to Europe's future. Within the U.S. Administration, the impetus behind the change was the failure to agree with the Soviet Union a joint line on the future of the European continent. Marshall's disappointment with the outcome of the foreign ministers' meeting in April 1947 led to his "determination to find a new approach to the problem of German recovery."[24] As a result, Kennan's Policy Planning Staff was set up in May to study European aid requirements, adding to the work already being done by the State-War-Navy Coordination Committee and the State Department's new committee on the Extension of U.S. Aid to Foreign Governments. By mid-May, Kennan's report, which recommended a first set of steps toward a Europe-wide market, with a customs union as a longer term goal, was making an impact in draft form. This was one of several papers that fed into Marshall's famous speech at Harvard in June.[25] Although Marshall himself did not deal directly with the integration issue, the speech was clearly informed by the debate.

Defining a U.S. line on European recovery meant reconciling two different perspectives on European reconstruction. The first came out of the War Department and was found in the Hoover Report issued in March 1947. Here, it was argued that the only way to revive the European economy was to put every effort into revitalizing German industry in order to create a self-supporting (West) German state. The Army was particularly keen on this approach as a way of keeping down the costs of Occupation. The second perspective was rather more cautious, and was found in the State Department's line that a "balanced recovery" in Western Europe should involve paying as much attention to security considerations and the potentially negative effects of German reintegration as to reviving the German economy, thereby taking into account both German and wider European concerns.[26] The European integration argument came to be favored as a way of achieving this goal.

On European integration itself, the U.S. Administration was split initially between the "free traders" and the "planners." In the former camp (with William Clayton) the idea of a customs union was supported, but with hostility toward any form of preferential agreement within Western Europe (and this covered Britain's imperial preferences, too). As for the planners, they were prepared to rely on supranational government intervention as a means of enhancing levels of West European production. The latter camp eventually gained the upper hand.[27]

Indeed, it is not surprising to find the argument for a more planned form of European integration taking hold so quickly in the State Department when we consider the role played by junior officials in promoting this new approach. Officials such as Charles P. Kindleberger, Ben T. Moore, Harold van B. Cleveland, Miriam Camps, and Joseph Jones, some of whom had earlier been involved in regional planning through United Nations agencies,[28] were keen on the idea of a supranational solution to Western Europe's problems. It was these officials who were drafting speeches for Acheson and Marshall in 1947 and who wrote the influential June 1947 memorandum that set out the State Department's position.

One of the key assumptions upon which U.S. support for European integration was premised was that the British would be involved in any West European integrative exercise. Britain, it was believed, would act as a counterbalance to Franco-German involvement in any such project. However, given British reluctance to get involved, this U.S. line clearly hindered efforts at creating any sort of supranational European organization. Acheson's policy reformulation in 1949 was to acknowledge this constraint, while at the same time reassessing the roles to be played by France and Germany in any future West European integration process. In recognizing that in the short term Britain would be prepared to give up neither its global interests nor its self-perception as a world power, U.S. support for European integration took a new turn. This new approach "would be built on a Franco-German rapprochement and would have British and American support in the form of military guarantees, economic collaboration and other measures that stopped short of merging sovereignties."[29] Henceforth the American line was to rely on British cooperation in a multilateral framework within which a more profound European integration would be encouraged.

Encouraging Integration: Putting the Plan in Practice

From the start, Marshall Aid was to be a temporary program of support. This was essential not only to provide a longer term justification for the aid as an investment in Western Europe's and indeed in America's future, but also to emphasize that while the United States was prepared to "pump-prime" the West European economy, it was still up to the West Europeans themselves to regulate their internal recovery and reconstruction. As such, the aid was intended to offer a "cure rather than a mere palliative."[30] This was premised on the understanding that the impediments to economic recovery were temporary "bottlenecks," not permanent blockages.[31]

Second, and perhaps most important, a central plank of the U.S. strategy (and indeed of Marshall's speech) was that the West Europeans would themselves be responsible for much of the operation of the Plan. They would be responsible for deciding the level of aid to be granted (at least in the first instance) and they should also coordinate its distribution. This approach came as a surprise to the West Europeans, replacing as it did the preferred bilateralism of the first years of the post-war period. It was a u-turn that was not entirely welcome. The Americans insisted that a collective and unified approach to the allocation of aid was a prerequisite for the granting of any financial support, that there would be no national shopping lists, and that American involvement in the program would be kept to a minimum at all stages. However,

> The proposal that grants to European countries should be made conditional on their accepting measures of integration was not accepted. It was rather a question of using the influence that aid gave to those administering it to push in directions they thought important.[32]

Above all, the Americans did not want to be seen to be dictating to the West Europeans,[33] although it was made crystal clear that Congress was very keen on the idea of European integration and that in order to get congressional support for any aid there was no option but to cooperate.

Third, the United States placed a great deal of emphasis on the institutionalization of cooperation. Not only was it clear that the West Europeans must cooperate, but that that cooperation should be structured in such a way as to leave a permanent imprint on the Western European polity. Pressure came directly from Congress when they agreed the first year of aid.[34] Initially, the United Nations Economic Commission for Europe (UNECE) was to be the coordinating body. It was more than symbolic that this idea had been dropped by 1947, as this date marked the start of a new security order in Western Europe, characterized by something other than four-power cooperation and anti-German treaties.[35] Pressure on the West Europeans to create the Organization for European Economic Cooperation (OEEC) out of the informal Committee for European Economic Cooperation (CEEC) saw the Americans trying to keep up the political momentum that had begun with the Marshall Plan proposal.[36] In any case, there were fears of Soviet obstructionism if the ECE was used.

Within this institutionalized framework, the United States was particularly keen to see a long-term planning strategy emerge that would sit alongside the short-term objectives that were inevitably easier to achieve. Marjolin points to the irony of this U.S. approach when he says that "there was something of a paradox here: it was curious, to say the least, that the United States, whose philosophy was essentially liberal, should seek to impose authoritarian planning on Europe,"[37] although this was itself a matter of debate within the U.S. Administration.

Fourth, despite apparent U.S. support for European-level central planning, it was clear that European integration was expected to sit within an economic framework of multilateral trade liberalization.[38] This, too, was as much about politics as it was about economics. It is sometimes easy for West Europeans to forget that the U.S. strategy in promoting Marshall aid was intended to foster closer collaboration between the United States and Western Europe, as much as it was intended to encourage internal West European cooperation. Even so, at the time, it was not always clear how compatible the "regional" and "universalist" strategies would be in practice.

"The US was both a lobbyist for a united Europe and a role model."[39] Yet the U.S. vision of an integrated Europe remained vague in the absence of a consensus on how a united Europe might look. What was being promoted here was a trend, a process of change, or a policy direction rather than a specific vision of West European union. As such, while it is clear that there was a U.S. policy on Western Europe at this time, it is not so easy to define a coherent U.S. line on European integration. This policy flexibility allowed the West Europeans a great deal of maneuver in responding to the U.S. policy.

West European Responses

American policies toward European integration at the time of the Marshall Plan provide us with useful insights into U.S. motives vis-à-vis Western Europe in the late 1940s, allowing comparisons to be drawn between intentions and eventual outcomes. However, inherent in those policies and in the Marshall Plan itself was the understanding that the West European response would carry the most weight in both implementing the Plan and in providing the context within which that implementation would take place. Indeed, it was to be the interplay between the policy of American decision makers and the West Europeans' reaction to and interpretation of that policy that would define the extent to which the Marshall Plan and European integration would go hand-in-hand. While

> Americans like to believe that the Marshall Plan was a timely, generous and extraordinarily successful act of statesmanship that forced France, Germany, Britain, Italy and the other Europeans to cooperate and in the process saved Western Europe. That stretches considerably. The United States played a role, but was not the creator of modern Europe.[40]

Although the immediate West European response to the Marshall Plan was overwhelmingly positive, the reaction to the integration strategy within it was largely one of skepticism.[41] This is not to say that this skepticism existed across the board. There were groups and individuals who saw that U.S. objectives might be harnessed to support their own preferred (and often prointegration) vision of Europe's future.

However, what the West Europeans wanted first and foremost was the financial aid. The rest of the package could be taken or left. In practice this meant that the West Europeans supported the American line only insofar as it allowed them access to the funds. Tolerating the U.S. prointegration line was especially important when it came to ensuring congressional support for the appropriations involved.[42] But this was not too painful a task for the large majority of West European governments in power in 1947, as there was in any case much support for interstate cooperation, as long as "integration" was left undefined and the United States took a back seat in pressing for any specific definition of that process.

Despite the influence of European movements and a pervasive hostility toward nationalism at this time, West European governments continued to see the world very much in terms of balance of power politics. Even though geopolitical realities had changed, the mindsets of the ruling elites had not. Postwar West European politics and the prospect of cooperation itself were still interpreted from a state-centric standpoint, so that "While Washington saw the Marshall Plan as a package for Europe, the assorted European recipients invariably sought to tailor their participation to their own national circumstances."[43] The United States recognized this as early as July 1947 and even considered drawing back from their initial decision, which compelled the Europeans to decide for themselves.[44]

In some instances, the Marshall Plan seemed only to highlight the differences between government positions. This was especially true on the subject of Germany's reintegration, but it also applied to European economic integration.[45] Fervent nationalism may well have been discredited after 1945, but the West European state system, although much weakened and in some cases destroyed altogether, was beginning to reassert itself. The fact that the problems faced by West European states after 1945 varied considerably made a concerted approach to European recovery more difficult, and while it was acknowledged that national recovery and European recovery were to be inextricably tied together, it was not clear how the two sides of the postwar coin would in practice be linked. This dilemma had to be worked out through a process of policy compromise and convergence that would continue to place the national dimension center stage. This was the line taken by the

French Government within the framework provided for by its Monnet Plan.[46]

Thus, a differentiation of national problems led to a differentiation of national responses. This had three effects. First, European integration began to look very much like an *externally imposed* policy, a policy justified only insofar as it allowed for the receipt of U.S. aid. Second, increasingly, European integration was defined as a foreign policy matter, rather than as an integral part of internal strategies for economic and political recovery. This may not be so surprising if Price is correct in stating that "The idea of close cooperation was ... clearer in the mind of Americans than of Europeans,"[47] even if, as we saw earlier in the chapter, the U.S. approach was itself rather vague and contradictory. European integration was judged positively by the large majority of West European governments as long as it did not impinge on issues of national sovereignty, which in practice implied that it could not impinge of a government's freedom of maneuver. Thus, for most Marshall aid recipients, integration came to imply little more than intergovernmental cooperation, so that the Marshall Plan failed to break down national barriers in the way the United States had hoped.[48] Third, however, it can be argued that the differentiation allowed for within the Marshall Plan framework also had a more positive dimension. For some, the Plan's very success rested on its flexibility. In this sense, while the Plan did not force the West Europeans to commit to any form of supranational or federal union, it did promote an ethos of cooperation that could find support across a large number of states.

Thus far the West Europeans have been "lumped together" in a way precluded by the very differentiation alluded to above. In practice, it is difficult, if not impossible, to sustain such across the board generalizations. For a start, even if the majority of governments favored a looser cooperation as against a tighter supranational or federal form of integration, there were numerous groups in Western Europe advocating and working for the creation of some sort of United States of Europe. Ideas about European integration had been circulating freely within Europe during the war and were openly discussed, at least at elite level. And at governmental level, the setting up of a West European customs union, covering not just the Benelux countries but also France and Italy, was very much on the political agenda in 1947–48.[49] However, this enthusiasm for customs union began to peter out toward the end of 1948, even if the OEEC did agree to set up a study group to gather relevant information on the project.[50] The requisite political will for such an integrative move was still lacking at this stage.[51]

National Perspectives

While Marshall aid was crucial in helping the Germans to resolve their industrial problems (with, for example, coal production still only 45 percent of prewar levels in 1947), the political and symbolic impact of the Plan also left a critical legacy. "Instead of exacting reparations, as after 1919, it offered precious start-up capital. Instead of imposing a discriminatory regime, it opened the door to rehabilitation."[52] In Duchene's words, "West German recovery was implanted in the Marshall Plan like the yolk in the egg."[53] Although Germany was not invited to the meeting that set up the CEEC in 1947, its requirements were included in the European Recovery Program (ERP) sent to Washington at the end of September 1947. "This was the first sign of a reintegration of Germany into the concert of European nations."[54]

Clearly the Americans had more influence over West Germany than over any other West European state as they strove to encourage support for European integration. On a practical level, too, it was easy for the Americans to administer Marshall aid as it flowed into the three occupied zones. The United States was thus able to use its influence to strengthen the political and economic forces that favored integrationist solutions to West Germany's postwar recovery. This was not difficult given support for integration in the Parliamentary Council that drafted the (constitutional) Basic Law, and the fact that later on "the Adenauer government came to see European integration and Germany's return to international respectability as identical."[55]

It was recognized that if the overbearing economic constraints imposed on West Germany by the Allies were to be lifted, European integration was to be the means by which this would happen.[56] This marked the beginning of a German identification with European integration that would endure for at least as long as the Cold War. This association allowed West Germany to begin to regain its credibility. It opened the door to German control over its own industrial production, and the normalization of relations with the French.[57] It is also worth remembering that the West German Basic Law, which was signed in 1949, included a provision (Article 24), which allowed for the transfer of sovereignty to international organizations. It is interesting that the Germans used their commitment to European integration as a stepping-stone to regaining their sovereignty. After all, tying in the short-term, their new-found sovereignty to such a commitment could in the longer-term imply a sharing or even, some would say, an undermining of German sovereignty as the process of European integration deepened.

Inevitably there were some tensions between the Germans and the Americans at the end of the 1940s, largely over the form that economic reconstruction should take. But these did nothing to undermine the belief that "along with the presence of the American Seventh Army, the Marshall Plan was the most important symbol of America's commitment to the survival of the Federal Republic."[58] Indeed it is certain that "Germany's integration into Western Europe and the Atlantic Community still stands as one of the central achievements of the Marshall Plan."[59]

In Italy, the economic and the political situation in 1947 was extremely unstable. With the lowest per capita food levels in Western Europe and the largest Communist Party in the West,[60] the Americans were desperately keen to do whatever was necessary to guarantee political stability. The Italian Government, and De Gasperi in particular, after his resounding election victory in April 1948, made full use of Italy's unstable condition to win U.S. financial support. This was not difficult to do. De Gasperi recognized that the United States was dependent upon him if they wanted to keep the Italian Communists out of power. This gave him a certain freedom of maneuver. Like the Germans, the Italians also saw in European integration a way of solidifying the foundations of the Italian state. But while the prointegration rhetoric was strong, the Italian commitment to taking more concrete steps toward economic integration (such as customs union) was somewhat ambivalent at this stage.

In Scandinavia, there was some concern about the security implications of Marshall aid and a fair amount of skepticism about the integrative assumptions underpinning it. This ultimately led Finland to reject the U.S. offer. While the other Scandinavians accepted the loose ties of the OEEC in exchange for the economic benefits that Marshall aid would bring, they remained rather reluctant participants even in this intergovernmental form of institutionalized cooperation.

By contrast, the Benelux countries were the most enthusiastic supporters of European federalism, and as such they were perhaps the only Marshall Plan countries to accept unequivocally that European integration was a priority worth placing over and above that of national sovereignty.[61] They saw the advantages that European integration could bring to their small but internally stable countries and supported U.S. policy wholeheartedly, even if they lacked the political clout to persuade their fellow West Europeans to follow suit.[62]

In France, Marshall aid was used to boost the postwar modernization drive. But economic effects aside, the Plan had a phenomenal political impact on French policy toward West Germany and thereafter on the future development of European integration. Like the Italians, the French had used the communist threat to win financial support from the United States. However, at the same time they continued to take a repressive line on German economic recovery. The premise on which French policy had been based was the destruction of German industrial and military might, and the construction of a revitalized French economy that would itself act as the motor of West European recovery. The Monnet Plan was designed to achieve this objective. However, with American intentions toward German reintegration becoming increasingly clear, a French strategy of this sort was soon out of the question. The French had lost the argument and as such were forced to reassess their approach toward West Germany. This meant having to accept that their economic fate was inextricably tied to that of their former adversary, and coming to terms with the notion that only together would they be able to determine the economic and political fate of Western Europe.[63]

This is not to say that the French Government in any way played down its own interests when faced with an American policy that seemed incompatible. Although the first impulse was to resist, the second was to find a more effective if circuitous route by which to achieve the same or at least similar policy ends—that is, to create security safeguards against any future German aggression. "Time was running out for the French. They had to strike a deal with the Germans while they still had the upper hand, and they had to do so even if it meant risking the future of Anglo-French cooperation, on which they had earlier built their hopes for security."[64] In this, the position of the Ruhr (that is, the industrial potential of a revitalized West Germany) would remain central, although France's repressive policy had to change.[65] With policy on West Germany's future still undecided at the end of the 1940s, the door was open to the Franco German initiative that became the European Coal and Steel Community (ECSC). It is interesting to reflect that the ECSC setup was not dissimilar to plans for an international Ruhr authority that had earlier been posited by the French.[66]

It is perhaps ironic that while the idea of a united Europe was for the French a safeguard against dependence on the United States,[67] it fulfilled the central plank of American foreign policy toward Western Europe after 1945. Indeed, Schuman's words in 1950 sounded remarkably like those that had been emerging from Washington in earlier years. This irony was not lost on Foreign Minister Georges Bidault, when he told the French National Assembly that "We need the United States in order to do without it."[68]

The American assumption before 1949 was that Britain had to be a part of any effort to integrate Western Europe. But with Britain still clinging to the illusion that it remained a world power, it is not surprising that the U.S. approach was unwelcome there. Many in the British Government were unhappy at being thrown into a prospective union with the (defeated) West Europeans.[69] Britain thus considered herself to be a special case. The Labor Government was particularly keen to avoid any restrictions on the country's sovereignty, which could threaten radical economic plans, the preservation of the sterling zone, and existing relationships with Empire and Commonwealth. This irritated the Americans immensely. Given this irritation, it is interesting that the British were also keen to preserve those wartime channels of bilateral communication that had been established with the United States, in the belief that the pre-1945 "special relationship" could persist into the postwar era. At the same time, the British Government were also committed to keeping the United States engaged in Western Europe.

It was on the issue of currency convertibility and the freeing up of trade and payments, however, that the British dragged their feet the most.[70] This clashed full on with the U.S. vision of a multilateral trading order that would provide the context for an integrated Western Europe. Without a British commitment, U.S. policy toward Western Europe seemed doomed to fail and as a result the U.S. Administration continued to place Britain under some pressure to comply with the U.S. policy line—without much success. From the start it was clear that the British attitude toward integration was very different from that of the United States.[71] For example, once the OEEC was set up, efforts by the Americans to introduce some sort of supranational or majority voting element within the organization fell on stony ground, largely because of British opposition.

But it is too simplistic to see the British approach as merely hostility toward any integrationist proposal. The British position essentially comprised a lowest-common denominator policy, which emerged out of disputes within the British Government itself. There were a number of different strands of opinion on integration within Britain in the late 1940s. Bevin, as Foreign Minister, together with the Foreign Office, was in fact quite sympathetic to the customs union ideas that were circulating in 1947. The economics ministries, by contrast, did not share any of this enthusiasm.[72] Bevin's approach was rather ingenious, linking together a potential Commonwealth union with a customs union in Western Europe. This would have inevitably placed Britain in a pivotal position. Yet it came to nothing. Once the disputes had been ironed out, a much smoother and more unified British approach to integration emerged. This was positive, in principle at least, about reducing tariffs and liberalizing trade, if in a gradual (or simply slow) and pragmatic fashion, but it had little time for customs unions and supranationalism.[73] It certainly did not involve any easing of the British commitment to the preservation of their sovereignty at all costs.

American determination to drag Britain into an integrated Europe thus made the very goal of integration impossible. It was not until European integration and British participation were detached from each other in 1949 that the door to a tighter, more supranational form of integration opened. In the meantime the American commitment to British participation up until 1949 had left its mark in the form of the OEEC, as a truly wider but weaker organization than the United States had originally envisaged. Altiero Spinelli, as a committed federalist, was critical of Americans on this count, arguing that the United States could have forged a direct link between Marshall aid and an integrated Europe had they pushed the West Europeans a little harder, and had they earlier understood the intransigence of the British position.[74]

Even though Britain was the main barrier to the creation of a supranational OEEC and the establishment of a more direct link between the Marshall Plan and European integration proper, it would be unfair to blame only Britain (and U.S. reluctance to understand fully British intransigence) for the constraints placed on the European integration process in the late 1940s.[75] Efforts to construct a customs union with merely a subset of Marshall Plan states came to nothing at this point, and all states involved in the OEEC assessed the merits and demerits of European integration from their different national standpoints.[76] Some simply came to more prointegration conclusions than others.

The OEEC and European Integration

While the importance of the national dimension is beyond dispute, the very fact of the OEEC's existence should not be undervalued. Even though the level of coordination fell short of what was originally planned for the organization,[77] this was largely because it was left up to its 16 member states to operationalize. Even if the Americans were wrong in believing that this organization could eventually support a tighter process of integration, the establishment of a permanent West European organization was quite an achievement, although the organization itself was unequivocally intergovernmental in form. Hence, it is worth reviewing in brief the form and achievements of the OEEC.

The Organization for European Economic Cooperation was set up in April 1948 with its governing body and central institution the Council of Ministers. This body was made up of one representative for each member state and it met weekly on the official level, with ministerial gatherings about four times a year. It dealt mainly with general policy issues and administrative matters. At the time of its inception, France had wanted some sort of supranational component established alongside the intergovernmental Council, which would possibly have involved the Secretariat-General taking decisions in his own right. This did not meet with unanimous approval, however.[78] Instead, a small Executive Committee of five national officials was set up. This was headed by a Director-General, and its work was supported by a number of specialist committees, some of which (like the European Payments Union) were eventually hived off from the OEEC. The only small concession to Monnet's vision of a supranational organization was that the secretary-general was given the right *ex-officio* to initiate proposals, even if this amounted to very little.[79] The Executive Committee was also able to take delegated executive decisions, although in practice this gave it no real autonomy.

Central to the operation of the OEEC was the Council's reliance on the unanimity principle for all votes taken, although opt-outs from decisions were also possible. This decision-making procedure had been insisted upon by the United Kingdom, the Netherlands, and the Nordic states, despite tentative American suggestions that some sort of limit should be placed on national vetoes.[80] The Americans were in a difficult position in making suggestions of this sort. While they were not happy with the constraints the member states had placed on the OEEC's autonomy, they did not want to interfere in its operation, as this might further undermine the organization's independence. The reality of the day-to-day operation of the OEEC was that decisions were effectively taken along Franco-British lines, with the Americans acting as umpires in disputed cases. While the smaller countries were able to protect their own interests, they tended to be more reactive in their OEEC involvement.[81]

The OEEC has been judged by some to be a phenomenal achievement in its own right. Marjolin, the first secretary-general of the OEEC wrote that the Organization was "the most dazzling political and economic success in the history of the western world since 1914."[82] Ironically, this success could be judged to be a function of the very intergovernmental characteristics that others would be all too ready to criticize. However, at a time when "collaboration" was viewed with suspicion, the institutionalized yet voluntary nature of the OEEC allowed for a gentle introduction to a new and rather more formal exercise in interstate cooperation.[83] Even so, when addressing the impact that its existence had on the future European integration process, less hyperbole is usually the order of the day. Dinan was fairly upbeat when he called the OEEC a "trigger of debate."[84] By contrast, it is reported that Monnet was more likely to judge the OEEC as a "trigger of crisis," in other words as a prompt for French action and as an example of how *not* to build a new Europe. Monnet's hostility toward (and, we assume, disappointment with) the OEEC never left him. He talked of the OEEC as "the opposite of the Community spirit,"[85] and Duchene reports that "in later years, whenever he said of something that it was 'an OEEC affair' he meant nothing would come of it."[86]

But perhaps the most important weakness of the OEEC from a European integration perspective was its short-termism, that is, its inability to allow for a more visionary program of action on economic growth and industrial development among its participant states.[87] Although Marjolin says that he tried to give the Americans what they wanted on this score, the objective of long-term planning was never delivered, and by early 1949 the OEEC had lowered its sights considerably.[88] The United States agreed to this as they realized that these plans would in any case have perpetuated national barriers to trade. Thus, rather than as an agent of cooperation, the OEEC is remembered as an agent of liberalization. Its success in liberalizing trade and payments, albeit with limitations, was the legacy it left on the European economy, and indirectly, on the European Community.[89]

The OEEC was the first West European organization to institutionalize intergovernmental cooperation after World War II, and for that it could be termed a landmark in interstate relations and a stepping-stone toward European integration. It is not convincing to claim that there was a direct institutional legacy granted by the OEEC to the European Community, however. Yet, neither is it sufficient to claim that the OEEC was nothing more than a false start in the history of European integration. Rather, a more constructive way of interpreting the OEEC's role is called for: as an indirect influence on the European integration process of the 1950s insofar as it provided a framework for socializing West European elites into new ways of working[90] and of familiarizing them with the practice as well as the language of European integration. As Price states:

> Instead of action for, or in place of, national governments, the OEEC sought to promote understanding between governments, to coordinate

their policies and actions, to foster mutual aid, and, frequently, to influence their decisions by bringing to bear the thinking and judgement of
delegates and technicians from other countries.[91]

Only in this sense could the OEEC be judged a stepping-stone to
European union.

Conclusions

In seeking to address the relationship between the Marshall Plan and the
European Economic Community there are a number of interrelated
conclusions that this chapter draws. The first and perhaps central
conclusion is that the Marshall Plan did not lead directly to the establishment of the European Community. The juxtaposition of U.S. enthusiasm for integration and the disinterest (or self-interest) of the West
Europeans in the late 1940s, the lowest common denominator preference for cooperation over integration, and the loose intergovernmental
structure of the OEEC that failed to promote either supranationalism or
any concrete sense of European community, all point to the weaknesses
in any argument that would claim a direct link from Marshall Plan to
European Community. So while it is certain that the Marshall Plan and
the OEEC achieved many important economic and political ends, from
this standpoint European integration was not one of them.

Yet, the indirect influences on the later European integration process
were manifold. There is a tendency now to forget or at least to undercs-
timate the novelty of the Marshall Plan and the fact that it "constituted
a total departure from past European practice,"[92] that it was "something
quite new to Europe"[93] and that it was "singularly audacious" in its
operation.[94] This is especially clear if we focus only on institutional
outcomes. It is possible, therefore, to highlight a rather different set of
effects that arose out of the Marshall Plan and the OEEC: the gradual
reinsertion or reintegration of West Germany into the West European
fold; the improved economic conditions that made future efforts at
cooperation more promising; the establishment of transnational elite
contacts, both formal and informal,[95] which induced a process of
transnational socialization in favor of further cooperation; and the
creation of a precedent for institutionalized multilateral cooperation in
place of the earlier preference for ad hoc bilateralism. As Urwin notes,
the "OEEC played a major role in driving home the realization that the
European economies were mutually dependent, and that they prospered
or failed together."[96] It raised the issue of European integration as one

to be taken seriously—after all, the American Administration supported it—and one that would continue to be inextricably tied to matters of collective security.[97] One might also point to an emerging sense of optimism and self-confidence that arose out of the above changes, to the extent that they provided the West Europeans with a "psychological blood transfusion."[98] In Marshall's own words, "The remedy lies in breaking the vicious circle and restoring the confidence of the European people in the economic future of their own countries and of Europe as a whole."[99] It is in this sense that we might agree that "the Schuman Plan and the EDC proposal couldn't have developed without the ground being prepared and fertilized by the Marshall Plan endeavors."[100]

Moreover, it is also important in a more negative sense to see the Marshall Plan's failures and weaknesses as additional indirect influences on the setting up of the European Community. The inability of the Marshall Plan and the OEEC to respond fully to French security concerns that still viewed West Germany as a regional threat was particularly important in laying the ground for the Schuman Plan in 1950. While American and French interests frequently diverged, it was a growing acknowledgment of the need to counter American enthusiasm for West German reintegration (and the perception that this took precedence over French security concerns), which ultimately led the French to seek to establish the very institutional integrative framework that the Americans themselves had hoped for. This convergence was a convergence of means but not of ends, which (with the benefit of hindsight) did not bode well for the future of Franco-American relations. Likewise, when talking of the negative aspects of the Marshall Plan, we might also point to the late recognition by the Americans that the British would not shift from the intransigent position they had adopted toward supranational integration. The eventual realization that the British position was not going to change, along with a more widespread acknowledgment of all West European states' positions on European integration, allowed for the start of a process in the early 1950s that would ultimately involve only six of the original Marshall Plan recipients.

> Finally, Price helps us to draw together these conclusions when he says that: The OEEC stood out as the first organization through which the disintegration of western Europe into autarkic islands had been checked and a reverse trend established. During the transition both immediate economic necessity and temporary American aid were important contributing factors. With advancing recovery these factors receded in importance. That the trend did not then collapse seems to have been due chiefly to the successful *demonstration* given by the OEEC and other

emergent European institutions that positive benefits of distinct value to all members could be achieved by closer economic cooperation. ... Through consultations of unprecedented scope, continuity, and intimacy, and through the establishment and effective use of new cooperative institutions, undramatic but solid foundations were laid for further progress. Integration as a goal synonymous with unification—economic or political—was still far from realization. But integration as a continuing dynamic process of joint effort to deal with common problems through reason and consent had become a new reality on the European scene.[101]

One can say then that the indirect influence of the Marshall Plan was to be found in the demonstration effect which it provoked.

Thus, any understanding of the Marshall Plan's impact on the European Community must by necessity consider both the vision and policy of the U.S. Administration from early 1947, together with the response of individual West European governments. In addition, both the negative and the positive direct consequences of the Marshall Plan must also be taken into consideration. To reiterate, while it would be misleading to see a direct link between the Marshall Plan/OEEC and the ECSC/EEC, the events of 1947 certainly did put Western Europe on a path that would lead them toward further integration. We will never know for sure whether a rather different U.S. policy in the late 1940s would have directed Western Europe to a very different future.

Notes

1. Madeleine K. Albright, "Time to Finish the Job for All Europe," *International Herald Tribune*, May 28, 1997.
2. Derek W. Urwin, *The Community of Europe* (Harlow: Longman, 1991), p. 19.
3. Urwin, *The Community of Europe*, p. 15.
4. Urwin, *The Community of Europe*, p. 17.
5. Michael J. Hogan, "European Integration and German Reintegration: Marshall Planners and the Search for Recovery and Security in Western Europe," in C. Maier and G. Bischof, eds., *The Marshall Plan and Germany* (New York: Berg, 1991), p. 3.
6. Urwin, *The Community of Europe*, p. 16.
7. Charles S. Maier, "Supranational Concepts and National Continuity in the Framework of the Marshall Plan," in S. Hoffman and C. Maier, eds., *The Marshall Plan: A Retrospective* (Boulder, CO Westview Press, 1984), p. 29.
8. M. Beloff, *The United States and the Unity of Europe* (Washington, DC: The Brookings Institution, 1963), p. 16. Hogan, "European Integration and German Reintegration," p. 115.

9. Hogan, "European Integration and German Reintegration," p. 116.
10. Urwin, *The Community of Europe*, p. 21.
11. Lewis, "Hard Lessons." This was confirmed with the appointment of Averell Harriman as first Special Representative and Paul G. Hoffman as head of the ECA. Both wanted to see a refashioning of Europe's socioeconomic structure, according to Stirk, *A History of European Integration*, p. 91.
12. Hogan, "European Integration and German Reintegration," p. 116.
13. Beloff, *The United States*, p. 13.
14. Urwin, *The Community of Europe*, p. 18.
15. Hogan, "European Integration and German Reintegration," p. 142.
16. Hogan, "European Integration and German Reintegration," pp. 115–16.
17. Hogan, "European Integration and German Reintegration," p. 8.
18. R. Mayne, *The Recovery of Europe 1945–73* (New York: Anchor Books, 1973), p. 151. Beloff, *The United States*, p. 35, argued that this ambivalence persisted to some extent as there were some criticisms that European integration allowed for "French escapism" and was in opposition to atlanticism.
19. Desmond Dinan, *Ever Closer Union: An Introduction to the European Community* (London: MacMillan, 1994), pp. 17–18.
20. P. M. R. Stirk, *A History of European Integration since 1914* (London: Pinter, 1996), p. 88.
21. Beloff, *The United States*, p. 14.
22. Stirk, *A History of European Integration*, p. 88.
23. John W. Young, *Britain, France and the Unity of Europe 1945–1951* (Leicester: Leicester University Press, 1984), p. 67
24. Michael J. Hogan, "European Integration and the Marshall Plan," in S. Hoffmann and C. Maier, eds., *The Marshall Plan: A Retrospective* (Boulder, CO: Westview Press 1984), p. 3; Beloff, *The United States*, p. 14.
25. Hogan, "European Integration and the Marshall Plan," p. 5.
26. Hogan, "European Integration and German Reintegration," p. 122.
27. Stirk, *A History of European Integration*, p. 91.
28. Hogan, "European Integration and the Marshall Plan," p. 4.
29. Hogan, "European Integration and German Reintegration," p. 164.
30. George C. Marshall, commencement address, Harvard University, June 5, 1947, printed in the *International Herald Tribune*, May 8, 1997.
31. Maier, "Supranational Concepts," pp. 29–30.
32. Beloff, *The United States*, p. 33.
33. Robert Marjolin, *Memoirs 1911–1986* (London: Weidenfeld and Nicolson, 1989), p. 189.
34. Marjolin, *Memoirs*, p. 188.
35. Young, *Britain, France and the Unity of Europe*, p. 65.
36. Duchene, *Jean Monnet*, p. 168.
37. Marjolin, *Memoirs*, p. 200.

38. H. B. Price, *Marshall Plan and its Meaning* (Ithaca, NY: Cornell University Press, 1955), p. 350.
39. P. Duigan and L. H. Gann, *The United States and the New Europe 1945–1993* (Oxford: Blackwell, 1994), p. 40.
40. Ambrose, "When the Americans Came Back."
41. Hogan, "European Integration and German Reintegration," p. 126.
42. Mayne, *The Recovery of Europe*, p. 133; Stirk, *A History of European Integration*, p. 92.
43. Barry James, "National Sensitivities vs. U.S. Goals," in the *International Herald Tribune*, May 28, 1997.
44. Stirk, *A History of European Integration*, p. 91.
45. Young, *Britain, France and the Unity of Europe*, p. 69.
46. Marjolin, *Memoirs*, p. 182.
47. Price, *Marshall Plan*, p. 347.
48. Dinan, *Ever Closer Union*, p. 18.
49. These fell under a variety of sobriquets such as Fritalux, Finebel, and Fritnebel. See Price, *Marshall Plan*, p. 351.
50. Duchene, *Jean Monnet*, p. 185; Young, *Britain, France and the Unity of Europe*, p. 68. Young says that the French were keen on the customs union idea both to impress the Americans and because the economic integration idea had already taken hold.
51. Mayne, *The Recovery of Europe*, p. 154.
52. Josef Joffe, "For Germany, Priceless Gift of Pardon," in the *International Herald Tribune*, May 28, 1997; see also Price, *Marshall Plan*, p. 349.
53. Duchene, *Jean Monnet*, p. 184.
54. Marjolin, *Memoirs*, p. 183.
55. Schwarz, "European Integration," p. 214.
56. Maier, "Supranational concepts," p. 35.
57. S. Bulmer and W. Paterson, *The Federal Republic of Germany and the European Community* (London: Allen and Unwin, 1987), pp. 5–6.
58. Schwarz, "European Integration," p. 214.
59. Thomas Schwarz, "European Integration and the 'Special Relationship': Implementing the Marshall Plan in the Federal Republic," in C. Maier and G. Bischof, eds., *The Marshall Plan and Germany* (New York: Berg, 1991), p. 212.
60. James, "National Sensitivities."
61. Hogan, "European Integration and German Reintegration," p. 128.
62. Maier, "European Integration and the Marshall Plan," p. 35.
63. Duchene, *Jean Monnet*, p. 184.
64. Hogan, "European Integration and German Reintegration," p. 168.
65. Duchene, *Jean Monnet*, p. 184; Dinan, *Ever Closer Union*, p. 19.
66. Hogan, "European Integration and German Reintegration," p. 167.
67. Jean Monnet, *Memoirs* (London: Collins, 1978), p. 272.
68. Quoted in James, "National sensitivities."

69. Young, *Britain, France and the Unity of Europe*, p. 67.
70. Maier, "Supranational Concepts," p. 33.
71. Hogan, "European Integration and German Reintegration," p. 151; Stirk, *A History of European Integration*, p. 98.
72. Young, *Britain, France and the Unity of Europe*, p. 69; Hogan, "European Integration and German Reintegration," p. 128.
73. Young, *Britain, France and the Unity of Europe*, p. 119; Beloff, *The United States*, p. 92.
74. Cited in W. Wallace and J. Smith, "Democracy or Technocracy? European Integration and the Problem of Popular Consent," *West European Politics*, Vol. 18, 1995, pp. 137–57; see also Beloff, *The United States*, p. 31.
75. Mayne, *The Recovery of Europe*, p. 156.
76. Hogan, "European Integration and German Reintegration," p. 128.
77. Urwin, *Community of Europe*, p. 19.
78. Urwin, *Community of Europe*, p. 19; Marjolin, *Memoirs*, p. 189.
79. Duchene, *Jean Monnet*, p. 169.
80. Duchene, *Jean Monnet*, p. 169; Marjolin, *Memoirs*, p. 189.
81. Marjolin, *Memoirs*, p. 192.
82. Marjolin, *Memoirs*, p. 175.
83. Urwin, *Community of Europe*, p. 21.
84. Dinan, *Ever Closer Union*, p. 19.
85. Monnet, *Memoirs*, p. 273.
86. Duchene, *Jean Monnet*, p. 169.
87. Arnold J. Zurcher, *The Struggle to Unite Europe 1940–58* (New York: New York University Press, 1958); Mayne, *The Recovery of Europe*, p. 147.
88. Marjolin, *Memoirs*, p. 200.
89. Urwin, *Community of Europe*, p. 21.
90. Price, *Marshall Plan*, p. 234.
91. Price, *Marshall Plan*, p. 350.
92. Duigan and Gann, *The United States*, p. 39.
93. Mayne, *The Recovery of Europe*, p. 146.
94. Valery Giscard d'Estaing, "The Seeds of European Union: Can 1997 Match Initiatives of 1947 and 1957?" in the *International Herald Tribune*, May 28, 1997.
95. Duigan and Gann, *The United States*, p. 40.
96. Urwin, *Community of Europe*, p. 22; Price, *Marshall Plan*, p. 347.
97. Duchene, *Jean Monnet*, p. 185.
98. James, "National Sensitivities"; see also Duigan and Gann, *The United States*, p. 39.
99. George C. Marshall, commencement address, Harvard University, June 5, 1947.
100. Price, *Marshall Plan*, p. 347.
101. Price, *Marshall Plan*, p. 356 (my italics).

CHAPTER 2

The Marshall Plan, Britain, and European Security: Defense Integration or Coat-tail Diplomacy?

Jolyon Howorth

The Marshall Plan aimed to persuade the Europeans to take responsibility for the organization of their own affairs. This was as true in the security field as in that of economic recovery. There was a widespread assumption in the immediate post-War years, both in the United States and in Europe, that European integration must involve (and ideally be led by) Britain. Moreover, integration was perceived in the first instance as being a security project. Bevin's initial long-term aim in August 1945 was an Anglo-French alliance as the cornerstone of European security. Such a European security entity—firmly allied to the United States—appeared to have the blessing of the major political leaders in both Britain and France, as well as the overt approval and encouragement of establishment opinion in the United States. Several factors combined to kill the scheme off. First, officials in Whitehall insisted that European security integration would undermine the United Kingdom's special relationship with Washington, despite the fact that many U.S. analysts argued that a European security entity was not only possible but essential. Such views were voiced by liberal internationalists as well as by republican conservatives and even isolationists. But Britain was also increasingly reluctant to abandon the Commonwealth in favor of an inchoate European project. Thus was NATO born. Yet the original thinking foresaw a balanced "twin pillar" alliance, involving U.S. front-loading while the Europeans gradually assumed responsibility for their own defense and security. As the key element in any defensive system for continental Europe, France saw itself, not unreasonably, as a legitimate spokesperson for the Europeans. Paris also recognized that the United Kingdom was an essential part of any European security structure and accepted that Britain would play a leading role. Had there been a serious effort on the part of London and Paris to coordinate their respective *European* policy, the alliance could have evolved into an evenly balanced structure. The crucial element in the collapse of any potential European pillar between 1947 and 1949 was the gradual withdrawal of British support for the project. The United Kingdom could not bring itself to play the European role that history and geography had carved out for it. That tendency was finally reversed fifty years later in 1998.

In March 1997, France and Germany formally proposed to their European Union partners the merging of the WEU and the EU in order to give greater organizational coherence, political credibility and operational impact to Europe's emerging common foreign and security policy (CFSP). The reaction of the conservative government of John Major was one of outrage. Foreign secretary Malcolm Rifkind, denouncing this "betrayal" on the part of his EU partners, threatened to veto the Treaty of Amsterdam, due to be signed in June, if this proposal was not dropped. Only weeks later, Major was defeated and the Blair government came to power. Despite a public relations campaign to suggest that Tony Blair was going to adopt a radically different attitude toward Europe, "New Labour," on the issue of EU/WEU merger, hardly differed from the previous line adopted by "Old Tory." The answer was "No!" Why?

The public facade of the U.K. rationale concentrated on the somewhat disingenuous argument that a reinforced WEU would be wastefully replicating the work of National Alliance Treaty Organization (NATO) or even seeking to supersede the Alliance. This argument is disingenuous in that NATO itself, at its January 1994 summit, had called for the development of a European Security and Defence Identity (ESDI) and had devised the military structures—Combined Joint Task Forces (CJTF)—which would facilitate such a development. In a series of interviews conducted in the Ministry of Defence and in the Foreign and Commonwealth Office in May 1997, the author discovered a less public argument behind U.K. reluctance to entertain closer links between WEU and the EU. A meaningful or powerful European security entity, Whitehall sources argued, would encourage American isolationism and lead to the disintegration of NATO. The worm in the apple is identified as "caucusing." This is traditional NATO-speak for meetings at which only Europeans are present. If WEU and the EU merged, such meetings would become not only inevitable but also indispensable. For Whitehall, therefore, a properly institutionalized ESDI, especially if it involved the merger of WEU and the EU, represents the supreme danger. Europe, it seems, must be maintained in a state of permanent minority and discouraged from pursuing any course that might lead to the development of greater equality or balance between the two sides of the Atlantic. This I have called coat-tail diplomacy. In reality, it, too, is largely a rationale that allows the United Kingdom to continue to hold out against the development it fought shy of in 1948: genuine European security integration.

And yet, 'twere not ever thus. When George Marshall made his Harvard speech on June 5, 1947, the dominant thinking in establishment circles on both sides of the Atlantic was quite different. The Marshall Plan in and of itself was, of course, not initially a plan for security in the military or defensive sense. But those dimensions, as most analysts now recognize, were fully implicit both in the plan itself and in the thinking behind it, as well as in the organization which derived from it. After Russia's refusal to be associated with the Plan, the security dimension became critical. Many commentators at the time shared the view of the Royal Institute of International Affairs specialist R. G. Hawtrey, that Marshall aid "was not directly related to the needs of defense, but it cannot be dissociated from them" (Hawtrey 1949: 15). Allen Dulles, in his apologia for the Marshall Plan, makes it explicit in the final chapter on "The Marshall Plan and Foreign Policy," that the economic and the security dimensions of the scheme were two sides of the same coin (Dulles 1948).

A Vision of European Autonomy

Marshall's own words reinforce the notion that the United States was inviting—indeed encouraging—the Europeans to get their act together. "It is already evident that, before the United States government can proceed much further in its efforts to alleviate the situation and help start the European world on its way to recovery, there must be some agreement among the countries of Europe as to the requirements of the situation and the part those countries themselves will take in order to give proper effect to whatever action might be undertaken by this Government. *This is the business of the Europeans. The initiative, I think, must come from Europe*" (my stress) (Documents 1949: 10). What was true of economic recovery was equally true in the realm of security organization.

The most perceptive Americans were well aware that any U.S. attempt to impose hegemony (even if that were the game plan) could prove counterproductive. The influential editor of *Foreign Affairs*, Hamilton Fish Armstrong, put it succinctly in the July 1947 issue of the journal. Fully aware that the crusading rhetoric of the Truman doctrine speech had fueled the flames of ideological controversy, Armstrong asked: "What should the United States do in order that when Europe makes a choice of social philosophies, it will judge our ideas on their merits?" The answer, he insisted, was to offer U.S. assistance for Europe to reemerge as an independent actor: "If the European economy is gradually to be revived and restored, it must be helped to reconstruct the plant that in turn will enable it *to be independent of us and to compete with us*" (my stress). Armstrong went even further: "We must encourage not merely enterprises which will be mutually profitable to Europeans and to us, but also those which will be profitable to them and to third parties; for Europe will resist becoming the satellite of American capital and industry, even in order to live, and in broad terms it is not to our advantage that she should so become even if she would" (Armstrong 1947: 546). Dulles was equally explicit: "The recovery of Great Britain and of certain other west European countries, and their ability to pay their own way in the future, is tied in with their recovery as maritime nations. That recovery will spell increased competition for our own merchant marine. Here is a tangled issue which will require real statesmanship. We should face it boldly, for as we start to restore Europe, *we must recognise that we are building up competition for ourselves.* ... This dilemma is inherent in the entire Marshall Plan. The Plan presupposes that we desire to help restore a Europe which can and will compete with us in the world markets and for that very reason will be able to buy substantial amounts of our own products" (Dulles 1949: 93 (my stress)). A somewhat separate but parallel point was stressed by Henry Stimson: "As we take part in the rebuilding of Europe, we must remember that we are building world peace, not an American peace. ... Our cooperation with the free men of Europe must be founded on the basic principles of human dignity, and not on any theory that their way to freedom must be exactly the same as ours. We cannot ask that Europe be rebuilt in the American image" (Stimson 1947: 11–12). The most explicit apologists of the Marshall Plan were therefore also the most explicit in recognizing that European autonomy and self-sufficiency were not only the ultimate object of the exercise, but also the litmus test by which to judge its success.

In the subsequent wrangling over the precise balance of the Euro-American relationship, and in particular over the degree of genuine

European autonomy in both economic and security matters, these principles were, of course, to come under great strain. Realism did not simply take fright before such idealistic expressions of interdependence. But the fact remains that the entire diplomatic and institutional nexus stemming from the Marshall Plan, including the drafting of the Brussels Treaty, the establishment of the OEEC, and all that followed in their wake, was explicitly predicated on the belief that Europe should recover her autonomy. How does all this relate specifically to security?

Blueprints for a West European Bloc—and British Ambivalence

During the closing months of the War, blueprints for a West European security bloc had been developed in multiple centers—Norway, Holland, Belgium, France, and also London (Young 1984: 5). Virtually all these different projects attributed to the United Kingdom, usually in association with France, the responsibility for leading such a military alliance. At first, the British seemed keen. Certainly, in the immediate postwar years, Britain saw closer association with the continent as being essentially a military question (Young 1984: 7), while most continentals were already thinking in terms of economic and even political integration. One major exception at this point seems to have been Anthony Eden, whose writings and speeches spoke only of the Commonwealth and Empire and totally ignored Europe (Eden 1947). But both Attlee and Bevin were clearly in favor of greater European integration, even though Attlee at least was uncertain how far Britain could take the lead (Harris 1982: 314–15). Bevin's long-term aim, as expressed at a Franco-British summit in August 1945, was "extensive political, economic and military cooperation throughout Western Europe with an Anglo-French alliance as a cornerstone" (Young 1984: 14). However, throughout 1946, Franco-British differences (over the Levant and Germany) served to delay the signing of any such pact, and, in parallel, the United Kingdom found itself increasingly siding with the United States over the shape of the postwar world—particularly over German policy. The United Kingdom was especially keen to ensure that U.S. commitment to European security be made permanent through the four-power agreement on demilitarization and containment of Germany, which then-Secretary of State James Byrnes had proposed in mid-1946.

It was here that the first seeds of British doubts about the very wisdom of a European security capacity seem to emerge. Political leaders such as Attlee and Bevin, while genuinely keen to pursue the

European bloc idea, were nevertheless cautious—if only to the extent that they considered "Big Three" politics as an even higher priority. But it is important to recognize that, at this stage, they did not tend to see the "European option" and the "Big Three option" as contradictory or incompatible. Whitehall, however, did. Many officials in the Foreign and Commonwealth Office (FCO), Ministry of Defense (MOD), Treasury, and Department of Trade (DOT) warned in strident terms that Washington would perceive the European option as incompatible with the more global order that the United States was pursuing (Young 1984: 39). This was to become the crucial argument that underpinned coat-tail diplomacy. It is highly significant that the one major issue on which the drafts of the Franco-British Dunkirk Treaty of 1947 generated serious disagreement between Paris and London was the likely impact on the United States of too strong a commitment to Franco-British solidarity against Germany. Whereas the French wanted the treaty to guarantee against the mere threat of German aggression, the British wanted this watering down to a guarantee against the reality of direct aggression. In the event, a compromise was found that spoke of a "threat ... arising from the adoption by Germany of a policy of aggression" (Documents 1949: 5–8). Whitehall now for the first time openly expressed the fears that were still being voiced during interviews in May 1997: too strong a commitment on the part of the Europeans would lead to U.S. isolationism. While this argument was not entirely devoid of foundation, the reality was much more complex.

It is interesting to note that the Russian position on the Western bloc was by no means as rigid or even hostile as is often argued. Bevin obtained early assurances from both Molotov and Stalin that Moscow had no fundamental objections. However, Churchill's 1946–47 crusade in favor of European union was interpreted in Moscow as a hostile pact directed exclusively against the USSR (Galin: 47). As the Cold War took shape, this latter interpretation came to dominate. But, although in the earlier period Bevin had been keen not to upset Moscow, concerns about Russian reactions to a West European bloc shifted in focus. The question in 1947–48 became: Would the Soviets be more or less likely to attack Western Europe if the prevailing security entity were: (a) a West European bloc or (b) an Atlantic bloc? The answers were never clear.

Nevertheless, by the time the Dunkirk Treaty was signed in March 1947, Bevin (as opposed to his civil servants) was becoming much keener on promoting the European bloc. He initiated bilateral discussions with Belgium and Holland with a view to forging a West European alliance. By May 1947, with the Byrnes notion of a four-power agreement scuppered at the Moscow Council of Foreign Ministers (CFM) talks, Bevin—according to Young—believed that "since the Americans were predominant in the Western hemisphere and the Russians in Eastern Europe, Britain ought to look to her own security and begin to organise Western Europe with determination" (Young 1984: 60). The notion was even beginning to find favor with the military, who saw the advantages of conferring on the United Kingdom a deep-continental defensive perimeter. In other words, many of the objective foundations for a West European security system had begun to fall into place by the time Marshall made his speech. What was lacking was military equipment and hardware. When Bevin met Marshall later in 1947 to discuss the security dimensions of European cooperation, the U.S. Secretary of State specifically proposed to his British counterpart that the Europeans—including Britain—adopt the same approach on security as had been adopted for the economic aspects of recovery: form a strictly European alliance in the first instance and then discuss with Washington the requirements for additional U.S. support (Young 1984: 79).

Ernest Bevin: Closet European or Resolute Atlanticist?

In a recent general survey of "Britain and European Unity," John Young has outlined the parameters of a latent controversy over Ernest Bevin's real security intentions. While traditional historiography, including the work of Bevin's official biographer (Bullock 1983), has tended to dismiss his European policies as either lacking in substance or little more than a short-term flirtation or even a smokescreen for a more deeprooted Atlanticist ambition, recent work has tended to concur with the view of Bevin's first biographer, Francis Williams, who insisted on the reality of his "Third Force" vision. Historians as diverse as Avi Schlaim, Geoffrey Warner, Robert Holland, John Gaddis, Kenneth Morgan, and John Kent, as well as Young himself, have stressed the seriousness and relative sophistication of Bevin's European aspirations (Young 1993: 14–18). In 1946–48, Bevin developed his vision of a Western [European] Union "based on the Anglo-French *entente*, but including Belgium, the Netherlands, Luxemburg, Eire, Portugal and perhaps Italy as well" (Morgan 1984: 273). Moreover, there was, at this stage, no presupposition on his part that such a new European political grouping would automatically lead to an *Atlantic* alliance (Morgan 1984: 267). There was certainly no intention, either in the mind of Bevin or in that of Bidault, that "Western Union," however it developed, would become permanently subordinated to a hegemonic United States. John Gaddis cites a secret cabinet session in March 1948 whose conclusion was that the United Kingdom's "ultimate aim should be to attain a position in which the countries of Western Europe should be independent both of the United States and of the Soviet Union" (Gaddis 1985: 78). If Western Union led to a some sort of alliance with the United States, so much the better. But it was unequivocally something the Europeans were going to do for themselves anyway. John Kent and Michael Hogan have demonstrated that Bevin had in mind the creation of a tightly knit West European economic and security system with the potential for considerable autonomy from the United States—what Hogan has called "the Middle Kingdom." Moreover, this embryonic ESDI was to involve no small measure of supranationalism (Hogan 1987: 114–18). However, it is important to note here that these plans also involved attempts to integrate the Commonwealth into the European structure. Bevin in particular was convinced that the combination of Western Europe, the Mediterranean, the Middle East, and Africa would be an unassailable force in the world: "If we only pushed on and developed Africa, we could have [the] U.S. dependent on us and eating out of our hand in four or five years," he told Dalton in October 1948 (Gupta 1975: 305–6). It was, in large part, because of this chimeric distraction that Britain failed to treat Europe with the sense of priority or focus that it merited in these crucial years.

Although, at this time, the French were, if anything, keener than the British on precipitating an American alliance, neither Paris nor London believed that an Atlantic alliance would lead to a dependent Western Europe. Nor is there any serious evidence, as it was once asserted, that Bevin's espousal of European union was primarily a tactical ploy aimed at securing American commitment. On the contrary, both Bevin and Bidault believed in the eventual creation of a "strong, independent Western Europe, able to stand alone without American support" (Young 1984: 78)—even though it was equally assumed that the two sides of the Atlantic would remain firm partners. Between Summer 1947 and Spring 1948, Bevin pursued his European vision with energy and determination. According to Milward, he envisioned "a European customs union as not merely a desirable but a necessary basis for the western European defensive alliance which had assumed such high priority in his policy." Against him were ranged the "implacable opposition" of his economic ministers and the "almost unanimous opinion of civil servants" (Milward 1984: 235–36). Bevin rode roughshod over the petty objections and generally negative attitudes of his officials as well as protesting against the objective Gallophobia of the chiefs of staff. Above all, he insisted on pushing forward the embryonic military alliance between the

United Kingdom, France, and the Benelux countries. The spirit of the time was well expressed by Sir Harold Butler, minister at the Washington embassy: "The most significant change is the revival of the Western European will to live. … For that the Marshall Plan must be regarded as mainly responsible. It was not, however, the offer of further American aid which revived the drooping spirits of the Europeans. They had no reason to think that by themselves more billions of dollars could be more than a temporary palliative. What stirred them to action was the notion that, by working together, they could use this American grant to lay the foundations of a new European system. … It may safely be said that without the Marshall offer, the unitary movement in Europe would not have been launched" (Butler 1948: 609). A potentially autonomous European security entity appeared to have the blessing of the major political leaders in both Britain and France. Moreover, it appeared to have the overt approval and encouragement of establishment opinion in the United States.

The Brussels Treaty produced the bases for precisely such a security system. It is by no means coincidental that Brussels wrapped up in one general package a European cooperation program covering defense, security, trade, economics, social policy, and culture. In many ways, the Brussels Treaty, rather than the Coal and Steel Community, should be seen as the foundation stone of the European Union. By the spring of 1948, it was obvious to everybody that, in the words of James Reston, "the economic recovery of Europe and the military security of Western Europe were inseparable" (Reston 1948: 35). There were no illusions in Washington about the ongoing political implications of the Marshall Plan and the Brussels Treaty. As Stacy May, formerly of the Council of National Defence, made clear in April 1948: "No sober appraisal of the Program can afford to ignore its continuing implications. For the nations of Western Europe it means a commitment to collaborative action that must continue far beyond the restoration of the pre-war status quo. Carried to its logical conclusion, it calls for a degree of economic and perhaps of political unity in Europe that has never been attained in the past." And May went further still in concluding that "it is our continuing objective to help Europe attain such a degree of effective unification that she can hope to avoid the recurrence of war." If America could do that, May wrote, "we shall have advanced far on the road to political maturity" (May 1948: 458).

Nor was such a project viewed with trepidation in Europe. After the signature of the Brussels Treaty, both Bevin and Bidault seemed determined to convert the pact into the much discussed framework of

Western Union. There is no doubt that the escalation of the Cold War throughout the year raised new and more complex questions about what we might call, in shorthand, the "Brussels process." However, the questions being asked in most chancelleries were not those that appear to have exercised the officials in Whitehall (to do with U.S. nervousness about the rival claims of a European security entity, or to do with the prospect of resurgent U.S. isolationism). The new questions had to do with the nature of security relations between the emerging European bloc and the United States, and more specifically about the connection between that relationship and the United Nations global mandate—an issue to which I shall return. However, it is essential to recognize that, as distinct from the grand globalizing visions of leaders such as Bevin and Bidault (and de Gaulle), when it came down to the details, French and British officials had radically divergent agendas.

A case in point was the location of the mechanisms agreed for implementation of the Brussels Pact. The United Kingdom (supported by Holland) was insisting on the new security institutions being based in London. The French, not without logic, argued that the defense of continental Europe (which was presumably what was at stake) could not be organized from an offshore island. Although at one level this might seem like a petty difference reflecting little more than nationalistic motives, the difference is highly symbolic of the distinct ways in which the British and the French saw the military problem. It was rather like the discussion between the chicken and the pig over their respective attitudes toward bacon and egg as a breakfast dish: the one was merely involved, the other was fully committed. U.K. claims to be the nerve center of a European defense were rapidly revealed to be flawed when Attlee and the air and navy chiefs—citing the Dunkirk precedent—initially refused to agree to commit British troops to the defense of continental Europe. It was only after strong intervention from Montgomery and Bevin himself that such a commitment was made—in May 1948 (Young 1984: 90). Both De Gaulle and Bidault and others (Soustelle 1948) constantly argued that, while the United Kingdom was vital to the defense of Europe, it made little sense to centralize the planning for such a defense in London rather than in Paris (De Gaulle 1990. II). This issue is an early indicator of a significant difference of approach between London and Paris: the chicken and the pig!

In any case, the increasingly visible military weakness of the European powers was making the case for an Atlantic alliance more and more compelling. On this, the British were being less than transparent. Since mid-1947, the French had been pressing Washington for staff talks leading to a military alliance. In discussions with their French colleagues, the British supported this idea. Yet, while ostensibly talking to the French about ways and means of bringing in the Americans, the British were, at the same time, holding their own secret talks with the United States and Canada about a future alliance (Wall 1991: 134). Moreover, it seems clear that traditional Francophobia within the U.K. armed services was a factor in persuading the Americans to keep the French out of these preliminary talks as long as possible (Wall 1991: 134–35; Young 1984: 91–92). It was particularly hypocritical of the British to consider the French as being "soft on communism" when one of the U.K.'s negotiators in the Washington talks was a Soviet spy, Donald Maclean. Already, despite Bevin's repeated statements of commitment to a *European* security entity, the United Kingdom was demonstrating its inability to take that commitment beyond the level of rhetoric or hype. One of the reasons for this rather underhand behavior was that the British were becoming uneasy about the extent to which Washington had already begun to view the United Kingdom as little more than an integral part of its European policy. Both the Marshall Plan and the Brussels Pact fed into a growing U.S. approach that viewed the whole of Europe, including the United Kingdom, as a single undifferentiated unit.

Another stumbling block was the American pressure (backed by France) for a permanent body in Europe to manage Marshall aid. The French were just as convinced as the Americans that only a genuinely independent planning body (such as those being dreamed up by Jean Monnet for other purposes) could lead to a fully efficient economic recovery. The British, citing "sovereignty," insisted on intergovernmentalism. Thus it was that when OEEC was established, it was on intergovernmental bases. It should be noted that the British were not afraid of standing up to Washington on a fairly crucial strategic issue, which also risked fueling the flames of isolationism, when they felt so inclined. The real reason for Britain's Euroskepticism, as with other aspects of policy, had to do with an underlying British hostility to integration—as opposed to cooperation.

European Strength and American Isolationism

While there were (and evidently still are) numerous mandarins in Whitehall who believed that Washington would look down with disfavor on the prospect of European security autonomy, voices echoing those concerns from across the Atlantic are hard to discern. Typical of the U.S. view was the first serious assessment of the security situation, published by *Foreign Affairs* in April 1948. Under the title "How strong is Britain?," a rising young analyst called Bernard Brodie did not mince his words. Signaling for the first time to the foreign policy establishment that "the star which shone so brightly is now revealed as a nova in descent," Brodie made it clear that there was no way in which the United Kingdom could henceforth "maintain an adequate national defense." He noted with regret that the British defense establishment were at that time obsessed with the idea of compensating for British decline by creating an integrated "imperial defense system," a notion which Brodie dismissed as "a pipe dream." He conjectured that, if the United Kingdom was to attempt to build up an adequate national defense capability over the coming 10 to 15 years, it could only be done at the price of massive dependency on U.S. subsidies: "Such an enterprise might indeed be a good investment for the United States to make in its own national security, but it is not likely to prove politically acceptable." In other words, in the view of this rising defense analyst, U.S. underwriting of U.K. security requirements alone—never mind the rest of Europe—was unlikely to be acceptable. Brodie's conclusion was unequivocal: "The United Kingdom still enjoys the position of leadership ... among the countries of Western Europe. Her collaboration is therefore indispensable for the essential task of organising the democracies of Western Europe into some kind of unified security system. Taken together, these countries dispose of a population and fund of resources quite adequate to make them a real counterpoise to Soviet power. ... Historically, they have not demonstrated remarkable unity in their foreign and security policies, but the circumstances of today may warrant expectation of drastic change in those respects. If among those circumstances we can presuppose an American policy which follows in general the pattern laid down by the European Recovery Program as originally conceived, the prospects are good that economic viability and strategic cohesion in Western Europe can both be accomplished. From the military point of view, that would be a gain of fundamental importance. It would be absurdly wrong to assume that the Soviet Union is so strong and western Europe inherently so weak that Soviet armies could overrun the latter area at will" (Brodie 1948: 432–49). But these views were not just voiced by liberal internationalists. Ironically, republican conservatives and even isolationists—men like Taft and Hoover—argued with equal conviction that U.S. backing for European security should be proportionate to the degree of genuine European security integration that already existed (Hogan 1987: 385). John Gaddis has confirmed this mood, noting that both Acheson, on becoming Secretary of State in 1949, and his main intellectual advisor, George Kennan, still hoped to create a unified Europe able to stand on her own feet. As preparatory discussions took place on the nascent Atlantic Alliance, "there ensued ... the most thorough analysis yet carried out in Washington on the question of what the United States really wanted in Europe: an independent, self-reliant aggregation of power comprising as much of Europe as possible, or a sphere of influence closely linked to Washington. Most U.S. analysts appear to have favored the former. It was British reluctance to embrace Europe which ensured that what emerged was the latter (Gaddis 1985: 76–80). In the debates within the U.S. security establishment, articulation of the notion that a strong Europe would encourage the U.S. to withdraw into isolationism is extremely hard to detect.

To be sure, residual advocates of traditional isolationism were still vocal in the remoter parts of the American heartland—men such as Senator James Kem (Missouri), William Jenner (Indiana), and George Malone (Nevada). But by 1948, establishment opinion was swinging massively in favor of the United States assuming fully its historic responsibilities. This swing was already visible in the 1945 speech made by Senator Tom Connally during the Senate debate on ratification of the United Nations charter. In impassioned tones, he warned against any repeat of the isolationist errors of the past. But he need hardly have worried about the outcome. According to Robert A. Divine: "By June of 1945, the internationalists had created such overwhelming public support that approval of the United Nations charter was a certainty" (Divine 1967; Siracusa 1978: 102). Henry Stimson confirmed that isolationism was no longer even an option for the United States: "Americans must now understand that the United States has become, for better or worse, a wholly committed member of the world community. ... It is the first condition of effective foreign policy that this nation put away for ever any thought that America can again be an island unto herself. No private program and no public policy, in any sector of our national life, can now escape from the compelling fact that, if it is not framed with reference to the world, it is framed with perfect futility" (Stimson 1947: 11–12). Isolationism, by 1947, faced "a bipartisan alliance of liberal internationalists drawn from both political parties, from the major trade unions and from the multilateral bloc of capital-intensive firms and investment banks" (Hogan 1987: 381). The use of the "isolationist scarecrow" was, at best, disingenuous, at worst devious.

The Creation of NATO and Euro-American Balance

The Vandenberg Resolution, as well as the Senate Foreign Relations committee report on it, were explicit in stating that the aim of American support for the Brussels Pact was to promote "self-help" among the European signatories. The nature and status of the projected American connection transpires from the language of these documents, which was peppered with words such as "association" and "cooperation." Although there were those who could see already that a hypothetical NATO would probably involve U.S. hegemony through "a large military establishment with a large standing army" (Reston 1948: 38), the tenor of the debate in 1948 and 1949 suggested much more in the way of U.S. front-loading of European allies who would gradually be able to take on their own security (Eliot 1949: 645–48). Even after the Vandenberg resolution had passed Congress, progress was exceptionally slow on the creation of the Atlantic Alliance. This was due in large part to growing differences of perception in Paris, London, and Washington as to what the exercise was really all about. In these debates, the positions of Paris and Washington were based on a relatively lucid view of the strategic requirements of France and the United States. The British position, however, reflects the intrinsic ambivalence of the United Kingdom about the political implications of security integration per se. There is no doubt, as many analysts have demonstrated, that French negotiating skills were lacking in refinement. The French felt misunderstood, undervalued, marginalized, and panicky. Intelligence reports based on worst case scenarios predicted the Red Army could be in Bordeaux within weeks. Traditional French *self-perceptions* suggested that the rest of the world should take notice of France's point of view. Hence, the frequent incidents of bombast, hubris, and arrogance, which from time to time led to French threats to withdraw from the discussions—as if France were doing the U.S. a favor rather than the other way around! Two issues in particular highlight the differences. The first had to do with the U.S. preference for the careful negotiation of a lasting and long-term alliance, whereas the French priority was for immediate American delivery of military hardware. This difference of opinion is understandable and, with hindsight, relatively insignificant. More telling was the American perception of the strategic contours of European security, which initially concentrated more on the North, including Scandinavia. The French view prioritized central Europe and the Southern flank and saw the inclusion of Italy, as well as France's North African departments, as essential. The British oscillated between these two positions, at first siding with the

Americans, only to find Washington gradually shifting over to the French position. Indeed, the Atlantic Alliance, when it was eventually signed, corresponded almost entirely to the blueprint that Paris had laid down from the outset (Wall 1991: 146; Bozo 1991: p. 32–33). The United States considered France to be the bulwark of European defense and over 50 percent of all military aid to the NATO countries was earmarked for France. The fact that France eventually frittered away this advantage through its Indochina quagmire does not alter the underlying reality that, as the French had always argued, an integrated defense of Europe had to consider France as the cornerstone. Washington fully recognized that, but the United Kingdom refused to.

This leads to the central issue at the heart of the dilemma over European security integration. Throughout the negotiations, France had insisted on the alliance being seen as a reasonably balanced structure between Washington and the Brussels Pact countries. As the key element in any defensive system for continental Europe, and as a former great military power, the French saw themselves, not unreasonably, as legitimate spokespersons for the entire Brussels process. They also recognized that the United Kingdom was an essential part of any European security structure and accepted that Britain would play a leading role. Had the British also seen things in this light, and had there been a serious effort on the part of London and Paris to coordinate their respective European policy, there is reason to believe that the alliance could indeed have evolved into a more balanced structure. Certainly, French insistence on being part of NATO's executive command structure was an entirely reasonable proposal. The Brussels Pact was not intended—by Washington any more than by "Brussels"—to lead to a situation in which the United States effectively took over responsibility for the security of Europe. But without tight European coordination, particularly between the British and the French, the Brussels Pact risked being stillborn. Although, in October 1948, a strategic plan was adopted that, in theory, allowed the Brussels Pact countries to envisage a forward, Eastern defense of continental Europe, control of the Mediterranean and air superiority, everything depended on U.S. military supply. A command structure was established but, perhaps inevitably, the British and the French managed to quarrel over appointments. In particular, Montgomery's insistence on assuming the title of Commander-in-Chief of the forces of the Western Union, rather than "merely" Chairman of the Commanders-in-Chief Committee, was bitterly resented by his immediate subordinate, the French General de Lattre. American commentators understood the sensitivities involved. As George Fielding

Eliot remarked, "The security of France cannot be committed to the hands of a general representing a nation which, however powerful at sea and in the air, is not prepared to make a major and immediate contribution to the armies which must secure France from being invaded again" (Eliot 1949: 646). Whether or not, other things being equal, the Brussels process could have led to its initial goal of a balanced, two-pillar defensive structure with the United Kingdom and France playing an important commanding role in the generation of a European security entity, tied in to a nonhegemonic American alliance, must remain an open question. However, it did not. Several factors in particular conspired to ensure its failure.

Arguably the most critical factor was the withdrawal of British support for a European security order. As Sir Harold Butler, minister in the Washington embassy, had written in July 1948, one essential prerequisite for European union was "the whole-hearted participation of Britain." The problems of European recovery, and particularly the problem of Germany, argued Sir Harold, could only be solved "if Britain became an integral part of the European system. Mr. Bevin's vigorous lead in convening the 16 nations and in promoting the Brussels Treaty was therefore decisive. With British participation, the problem became soluble" (Butler 1948: 612). However, by late 1948, Bevin's enthusiasm had begun to be worn down by the entrenched anti-Europeanism of the Whitehall machine, and the widespread and highly atavistic little-Englandism of the Labour party had come back into its own. More crucially, another debate began to rage that pitted "Europeanists" against "Globalists," thereby securing the victory of "Atlanticists." During the discussions on the Brussels Pact, a number of British commentators argued that the creation of "regional pacts" would undermine the global security objectives of the United Nations. Examples of such critics were Lord Altrincham and L. S. Amery, former minister for the Colonies and Dominion affairs (Altrincham 1949). What these critics were in fact arguing, in this roundabout way, was that Britain should concentrate on the Commonwealth, which had a "global" span, rather than Europe, which ran the risk of being perceived as an anti-Soviet bloc. This line of argument was both disingenuous and destructive. It was disingenuous because its advocates knew full well that the alternative to Brussels was an Atlantic alliance, which would have no more relevance to the Commonwealth (apart from Canada) than would the Brussels Pact. It was destructive because it did provide ammunition, within the United States, to those who continued to believe in the global remit of the United Nations and who were thereby led to see predominantly regional security arrangements as profoundly destabilizing. Such a view was forcefully and consistently put forward by none other than the editor of *Foreign Affairs*, Hamilton Fish Armstrong. However indirectly, these arguments served to discredit the embryonic influence of the Brussels Pact and to argue the case for a global security arrangement, or, as second best, an Atlantic alliance. Brussels and the United Nations (or Brussels and NATO) were now increasingly being seen as contradictory rather than as complementary security projects.

In any case, by the spring of 1949, both the United States and Great Britain had begun to reassess their fundamental diplomatic objectives: "Although, at first, Bevin saw the Atlantic Pact as a way to strengthen Western Europe, the success of the American Alliance, alongside other factors, was to lead him away from closer European unity after 1949 towards a new vision, which catered more for British links to America and the Commonwealth" (Young 1984: 107). Similarly, "a historic shift in American policy was taking place away from the European continent and France in favour of the special relationship with Britain and the Commonwealth. ... The State Department had adopted a fundamental policy change, recognising finally that Great Britain could not be coaxed into joining Europe" (Wall 1991: 155). According to Hogan, "the British codified their policy towards Western Europe in two papers approved by the Cabinet in October [1948]. The papers explicitly rejected supranationalism in favour of the principle known generally as the 'point of no return.' This principle held that Britian could not be drawn into Europe beyond the point where it could extricate itself safely, or at the expense of its economic well-being, its commitments to the Commonwealth, and its position as the pivot in a North Atlantic system of overlapping blocs." But Hogan goes on to add that it was not so much this statement of what may well have been long-standing British policy that was remarkable. Rather, "it was the assumption that British diplomacy now had support in Washington" (Hogan 1987: 275). This dramatic reversal of priorities was poignantly assessed in January 1950 by the French statesman Paul Reynaud who pleaded with Washington to use all its influence to keep the European show on the road. He went so far as to suggest that the United States should use the threat of the withdrawal of Marshall Plan credits in order to force the Europeans to maintain the unitary momentum. And he particularly regretted the volte-face of the United Kingdom. "I am not one of those who accept Great Britain's present attitude. In a unified Europe, France and England together could balance Germany's economic power. ... No matter how difficult Britain's managed economy makes European economic union, the project must be pursued with determination. There can be no 'Europe' without a close understanding between France and England. America's contribution should be to help create this. If she brought the British and French together, and then encouraged them both to reach agreement with Germany for the creation of a great, single market, the other countries of Western Europe would inevitably follow the lead. Such a great and sustained effort to aid in the creation of a new Europe would be not only sound politics but a fresh claim to glory for the American people" (Reynaud 1950: 264). His regrets were echoed by Sir Duff Cooper, former conservative minister and recent British ambassador in Paris. Writing in October 1950 about the lost chances for genuine European integration along the lines suggested by the Brussels Pact, Cooper concluded with these bitter words: "Five years have passed and with them has passed also Britain's great and, it is to be feared, her last opportunity. Her present government has paid lip service to the idea of a united Europe, but those who have been striving for it, and believe it to be a practical ideal, have found to their bitter regret that, at every effort that has been made to advance along the hard road, it has been the representatives of His Majesty's Government who have blocked the way" (Cooper 1950: 4). Cooper added that the United Kingdom's recent refusal to participate in the ECSC was the worst example of this bad faith: "By her refusal, she has not only forfeited her right and her opportunity to lead Western Europe, but she has also gravely endangered the success of the scheme." But Reynaud and Duff Cooper were voices crying in the wilderness.

The European Defence Community: Last Chance for European Security?

There remained one last chance to produce the momentum that might have led to the European security entity that seemed within grasp at the time of the Marshall speech. The Korean War led directly to a four-year debate on German rearmament. I do not intend to revisit the tortured debates on the formation of a European defense force embracing German troops. The well-known story has been told and retold a dozen times. But in the welter of detail, a significant element has been insufficiently highlighted. In all the original proposals, the basic objective had been to create a workable European pillar. This was true of the Churchill proposal for a European army put to the Council of Europe in August 1950; of the original American plan, known as the NATO plan, modified by the Spofford compromise; and of the Pleven plan for the European Defence Community (EDC). It was this aspect of the entire scheme that finally won Eisenhower round to the French plan in preference to the NATO plan: "Europe cannot attain the towering material stature possible to its people's skills and spirit so long as it is divided by patchwork territorial fences. ... In the political fields, these barriers promote mistrust and suspicion. ... But with unity achieved, Europe could build adequate security. ... The establishment of a workable European federation would go far to create confidence among people everywhere that Europe was doing its full and vital share. ... I tell you that joining Europe together is the key to the whole question" (Fursdon 1980: 119). There was no doubt at that stage that Eisenhower believed the United Kingdom should be an integral part of the scheme. What threw a spanner into the painfully elaborated negotiations that had eventually seen everybody converge on the Pleven proposal was the U.K. government's refusal to be part of it. On November 28, 1951, Anthony Eden, the new foreign secretary, made it clear that Britain would not join. Whatever one might think of the French proposals, or of subsequent French shilly-shallying over the EDC, it was this blanket refusal by the United Kingdom that effectively scuppered the entire project. Paul Reynaud immediately drew the inevitable conclusion: "If Britain refuses to join ... what a powerful argument for the European Army's opponents in Parliaments. ... Britain's refusal to be part would, I am certain, lead the French parliament to reject the European army, and no-one, in their heart of hearts, would blame it" (Fursdon 129). Subsequently, the French even modified their proposals in order to try to bring the United Kingdom—along with the Commonwealth—back into the EDC. Acheson put pressure on the British to accept (Fursdon 133). But they would not. Instead, they offered full support—from outside. The Europeans were even prepared to try to live with this, but the Labor Party then issued a statement to the effect that, if they were ever returned to power, they would not guarantee to be supportive because of their rejection of German rearmament. With collaborators like this, who needs allies?

It is not my intention to claim that the United Kingdom alone prevented the European pillar from developing. The EDC treaty was eventually signed and prospects for a viable force were not totally bleak, even with the U.K. opt-out. The French parliamentary vote was, at the end of the day, the deciding factor. But that vote should not be interpreted, as it so often has been, as a vote against a European security entity.

One other element is also often overlooked. The debate in France was not about a European defense as opposed to national independence. General de Gaulle's opposition to the EDC, which proved fatal to the scheme, was not based fundamentally on a predilection for something called "indépendancégrandeur." It was based on considerations of military effectiveness and was in fact very similar to the objections that had originally been raised by the Americans during the Spofford period. Jean Monnet had deliberately excluded all military men from the team, which stitched the plan together precisely because it was first and foremost a political project. De Gaulle simply did not think it would work militarily. His own proposals for a European army, with distinct national units, nevertheless called for a high degree of integration. For one thing, de Gaulle insisted that the United Kingdom must be part of the scheme. Second, he argued that "from the perspective of European defence, it is of the highest practical necessity that the countries involved should adopt the same strategic plans and should place in common all those resources which can be merged without depriving the various armies of their body and soul: infrastructure—that is to say, airports, ports and communications systems; the structure of combat units; weapons systems; the production of certain materials; command structures; joint general staffs etc., every means of cooperation which would allow for the ideal association of nations in a confederation of states" (De Gaulle 1990 II: 590).

European states all understood and accepted the need for a European Security Pillar. The United States urgently pressed these same states to create one. It was not for want of trying that the project floundered. It was not a simple task. There were many important differences of opinion within and among the European nations as to how such a security structure could be configured. But at the end of the day, the absolutely crucial factor in ensuring that it did not happen was that the United Kingdom could not bring itself to play the European role that history and geography had carved out for her. The U.K. preferred clinging onto America's coat-tails. As these lines were being written (March 1998), U.S. and British warships were steaming into the Persian Gulf to threaten Saddam Hussein with military retribution. Meanwhile, France (vociferously) and most other EU countries (more discreetly) were urging a concerted European diplomatic approach. Britain, under Tony Blair, held the presidency of the European Union. But when called upon to choose between an American "solution" and a European one, the United Kingdom, once again, had no hesitation in opting for the former. Why?

References

Altrincham, Lord (1949), "The British Commonwealth and Western Union," *Foreign Affairs*, 27/4.

Armstrong, H. F. (1947), "Europe Revisited," *Foreign Affairs*, 25/4.

Bozo, F. (1996), *Deux Stratégies pour l'Europe: De Gaulle, les Etats Unis et l'Alliance Atlantique*, Paris, Plon.

Brodie, B. (1948), "How Strong is Britain?" *Foreign Affairs*, 26/3.

Bullock, A. L. C. (1983), *Ernest Bevin: Foreign Secretary 1945–51*, New York, Norton.

Butler, H. (1948), "A New World Takes Shape," *Foreign Affairs*, 26/4.

Cooper, D. (1950), "The Plough and the Furrow," *Foreign Affairs*, 29/1.

De Gaulle, C. (1990), *Discours et Messages*, Paris, Plon.

Divine, R. A. (1967), *Second Chance*, New York, Oxford University Press.

Documents (1949), *Documents on European Recovery and Defence: March 1947–April 1949*, London, RIIA.

Dulles, A. W. (1948), *The Marshall Plan*, new edition, Oxford Berg 1993

Eden, A. (1947), "Britain and the Modern World," *Foreign Affairs*, 26/1.

Eliot, G. F. (1949), "Military Organisation under the Atlantic Pact," *Foreign Affairs*, 27/4.

Fursdon, E. (1980), *The European Defence Community: A History*, London, Macmillan.

Gaddis, J. L. (1985),"The US and the question of a sphere of influence in Europe," in O. Riste (ed.), *Western Security: The Formative Years*, Oslo, Universitetsvorlaget.

Galin, A. (1947), "Europe split or united?" *Foreign Affairs*, 25/3.

Gupta, P. S. (1975), *Imperialism and the British Labour Movement 1914–1964*, London, Macmillan.

Harris, K. (1982), *Attlee*, London, Weidenfeld and Nicholson.

Hawtrey, R. G. (1949), *Western European Union: Implications for the UK*, London, RIIA.

Hogan, M. J. (1987), *The Marshall Plan: America, Britain and the Reconstruction of Western Europe 1947–52*, Cambridge University Press.

May, S. (1948), "Measuring the Marshall Plan," *Foreign Affairs*, 26/3.

Milward, A. S. (1984), *The Reconstruction of Western Europe 1945–51*, London, Methuen.

Morgan, K.O., *Labour in Power 1945–1951*, Oxford, Clarendon.

Reston, J. (1948), "Prospects for Stability in our Foreign Policy," *Foreign Affairs*, 27/1.

Reynaud, P. (1950), "The Unifying Force for Europe," *Foreign Affairs*, 28/2.

Siracusa, J. M.(1978), *The American Diplomatic Revolution: A Documentary History of the Cold War 1941–1947*

Soustelle, J. (1948), "France, Europe and Peace," *Foreign Affairs*, 26/3.

Stimson, H. L. (1947), "The Challenge to Americans," *Foreign Affairs*, 26/1.

Wall, I. (1991), *The US and the Making of Post-War France 1945–54*, Cambridge University Press

Young, J. W. (1984), *Britain, France and the Unity of Europe*, Leicester University Press

N14
N44
H56
F35
93—116
61—90
US1

CHAPTER 3

Cooperation and Community in Europe: What the Marshall Plan Proposed, NATO Disposed

Robert Latham

In this age of humanitarian intervention and hopeful goals of European integration, the Marshall Plan is often held out as a historical beacon and symbol of international activism and engagement. This view fails to note that while the U.S. state invested funds and directly intervened in the political economies of European states and societies, it did so through supranational structures that were self-consciously designed to be non-political and temporary. The avoidance of thick political institutions was made possible by a heavy emphasis on private sector involvement in aid flows and management. The Marshall Plan itself, in this constrained form, could only as a result put integration on the agenda. The decisive forces shaping the long-term legacy of the Marshall Plan, that is, the emergence of the European Community—came from the realm of security, bearing on the formation of NATO.

O nce again the United States and Europe are caught up in a complicated mix of war, social reconstruction, and the hopeful goals of regional integration. Perhaps ironically, the very institutions that were a product of reconstruction and the pursuit of integration after World War II (the European Union and the National Alliance Treaty Organization) are central players today in the Balkans.

The recent military intervention of NATO in the Balkans—and the pursuit of postconflict reconstruction and integration especially through the EU—is lauded by some as a new post–Cold War departure in activism for the West. But I want to point out some historical reasons why we should be less hopeful about the possibility of a renaissance of engagement by the West. Indeed, we should recall that what makes the intervention in Kosovo stand out as exceptional, against the background of the past decade, is the rather poor record of the West in establishing serious commitments to the political and social development and security of countries not only in southeastern Europe but around the world that might help avoid crises such as Bosnia, Kosovo, and Rwanda.

In this context it is to be expected that the Marshall Plan would be held out as a sort of historical beacon and symbol for the type of international activism and engagement it takes to help fix problems around the world. We can take the establishment of the Marshall Plan—as well as the construction of NATO and the EU—as an instance of international activism on the part of the West. But we need also to consider how this activism was practiced and with what implications for the politics of the period. I will argue in this chapter that there was a minimal approach to aid and reconstruction shaping the formation of the Marshall Plan back in the 1940s. And this pattern had important implications for the relationship between the Marshall Plan and the construction of the European Community.

To take these claims seriously, we need to keep in mind three factors. In the first place, we cannot forget, as pointed out above and in other chapters in this volume, that the Marshall Plan was tied up in the complicated knot of security in Europe. Second, while the 1940s looks like a sort of "big bang" of international order building, in reality the United States was spending a lot of effort in figuring out ways to avoid committing itself around the world in all sorts of ways. Despite the activism we associate with the United States in Europe, that region was no exception. It is arguable that all the effort to minimize its formal, long-term commitments led the United States to quite a bit of intervention in the politics of Western European states.

Third, despite all the rhetoric of regional integration floating around at the time, Western European states were as self-regarding at mid-century as any other national state. But I would not want to emphasize this factor over the other two. While it may be tempting to look to the protection of each country's sovereignty as the reason why the Marshall Plan was limited in its construction, it's only a piece of the puzzle. Indeed, there were some quite significant countervailing trends operating at the time. The Counterpart system of funds, for example, enacted in a way that allowed considerable U.S. control over the expenditures of each participating country, was an incredible infringement on sovereignty. We also should not forget that Germany was still occupied.

The broader point is that it was the fateful mix of these three factors that would guarantee that the Marshall Plan itself could only, as my title suggests, put integration on the agenda. The decisive forces shaping the long-term legacy of the Marshall Plan—that is, the emergence of the European Community—came from the realm of security, bearing on the formation of NATO.

Reconstruction, Liberal Style

I will start with some basic background about how the Marshall Plan was designed. This will help illustrate how the United States attempted to minimize its engagements in Europe.

The logic behind the U.S. support for European integration can be viewed as an effort to build strength in Western Europe directly through relations of international economic exchange. A "coordinated European economy," as Acheson put it,[1] was thought to be able to increase simultaneously political, economic, and, ultimately, military strength in Europe as well as minimize the necessity of the U.S. state having to administer directly international economic processes in Western Europe. It would also limit some of the historic excesses of European nationalism and mediate the differences among European sovereign states over issues such as the incorporation of Germany into the West.[2] This, after all, was the significance of linking economic integration with political community, as Ernst Haas discussed in a seminal 1961 article on integration. For him, shifting loyalties and expectations to new common institutions could yield a political community where "there is likelihood of internal peaceful change in a setting of contending groups with mutually antagonistic claims."[3]

In its deliberations on the European Recovery Program (ERP), Congress had generally expressed a strong interest in seeing the program tied to a European commitment to integration. But Congress was only willing to offer encouragement for integration in the text of ERP legislation. It refused to make integration an outright requisite for extending aid, which might have required it to construct authoritative and broad-scoped external state organs for this purpose.[4] Legislators such as Republican Senator Taft, whose interests revolved around the internal state, and were thereby suspicious of any external state-building, resisted approving an ERP that would imply a permanent U.S. organizational commitment to Western Europe.[5] This resistance led policy makers to construct an external state program that can be described as **autoextinguishing**. That is, by fostering "self-help" and "mutual aid" for an integrating Europe, the necessity of externally deployed organs and aid would disappear, and the program would extinguish. Its very success would mean its demise. Thus, if minimalization was an important strategic logic of liberal order-building, then auto-extinguishment was an important tactic. It differed from the basic liberal faith in a self-regulating international economic system in that the necessity of significant involvement and regulation was acknowledged by most leaders—albeit to achieve conditions that ultimately were expected to obviate that necessity.

The reasonableness of auto-extinguishment was reinforced by the judgment of policy makers such as Kennan that the economic, and political, problems in Europe were temporary, and perhaps even only a matter of "bottlenecks."[6] Despite reservations in Congress regarding some European state planning projects, the program was designed to work through individual European governments, and, thus, remained consistent with the preservation of their relative autonomy. By sharing authority over functions such as the distribution of resources (e.g., counterpart funds) with European states, the United States had located a formula that appeared to integrate its hegemonic center with the liberal uniaxis in Europe in a manner that would fulfill the imperatives of auto-extinguishment (since European states were expected to become productive economic agents without the disciplining of the U.S. state).

Another dimension of auto-extinguishment—and minimalization more generally—was the reliance on private interests in the operation of the ERP, rather than just state organs (especially U.S. ones).[7] At its simplest, this meant that the ERP would rely on private channels for the procurement of resources rather than governments.[8] Far more complex was the participation of business representatives, especially of multinational corporations (MNCs), in "a host of private advisory committees," which had important policy-making functions.[9] They were also engaged in explicit campaigns to strengthen national economies and international exchange through efforts such as the Anglo-American Council on Productivity, composed of industry and labor representatives from both the United States and Britain.[10] Most important of all, the Economic Cooperation Agency (ECA), the administrative organ of the ERP, was set up as a temporary independent agency, rather than as a part of the State Department, which, Congress feared, would have made a far more institutionalized addition to the U.S. state. To top it off, the president of the Studebaker Corporation, Paul G. Hoffman, was called on to head the agency, instead of Undersecretary of State William Clayton and even Dean Acheson, who at that time had temporarily left public service.

Senator Vandenberg, who was a key player in the design and passage of Marshall Plan legislation, understood exactly what was at stake in building an ERP that was severely limited as an organ for coordinating and administering economic relations—if not also for achieving other political ends—on a more long-standing and broad-scoped basis. He boasted to a constituent that, in the ECA, Congress succeeded in finding "the most non-political organization which has ever been put together on a government project."[11] The point was to avoid an "international WPA," and the key to doing so was the program's administrative character.[12] As Vandenberg had put it at the beginning of 1948:

> The question of finding a satisfactory administrative formula is perhaps the biggest single conundrum which the Senate Foreign Relations Committee confronts. We all pretty well agree as to our general objective—namely, that the *business* side of this essentially *business* enterprise shall be under the effective control of adequate business brains which shall be specially recruited for the purpose. At the same time we all must agree that ERP virtually becomes the "foreign policy" of the Government in Western Europe for the next four years. Therefore, our "business administration" of ERP has got to be in successful liaison with the Secretary of State and the President wherever foreign policy decisions are involved. We cannot have "two Secretaries of State [author's italics]."[13]

As it turned out, the ERP did not become the "foreign policy" of the United States in Western Europe—the militarization of NSC-68 eclipsed it by 1950. What Vandenberg and other policy makers did not grasp in 1948 was that by limiting the construction of U.S. state organs operating overseas, they were limiting their options in responding to future tensions and weaknesses in Western Europe. The intractability of states regarding the issues of integration, for example, meant there was little chance of any real headway being made through the ERP. In effect, the minimal character of the ERP and its ECA could not contend with the political and economic issues in Europe, which included, besides the demanding question of Germany, the control of exchange rates. In addition, European states not only resisted the U.S. model of integration that was being pushed, but each state also had its own approach to integration. The reliance on private power left a limited range of political and economic institutional instruments directly in the hands of the U.S. state.

Turning to private power in the international realm in order to help set the terms of relations, however, was consistent with the general effort to construct a liberal order in the context of a plurality of

(Western European) states and other actors such as MNCs. The space opened for states and corporations in the ERP accorded with the principles of self-determination, liberal rights, and economic exchange. But this left a provisional ERP little leverage and room for maneuver.[14] As we shall see, the limited character of the institutional repertoire increased the salience of strategic-military relations as an available—and as it turned out propitious—basis for continuing the liberal order construction process.

Economics and Security

We need to probe deeper into the mix of economy and security to get at the full implications of the limits placed on the institutionalization of the Marshall Plan. To start, despite its association with the increasing salience of strategic concerns, the hard line that beginning to emerge in the Truman administration in 1946 did not represent a militarization of American foreign policy or of relations with Western Europe. Rather, the growing confrontation between the United States and the Soviet Union was not initially accompanied by the militarization of U.S. foreign policy or of the international relations of states in the West. Such militarization would emerge only at the end of the 1940s.

A strong indicator of the nonmilitarized dimensions of American foreign policy is the conscious commitment held until 1949 to employ economic means as the basis of containment.[15] Even as late as April 1949 most policy makers still agreed that "economic recovery must not be sacrificed to rearmament and must continue to be given a clear priority." In what has come to be known as "economic security," the United States was able to use economic aid as diplomatic leverage, while simultaneously aiding recovery on the national and international economic levels. Both functions, in turn, dovetailed with the containment goal of helping European states and societies resist the internal and external push and pull of the Soviet Union.[16] Economic security, for the most part, was based on the notion that economic recovery could generate political stability and undermine internal communist challenges and external Soviet pressures. This, of course, is the positive version of economic security, and its application was most notably associated with the ERP. The negative (or punitive) version of economic security stressed sanctions and was applied notably in Eastern Europe.[17]

Of course, the association of economics and security in the context of order-making is long-standing. Nineteenth-century Cobdenite propositions to the effect that "trade leads to peace" shaped the views of important U.S. policy makers, including wartime Secretary of State Cordell Hull, who decided as a congressman—as early as World War I—that "unhampered trade dovetailed with peace; high tariffs, trade barriers, and unfair competition, with war."[18] Wartime planners such as Hull and others expected to exploit this "law" in the post–World War II world. As one 1944 State Department memo put it:

> The development of sound international economic relations is closely related to the problem of security. The establishment of a system of international trade which would make it possible for each country to have greater access to world markets and resources would reduce incentives to military aggression and provide a firm basis for political cooperation.[19]

Before relations with the Soviets became confrontational, it was expected that those "sound relations" would compel the Soviet Union to be at peace along with the other united nations. As relations became increasingly confrontational, this inclusive logic to the application of economic security began to fade away. The exclusive logic associated with containment became prominent. Economic over military means could be emphasized in the securing of states along the liberal uniaxis.[20] The strategic power of U.S. economic predominance could be applied to contend with Soviet political challenges in a manner that appeared to be consistent with the building of a liberal order. Since policy makers had determined there was no immediate threat of war with the Soviet Union, this was a feasible course. Indeed, the whole logic of economic security was predicated on the notion that the investment was sound—one does not furnish a house about to be bulldozed.

A further advantage to this formula for containment was that it was more likely to appeal to members of Congress who advocated a probusiness approach to external affairs. In effect, by joining security and economy in efforts such as the ERP, the Truman administration was able to gain support for both the politicostrategic and economic dimensions of order-building.[21]

As this last point suggests, economic security did double duty by both containing Soviet pressures and building stable economic conditions and relations at the national and international levels. In doing so, economic security reinforced the economic importance of Western European states and societies.[22]

The resources made available to Western European states under economic security programs were designed to achieve political stability and allow states to work out their own social and economic agendas (within limits, of course). While this outcome enhanced collective self-determination, it also supported representative democratic practices by creating space for the demands of the democratic left. In Western Europe, economic security was also viewed by U.S. policy makers as a way to enhance "personal freedom and social equality."[23] In other words, creating a stable environment of economic growth would open up room for individuals and groups not only to survive, but to pursue their interests in the political as well as the economic spheres. It was thought that it would equally undermine those interests—such as European Communist parties—that sought to destroy such liberty enhancing conditions.

That there was great conceptual consistency between the strategy of economic security and the attempt to rebuild international order does not mean that tensions associated with the implementation of economic security did not arise. Western European states, as mentioned above, clearly objected to the potential for intervention inherent in economic security programs. Such objections plagued much of the history of the ERP. While Western European states may have wanted access to U.S. economic resources deployed in their region, they did not necessarily want the political intervention that accompanied dependence on a preponderant U.S. state.

U.S. policy makers discovered that the way to minimize such tensions was to limit the political dimension of the program. During the war, planners believed that the conjunction of political and economic concerns could be minimized in the classic liberal sense of separation: techno-market logics and expertise would triumph over sectarian, power interests. In a Senate hearing on Bretton Woods, Secretary of the Treasury Henry Morgenthau, Jr. claimed that "These are to be financial institutions run by financial people, financial experts, and the needs in a financial way of a country are to be taken care of wholly independent of the political connection."[24]

The application of economic security was increasingly focused on the technologies of ostensibly apolitical economic growth.[25] Constricting economic security this way served triple duty. First, states that were protective of their autonomy were willing to tolerate an increase in U.S. intervention along minimal lines. Second, this approach made it easier for Congress to accept a new U.S. interventionist role, because it at least would be expressly limited. Third, this approach provided a degree of closure for the fragile and vulnerable political relations emerging in the immediate postwar years. Production increases were emphasized over the political challenges of redistribution. Such "productionist" closure, as Charles Maier points out, not only headed off political challenges by groups associated with the democratic left such as unions, it also insured that such groups would not be able to abuse easily the opportunities economic growth opened up for them.[26]

Strategy and the Making of the European Recovery Program

Containing the ERP along the lines described above should not blind us to the very strategic aims to which the program was applied. These aims were quite consistent, from a congressional perspective, with the Marshall Plan's institutional constriction in that its purposes would thereby also be limited to the requirements of stability and security, rather than remain open to any political aims U.S. planners and Western European participants might themselves define. Indeed, as the Truman administration's effort to get congressional approval for the ERP discussed above shows, it was necessary to emphasize the strategic dimensions of the ERP, rather than the benefits ERP would be able to offer the U.S. economy once the program helped Europe to achieve economic recovery.[27]

The strategic ramifications of the ERP cut across a number of dimensions: orienting Western European governments and electorates toward the United States and the West in general (in part by avoiding the pull of markets in the East); removing the presence of Communists in the Italian and French governments; aiding the British ability to maintain their international commitments;[28] and increasing the incentive of, above all, the French to accept the integration of Germany into the fabric of Western European economic recovery.[29] Although neither integration nor a solution to the incorporation of Germany on a political level would be achieved, the Marshall Plan did force the Soviet Union to a clearly externalized position by virtue of its refusal to participate. I n addition, the consolidation to be achieved through the Marshall Plan made the continuation of East-West trade more palatable to U.S. policy makers by reducing the threat of a drift toward the East. And while the Marshall Plan further distanced the Soviet Union from the West and contributed to a stronger Soviet grip on Eastern Europe (as some policy makers had anticipated), the immediate formation of fixed blocs was avoided. With the continuation and even encouragement under the Marshall Plan of East-West trade, the possibility—however dim it was—of eventually bringing Eastern Europe into the liberal order was at least not completely ruled out.[30] As an initial (August 1948) draft of the most comprehensive statement of U.S. policy prior to NSC-68 put it:

> By forcing the Russians either to permit the [Soviet] satellite countries to enter into a relationship of economic collaboration with the west of Europe which would inevitably have strengthened east-west bonds and weakened the exclusive orientation of these countries toward Russia or to force them to remain outside this structure of collaboration at heavy economic sacrifice to themselves, we placed a severe strain on the relations between Moscow and the satellite countries and undoubtedly made more awkward and difficult maintenance by Moscow of its exclusive authority in the satellite capitals. ... The disaffection of Tito, to which the strain caused by the ERP problem undoubtedly contributed in some measure, has clearly demonstrated that it is possible for stresses in the Soviet-satellite relations to lead to a real weakening and disruption of the Russian domination.[31]

But the economic security pursued in the Marshall Plan embodied strategic considerations that extended beyond political-economic tactics.[32] Even if, as Milward puts it, the goals of the Marshall Plan were mostly political while the means were economic,[33] there were military dimensions embodied in the Marshall Plan as well. Even in its earliest conceptualization within the Truman administration, policy makers tied military-industrial capacity, strategic materials and manpower concerns into the politicostrategic goals of a recovery program in Europe. The "Special 'Ad Hoc' Coordinating Committee" claimed that:

> It is important to maintain in friendly hands areas which contain or protect sources of metals, oil and other national resources, which contain strategic objectives, or areas strategically located, which contain a substantial industrial potential, which possess manpower and organized military forces in important quantities, or which for political or psychological reasons enable the U.S. to exert a greater influence for world stability, security and peace.[34]

Provisions for the control of strategic resources were ultimately incorporated in Marshall Plan legislation. During the deliberations over the Marshall Plan in Congress, legislators as well as critical commentators, such as Henry Wallace and Bernard Baruch, observed that the commitment to economic security implied a commitment to military security. It was understood that once the United States was involved in the former, it had somehow taken responsibility for the region in all its strategic dimensions.[35]

The military aspects of the Marshall Plan, in practice, never formally extended beyond the provisions for strategic materials. But the introduction of military-strategic considerations into early policy formation, as well as congressional deliberations, reveals that the endeavor to limit the specific application of containment to the economic realm was, in the least, questionable. There was no specified limit to the containment doctrine itself. Military ramifications were not ruled out by the specifics of the doctrine itself. Moreover, the minimal character of the ECA as an external state organ meant that there would be little difficulty in shifting the emphasis in containment from the economic to the military. That is, the minimum invested institutionally via the ECA could only facilitate its transformation into the Mutual Security Agency.

The ERP and Military Security

In 1949, the perceived need to move substantially beyond economic measures took shape as the U.S. commitment to the North Atlantic Treaty (NAT) and the Mutual Defense Assistance Program (MDAP) provided 1.5 billion dollars in military aid to Western Europe. The latter has been described by historian Timothy Smith as "a significant step in the shift from an economic to a military emphasis in postwar United States foreign policy."[36] By 1950, military security would become the predominant form of containment in Western Europe. NATO evolved in January of that year into a formal military organization as the North Atlantic Treaty Organization. In general, European relations would be significantly militarized along the lines suggested in NSC-68. The remainder of this chapter will be dedicated to tracing the forces associated with integration and the Marshall Plan propelling this transformation.

We can begin by noting that Henry Wallace and Bernard Baruch were correct about economic commitments leading to military ones. By 1948–49, it was becoming clear to leading U.S. policy makers such as Acheson that "economic measures alone ... [were] not enough" to achieve the recovery program associated with economic containment. Undersecretary of State Lovett agreed in 1948 that support "in the security and military field" was necessary in order not to undermine the ERP. What Lovett saw as being at stake in such aid was "the psychological effect rather than the intrinsic military value."[37] In other words, Western European states and societies needed to obtain a higher level of strategic-military security in order to supplement the effort in the economic security program, to bolster politicostrategic security and to achieve a confident environment for investment. This view was rein-forced by a Central Intelligence Agency (CIA) report in early 1949 that argued that the benefit of military assistance "would be primarily psychological," in that "the will to resist is unlikely to outrun the visible means of resistance."[38]

When he learned of the intention to construct a formal North Atlantic alliance at the start of 1949, Vandenberg, in response to a constituent, had to grapple with the tensions in the move from economic to military security:

> There is no doubt about the fact that it is a "calculated risk" for us to even partially arm the countries of Western Europe. It also very much a "calcu-lated risk" if we do not. One risk will have to be weighed against the other. You suggest that it will be a safe thing to do "when the economic stability of these countries shall have improved." The basic question we have to settle is whether "economic stability" can precede the creation of a greater sense of physical security. I am inclined to think that "physical security" is a prerequisite to the kind of long-range economic planning which Western Europe requires. The fact remains that the problem is fraught with many hazardous imponderables.[39]

What is being questioned is not whether the effort to achieve "economic stability" must precede or be preceded by military security, but whether the endpoint of stabilization per se must be reached. Vandenberg assumes an initial commitment to economic stabilization. Indeed, for him it is the very problem of economic stabilization that raises the issue of military security.

In Western Europe, the development of a military containment program was situated within the context of economic security. The National Security Council (NSC) had insisted in mid-1948 that mili-tary assistance should be "properly integrated with the ECA."[40] While this may not have come to full fruition, by the first half of 1949, the United States did begin to coordinate economic and military policy. And the link between economic and military containment was not manifest only in the military assistance program and the North Atlantic Treaty (NATO) commitment. The very unity that the Marshall Plan was designed to generate was supposed to increase productivity to a level sufficient for a Western European rearmament that would not sacrifice economic recovery.[41]

At first glance, the emergence of military security within the context of economic containment merely appears to fit well with the initial strategy of developing strength in Western Europe. It was one more dimension—albeit a supplementary one—on which to construct strength. In another respect, however, the economic security program itself can be viewed as the very force that made military security appear to be necessary. The priority given to the economic security program made a U.S. commitment to underwrite military security for Western Europe appear compelling. U.S. policy makers believed that Western European states themselves would not be willing to compromise their economic recovery efforts by diverting resources to defense. Paul Nitze, the main author of NSC-68, and Kennan's replacement as head of the Policy Planning Staff, was convinced in 1949 that Western Europe feared that a compromise of economic recovery would decrease the popularity of existing governments.[42] (His fears appeared to be well grounded in that the government of French Prime Minister Robert Schuman fell in mid-1948 over the issue of increasing the military budget.) Given the minimal nature of the ERP program, there was little that could be done within the institutional frame of economic security to overcome this compromise. The inevitable conclusion from the perspective of Nitze is the kind of "substantial increase in military assistance programs" called for in NSC-68.

Thus, rather than viewing the ERP as having failed to provide security through economic containment, it might be more accurate to recognize that the very commitment to economic security was never far from—and even opened the way up for—a growing commitment to the application of military security in Europe, as Vandenberg had realized. This was why Vandenberg felt he was confronted with "many hazardous imponderables." Indeed, given that the underlying logic of security in Europe was the containment doctrine, there was no specified institutional frame for keeping it limited to economic means. A U.S. commitment to contain communism in Europe could not in practice be circumscribed to the economic sphere. This was very clearly articulated by the State Department just prior to the signing of the NATO:

The North Atlantic Pact is a necessary complement to the broad economic coordination now proceeding under the European Recovery Program. [t]he Pact and the ERP are both essential to the attainment of a peaceful, prosperous, and stable world. The economic recovery of Europe, the goal of the ERP, will be aided by the sense of increased security which the Pact will promote among these countries. On the other hand, a successful ERP is the essential foundation upon which the Pact, and the increased security to be expected from it, must rest.[43]

NATO and the Politics of International Liberal Relations

Prior to the Korean War, there were few effective measures taken to build an Atlantic military organization. This was true despite the emergence of a NATO and Mutual Defense Assistance Program. Military assistance only trickled in and French policy makers were hypersensitive about potential German rearmament and ambivalent about the alliance overall. In addition, given the explicit U.S. commitment to militarily aid and defend Western Europe that a NATO represented, Western European states were reluctant to commit their own budgets to defense. The U.S. commitment to provide military aid and a nuclear deterrent helped reduce differences over the formation of the alliance, such as those associated with French reservations. But it had exactly the opposite effect regarding the goal of building an Atlantic military organization: The incentive for Western European states to do so was diminished.[44]

The lack of any real military organization-building indicates that the priority Lovett assigned to the psychological over the military effects of a U.S. military commitment was on target. NATO's import at the point of formation was above all political. Indeed, Kennan had observed at the time that a commitment to nuclear deterrence in Europe could have been made without a formal defense treaty like the NATO. Especially since U.S. troops were already in Germany, there was "an adequate guarantee that the U.S. will be at war if they are attacked."[45] In any event, the nuclear deterrent, according to Kennan, could do little to stop a Soviet troop advance. The better strategy was to use military aid as a leverage to get Western Europe to plan collectively and organize for its own defense.[46]

While Charles Bohlen, Department of State Counselor, initially agreed with Kennan that a NATO was not necessary, since the likelihood of a Soviet attack at the time seemed very remote, he did come around to point out that it had decidedly political advantages, particularly in its ability to instill confidence among European policy makers in the U.S. commitment to defend Western Europe.[47] Kennan in the end went along with the NAT, but did so only reluctantly, and pointed out through a Policy Planning Staff paper that:

> the need for military alliances and rearmament on the part of the western Europeans is a *subjective* one, arising in their own minds as a result of their failure to understand correctly their own position. Their best and most hopeful course of action, if they are to save themselves from communist pressures, remains the struggle for economic recovery and for

internal stability. ... Compared to this, intensive rearmament constitutes an uneconomic and regrettable diversion of effort. A certain amount of rearmament can be subjectively beneficial to western Europe. But if rearmament proceeds at any appreciable cost to European recovery, it can do more harm than good.[48]

A subjective sense of confidence was only, for Kennan, a component of the wider interest in building strength in Europe that began with economic security. But what Kennan did not see at the time was that by legitimating the need for confidence, the United States was moving down a slippery slope, since—as a subjective phenomenon—its boundaries were dependent on the very European policy makers and opinion leaders who were demanding to be confidently secure. European confidence in a U.S. deterrent was a problem that would continually plague U.S. policy makers throughout the Cold War. But in the late 1940s, this problem was especially acute, given the possibility of resistance to external U.S. commitments by isolationist interests represented by Senator Taft. A formal commitment would instill confidence in Western Europe that a U.S. resolve to defend the region would not be undermined by U.S. domestic resistance. Western Europeans only had to look at the temporary status of the ERP and the struggle over that program to see how elusive such commitments could be.

Interestingly, Kennan's initial views about deterrence paralleled on one level Taft's alternative to a NAT: a "unilateral commitment to Western Europe" through the nuclear air power umbrella.[49] Although the administration achieved a congressional commitment to both a NATO and military aid—the latter of which Taft, unlike Kennan, was decidedly against—its reliance on deterrence as the chief element of U.S. strategic posture in Europe resembled isolationist military strategy. Deterrence, which became such a cornerstone of Western policy, did double duty in this context. It satisfied Western European policy makers who wanted to minimize the pressures on their states to provide for Western Europe's defense, at the same time that it was at least palatable to isolationist critics such as Taft who sought to keep budgets low and avoid an extensive construction of European military organization.[50]

More central to the concerns here is the overcoming of divisions that had become apparent in the ERP. The program was unable to provide the political context for the consolidation—or "solidarity," as one recalls Kennan had called for—that policy makers in general had taken to be a *sine qua non* of order-building.[51] Britain opposed economic integration; France was reluctant to accept a West German state integrated into

Western Europe; and continued economic difficulties coupled with the Czech coup—when in early 1948 a Stalinist leadership grabbed control from a more moderate government—had eroded European confidence among Western European governments that sufficient security institutions were in place to resist Soviet pressures.[52]

As implied in the above discussion, the issue of West German integration was central to the role of the NATO regarding liberal order-construction. It was, above all, the U.S. desire to reestablish strength in western Germany—which could help relieve the United States of much of its economic and military responsibilities in Europe—that had led to the problem of how to integrate this newly emerging state into Western Europe in the first place. Acheson was willing to rely on a NAT to assuage French fears regarding a revitalized Germany. The liberal West could add an important member, West Germany, without having to risk the exit of another important member, France. The acceptance of Germany was made tolerable within the institutional frame of a NATO, which assuaged fears of an independent West Germany threatening France.[53] European representatives themselves had lobbied Senator Vandenberg in the fall of 1948 for a U.S. commitment to the North Atlantic alliance to "protect economic recovery and integrate a restored Germany."[54]

What is at stake here is the endeavor to locate a common institutional arena that could serve as a forum for collaboration for Western liberal states. If this could not be accomplished through the ERP, then with the emergence of a NATO the common cooperative framework of the liberal world could be shifted onto the military plane. Ambassador Harriman said it best in 1949 in a meeting of U.S. ambassadors and other leading U.S. policy makers:

> We should have a fresh look at the whole problem of cooperation with our European partners. The mutual security commitments of the Atlantic Pact seem to offer the best basis on which to undertake a concerting of action. Much had already been done through ECA channels but this method would become less effective without concerted multilateral action, although the ECA approach will continue to be pushed vigorously until an alternative is agreed upon. The Atlantic pact machinery would provide *room* for three important aspects of controls which were necessarily absent from the ECA approach. These were: adequate emphasis on security and political factors and the tackling of control of industrial know-how.[55]

The formation of a NAT meant that Britain's resistance to pursuing economic integration—in part because of its Commonwealth

interests—did not necessarily have to lead to the absence of a collaborative institutional frame that was inclusive of all the major liberal states
in Europe. It is easy to forget—especially in the 1990s—that in the
immediate postwar years cooperation in Europe was hardly guaranteed.
As Harriman so clearly pointed out, the militarization of liberal relations that took place in Western Europe at the end of the 1940s opened
up the possibility of basing political-economic cooperation on military-
strategic collaboration.

Integration and Militarization in Western Europe

Reflect for a moment on the position of U.S. policy makers. They faced
a plurality of states, each with democratic publics, powerful interest
groups, and politicians in precarious positions of power. The policy
makers of these liberal states, therefore, had to ensure that their state
and society had the autonomy to set the terms of its social existence so
that the various interests could be navigated. If these states had been
nonliberal and authoritarian they would no doubt also seek to set those
terms autonomously as well. Indeed, it is not at all clear that negotiation
or cooperation would be any harder or easier, since centralized power
could easily lead to a recalcitrance over a given issue deemed vital that
may not be tenable in a liberal state. It is likely to depend on the specific
situation. The crucial difference for liberal states is that they comprise
multiple social and political domains within each of which actors must
be autonomous enough to shape and contest practices and relations. For
authoritarian states, facilitating the determination and contestation of
the character and terms of market relations, civil rights, and democratic
governance by relatively autonomous actors is a problem. For liberal
states, it is a way of organizing political life. If autonomy has any real
meaning for an authoritarian state, it is the autonomy of the state per se
that matters. The practical implications of this is that, for issue areas
such as trade, a liberal state has to come to terms with its own market
actors, their specific interests, and relations with other market actors
including labor and the perceived demands and interests of a broader
democratic public, and then deal with other states with the same pressures and so on. Of course, all states have domestic interests with which
to contend.[56] But only liberal states legitimize, within distinct limits,
the relative autonomy of different actors across a wide array of domains
within which the question of justice and right are at least capable of
being politicized. They face the further problem that outcomes and
processes in one domain are intertwined with those of another, as any

politician who has had to explain economic crises to an electorate could attest. International order-makers are thus forced to devise mechanisms for allowing states to navigate these pressures. Yet, at the same time, the international coordination and construction of relations and policy—that is, order-making—must proceed, at least so that strength could be developed in the region.

This is the quandary. You get strength, based on the legitimacy of the very forces of liberal life discussed above, that can undermine strength and give one grounds for deep self-doubt and fear. We have states that want autonomy and yet lack confidence in their ability alone or together (through integration) to make themselves secure. States—coming back full circle—are not in a position to impose this security-making on societal actors who covet (along with policy makers) their economic development, the progress of which is in turn important for (economic) security.

As Harriman's comments earlier underscore, it must have been very tempting for U.S. policy makers to turn to the Atlantic alliance for a way to deal with these tensions. Many of the reasons why have already been considered. Indeed, it was exactly because liberal order-building engendered so many forces and tensions that there could never be any single force or factor to which the increasing militarization of relations could be attributed. This is the reason why I have adopted a functional approach. What would it mean to say that the militarization of the West was caused by something? As I hope the complexity of the above analysis conveys, that militarization was tied to so many processes and outcomes that looking for "the cause" of NATO is like looking for the cause of a state.[57] It is not just that things were over-determined. Western militarization was occurring in the variegated context of liberal order-building. Here and there, policy makers advanced militarization by such acts as reaching out for the political dimensions of NATO, avoiding unwanted consequences through military aid, "war-itizing" peacetime, and so on.

In the remainder of this section, I want to push the connection between integration and security a bit further to show that the transformation of the U.S. state into a predominantly military presence overseas—marked vividly, for example, by the displacement of U.S. economic recovery missions by U.S. military aid missions—flowed specifically out of the search for a way to come to terms with the quandaries inherent in the pursuit of strength.

To start, Vandenberg feared that U.S. military aid would undermine Western Europe's own efforts at security-building. The trick for him would lie in "making ... military aid wholly supplementary to the self-help and mutual aid defense programs of these other countries. In other words, it must be their last reliance rather than their first reliance in their own physical defenses."[58] Yet making it a "first reliance" was a compelling strategy in the context of the construction of international liberal order. Western European states would not have to face the pressures of constructing unified European strength. They could import it. By curtailing, as explored above, their own direct responsibility for their own security, and avoiding a program of extensive intra-European security cooperation to deal with both Germany and the Soviet Union, Western European states limited the necessity of having to make the greater sacrifices in state autonomy that would accompany an effort to build inter-European organs of military and economic power sufficient to resist perceived threats. The political effect of the U.S. nuclear deterrent was "to limit the extent of military, political, and economic cooperation and neglect the development of war plans."[59] Moreover, as a basic institutional frame, NATO could allay the tension between diverging state interests and the demands of economic and political collaboration inherent in an international liberal order. Instead of constructing an extensive cooperative institutional order, Western European states cooperated with each other and the United States just enough to help construct a militarized U.S. hegemonic center. While in the ensuing decades, Western European states did manage to cooperate in NATO, this cooperation was minimal in comparison to what would have been necessary without the United States. Even as late as the end of the 1980s, Barry Buzan could observe that "U.S. hegemony both underwrites much of the political and military coordination achieved by Western Europe, and prevents the development of higher levels of Western European cohesion."[60] Rather than displacing the political-economic integration that was the goal of the ERP—which was something that both Kennan and John Foster Dulles feared—it simply deferred it.[61]

It is important to keep in mind that NATO did not in itself prompt the integration of Western Europe. Rather, its ramifications for European integration was much more negative. First, it made it possible for Western European states to pursue integration in other dimensions to proceed without confronting head on in a compressed timeframe the pressures of more in-depth integration along political and economic lines.[62] In effect, by allaying these pressures and many of the differences between states in Western Europe touched on above, NATO left open the possibility of establishing economic cooperative institutions such as the European Coal and Steel Community that were integrative and yet violated only minimally sovereign state interests. NATO afforded states the time to work out differences between them.[63] This matters profoundly for liberal states, which face politically mobilized groups and democratic publics. Thus, cooperation could continue to take place in the wake of the ERP on an interstate basis, rather than necessitating supranational institution-building.

Second, it limited the necessity of Western European states themselves creating a strong link between the spheres of security and economy. That link turned out to be left, as Charles Maier points out, to the United States to make with limited success in the early 1950s in its effort to get Europe to increase its defense contribution.[64] By limiting cooperation mostly to the economic sphere, Western European states insured that it would take place in the context of interstate relations. It is the state in international liberalism that has stood at the juncture of international exchange and the national market economy. To have injected heavy demands for security cooperation into this configuration would have necessitated the construction of common security organs such as those associated with the failed European Defense Community (EDC), the French effort (beginning in 1950) to lay the groundwork for a cooperative European military force. It also would have required a coordination of fiscal and welfare policies that would have considerably constrained the scope of Western European states. With the United States taking responsibility for this linkage, Western Europe could trade off the necessity of constructing heavy, collaborative security mechanisms for lighter forms of U.S. hegemonic encroachments and interventions, which could be resisted without necessarily sacrificing European security. Harriman perhaps said it best when he argued at the fall 1949 meeting of ambassadors: "The Atlantic Pact concept should be the umbrella under which all measures agreed upon should be taken; that security, and not economic integration or political integration, should be the point of departure of our policy."[65]

In effect, what NATO did was provide a "space" for Western European states to work out their political and economic difficulties at both the national and international levels, especially, as Maier has observed, through the "politics of productivity." As an alliance in which power was overlaid from above by the United States, NATO removed much of the security question from the domain of democratic debate and contestation (an outcome that might have come back to haunt these states in the 1980s as pan-European social movements did contest "the security question" loudly). Indeed, this was a major political manifestation of the curtailment of direct responsibility for security in Western Europe. While Western European states would exercise influence over the character of NATO strategy and weapon deployments throughout the Cold War, ultimate responsibility for the production and maintenance of the security system per se, did not lie with these states.[66] As such, NATO permitted Western European states to narrow the content of interstate and society relations to the technologies of production and to mechanisms of liberal monetary and trade policy. These states would not need to depend on each other for much else. Acheson articulated this strategy in 1951 when he told Congress that "behind the shield of military power which we and our allies are creating, the techniques of growth and expansion are being maintained intact."[67] Indeed, the post–World War II period has witnessed in Europe the highest degree of institution-building in history, leading to the European Union. But the scope of such institutions historically has been mostly limited to technical-economic issues. (The difficulty of moving beyond this horizon formed in part the basis for a loss of faith in the possibilities of political integration in the 1960s.) This has preserved the sovereignty of the state over social and political policy. Given the common discipline of a cold war and the general reduction of interstate relations to political-strategic concerns, a narrow technological focus in the economic sphere, which, as Maier shows, reduced the vulnerability of liberal politics at the state level, was more tenable.

The provision of confidence through NATO and military aid represented a process of relieving Western European states of the necessity of having to provide for their own security. They did not need to become deeply involved in securing the region as might otherwise have been necessary. Strategy could be displaced to the global confrontation of the United States and the Soviet Union. Western Europe could concentrate on its domestic political and economic difficulties. As David Calleo points out, being distanced from "high politics" provided Western Europe opportunity to trade with Eastern Europe and the Soviet Union, since tensions were not as likely to interfere as in the case of U.S.-East trade. Calleo also shows that NATO allowed Western European states to free up resources not only for their own economic concerns, but also for their own military concerns: Britain could focus on Commonwealth defense, while France could focus on its colonies. And the emergent West German state had more room to consider rearmament within the NATO framework.[68] In response to this very possibility, France could successfully propose the Schuman Plan in order to forge common economic ties with Germany and the rest of Europe. NATO allowed for the European Coal and Steel Community to be separated from the direct pressures of security, and provided a common bond for economic integration.[69] Thus, the irony is that the militarization of Western European relations allowed states there to construct a space at the domestic and interstate levels that was distanced from the realm of security.

The reliance of the liberal world chiefly on U.S. military power and leadership meant that the transformation, from economic to military security could occur with a minimum of international institution-building, even cooperative military institution-building. In this transformation, the U.S. state in Europe was transformed from the ECA into the Mutual Security Agency and varied U.S. expenditures in the region were transformed into military procurements. Except for standard diplomatic machinery, the U.S. state in Europe was more or less reduced to NATO and covert organs such as the CIA. In this respect, the institutional legacy of the ECA was indeed limited as many in Congress had intended.

Conclusion

I recognize it is still too early to draw any definitive lessons from this history for current and future developments in southeastern Europe in the aftermath of war by NATO. However, we do need to be suspicious of claims that we are perhaps entering with a new century, an era in which wars are fought by the West to protect human rights and webs of political economic relations can be created to foster integration that make wars unthinkable. This chapter has tried to show that it is not that simple.

But it still not clear that policy makers—and even scholars—have much interest in confronting what 50 years of order-making could actually teach them. Those lessons seem to have been displaced by the euphoric myth that 1989 was a new "year zero" for understanding and ordering the world, and that the end of the Cold War also meant the end of the old order and the necessity to think hard about it.

Although we are in a political environment that is very different from the 1940s, many of the Cold War's essential components endure, including NATO, the perpetuation of a global U.S. military network, massive arms exports from the West, and a Europe still hesitant about providing for its own security. More generally, the construction of most of the pillars of contemporary international life depended, to varying degrees, on the early postwar effort to fashion an international order. These include the United Nations, a human rights regime, international economic institutions, European integration, decolonization, a proliferation of states, democratization, and liberalization. The eventful beginnings and unfolding of order-making in the middle of the twentieth century, within which the Marshall Plan was central, are therefore ignored at a cost.

Notes

1. Cited in Jones, *Fifteen Weeks*, p. 280.
2. For a discussion of the reasons for U.S. support of integration, see Rappaport, "The United States and European Integration," pp. 121–22; Hogan, *The Marshall Plan*, p. 90; Kaplan, *Community of Interests*, p. 7; and Calleo, *Beyond American Hegemony*, p. 30.
3. Haas, "International Integration," p. 366.
4. See Rappaport, "The United States and European Integration," p. 132.
5. Congressional resistance is considered in Ikenberry, "Origins of American Hegemony," pp. 388–89.
6. On the expectations of the disappearance of the ERP, see Arkes, *Bureaucracy*, pp. 203, 301; and Milward, *Reconstruction of Western Europe*, p. 169. The perception of the temporariness of Europe's problems and their status as an emergency discussed in Milward, ibid., p. 219; and Maier, "Supranational Concepts," p. 29.
7. On the ramifications of the business emphasis in the ERP, see Arkes, *Bureaucracy*, p. 329. See also Wilkins, *The Maturing of Multinational Enterprise*, pp. 287–323, on the general scope of the postwar activity of multinational corporations (MNCs). One area of MNC involvement not discussed here is the American occupation of Germany. See Eisenberg, "U.S. Policy in Post-War Germany."
8. See Arkes, *Bureaucracy*, pp. 157, 299, 215, 301, 325.
9. Hogan, *Marshall Plan*, p. 136.
10. See ibid., pp. 143–51, where many of the aspects of this participation—the chief goal of which was to incorporate labor into the recovery effort—are explored.
11. Vandenberg, *Private Papers*, p. 395.
12. Ibid., p. 382.
13. Ibid., pp. 392–93.
14. On the limited leverage of the ERP, see Milward, *Reconstruction of Western Europe*. p. 125; and Arkes, *Bureaucracy*, pp. 311, 326. The European resistance and alternatives is also discussed in Milward, pp. 120, 173; and Hogan, *Marshall Plan*, pp. 123–24.
15. Although this commitment has been recognized across the historiography of the Cold War, the most concentrated consideration is Pollard, *Economic*

Security, pp. 4, 55–57, 133. Pollard points out that the call for a milita-rized version of containment contained in the 1946 report to the president by Clifford, "American Relations," was shelved. The report (p. 479), however, not only recognized the value of economic security but argued that supplying "military support in case of attack is a last resort; a more effective barrier to communism is strong economic support."

16. Quote from Department of State, *FRUS, 1949*, Vol. 1, pp. 254–55. See also Pach, "Arming the Free World," p. 389; and Kaplan, *A Community of Interests*, pp. 21–22. The containment logic of economic security is considered in Messer, "Paths not Taken," p. 298; and, of course, Pollard, *Economic Security*, p. 133.

17. On Eastern Europe, see Lundestad, *America's Non-Policy Towards Eastern Europe*, p. 223.

18. Cited in Gardner, *Sterling-Dollar Diplomacy*, p. 9.

19. Cited in Pollard, *Economic Security*, p. 13.

20. Gaddis, *Strategies of Containment*, p. 83.

21. The dynamics of this concentration are explored by Freeland, *Origins of McCarthyism*, Chap. 5. See Arkes, *Bureaucracy*, p. 102, on the congres-sional probusiness approach in the Marshall Plan and its basis in the "trade leads to security" formula.

22. The commitment to work with Western Europe regarding both the domestic and international economic dimensions was predicated, in part, on its feasibility. In other words, economic and political conditions conducive to liberalization were already in place to some degree in Western Europe. In Asia, in contrast, a Marshall Plan-type program was rejected in part because of a perceived lack of feasibility. See Borden, *The Pacific Alliance*, p. 110.

23. Clifford, "American Relations," p. 479. See also Woods and Jones, *Dawning of the Cold War*, p. 155. Milward, *Recovery of Western Europe*, pp. 59–60, explores some of the reasoning behind integration as a spur to economic growth and, thus, "pluralist democracy" in Europe.

24. Cited in Gardner, *Sterling-Dollar Diplomacy*, p. 11. That type of faith was also echoed in the thought of David Mitrany; see his *Working Peace System*.

25. See Maier, "Politics of Productivity," p. 31; and Hogan, *The Marshall Plan*, pp. 134–51. Arkes, *Bureaucracy*, pp. 312–16, shows that while ECA head Hoffmann tried to emphasize that he was strictly interested in economic factors, he did realize that the ERP had a political dimension. The point is that the range of such a politics was constricted.

26. See Maier, "Politics of Productivity."

27. This constitutes the main theme of Freeland, *The Truman Doctrine and the Origins of McCarthyism*, Chap. 5; see also Jackson, "Prologue to the Marshall Plan."

28. Integration as a political goal of the Marshall Plan is considered in Milward, *Reconstruction of Western Europe*, p. 56. On the promotion of

U.S. interests in general, see Freeland, *Origins of McCarthyism*, p. 56; Block, *Origins of International Monetary Disorder*, pp. 83–84; and Kolko and Kolko, *Limits of Power*, pp. 436ff. The specific outcomes in Italy and France are detailed in Leffler, "Strategic Dimensions of the Marshall Plan," pp. 280–81; Jackson, "Prologue to the Marshall Plan," p. 1046; and Maier, "Supranational Concepts," pp. 32–33.

29. See Gimbel, *Origins of the Marshall Plan*, p. 4, on the incorporation of Germany; LaFeber, *America, Russia, and the Cold War*, p. 62; Maier, "Supranational Concepts," p. 31; and Leffler, "Strategic Dimensions of the Marshall Plan," pp. 282–83.

30. See Arkes, *Bureaucracy*, pp. 216–18, on the encouragement of East–West trade in the ERP. The dualistic multilateral and bipolar character of the ERP is discussed in Woods and Jones, *Dawning of the Cold War*, p. 246. The ramifications of the ERP for Eastern Europe as seen by the administration is treated in Lundestad, *America's Non-Policy Towards Eastern Europe*, p. 104; and Leffler, "Strategic Dimensions of the Marshall Plan," p. 283. In effect, a certain degree of closure was necessary regarding East–West multilateral economic relations before they could be carried on into the future.

31. "NSC-20/1, U.S. Objectives with Respect to Russia," reprinted in Etzold and Gaddis, eds., *Containment*, pp. 182–83.

32. The most complete treatment of these dimensions is Leffler, "Strategic Dimensions of the Marshall Plan," and idem, *Preponderance of Power*, Chap. 5. See also Jackson, "Prologue to the Marshall Plan"; and Ambrose, *Rise to Globalism*, pp. 92–93.

33. Milward, *Reconstruction of Western Europe*, pp. 5, 54.

34. "Report of the Special 'Ad Hoc' Committee of the State-War-Navy Coordinating Committee," April 21, 1947, in Department of State, *FRUS, 1947*, Vol. 3, pp. 204–19.

35. See also the comments by Jackson, "Prologue to the Marshall Plan," p. 1055. On strategic materials, see Kaplan, *Community of Interests*, pp. 13–14. Wallace and Baruch's observations are treated by Kaplan, p. 13; and Hogan, *Marshall Plan*, p. 94. The links between economic and military security made in the Senate are considered in Arkes, *Bureaucracy*, p. 110.

36. Smith, "From Disarmament to Rearmament," p. 359.

37. Acheson is quoted in LaFeber, "NATO and the Korean War: A Context," p. 463. Lovett is quoted in Pach, "Arming the Free World," pp. 364–65.

38. Cited in Smith, *The United States, Italy and NATO*, p. 105.

39. Vandenberg, *Private Papers*, p. 475.

40. "NSC 14/1," in Etzold and Gaddis, eds., *Containment*, p.130.

41. See Hogan, *The Marshall Plan*, pp. 313, 189, on the rearmament-integration link and coordination.

42. See May, "The American Commitment to Germany," p. 438.

43. Etzold and Gaddis, eds., *Containment*, pp. 158–59.
44. On these points, see Kaplan, *The United States and NATO*, pp. 4, 104, 128, 152, 173; idem, *Community of Interests*, pp. 74–76; Schwartz, *America's Germany*, p. 115; Ireland, *Entangling Alliance*, p. 183; Leffler, "Strategic Dimensions of the Marshall Plan," p. 295; Lundestad, "Empire by Invitation," p. 272; and May, "America's Commitment to Germany," pp. 432–33.
45. Cited in Kaplan, *The United States and NATO*, p. 71.
46. Kaplan, *Community of Interests*, p. 41.
47. Bohlen's views are cited in Folly, "Breaking the Vicious Circle," pp. 70–71; and Gaddis, *Long Peace*, Chap. 3.
48. Etzold and Gaddis, eds., *Containment*, pp. 154–55.
49. Taft's views are in Doenecke, *Not to the Swift*, pp. 162–63. On the way NATO overcame the potential for a return to isolationism, see May, "America's Commitment to Germany," pp. 431–36.
50. The extent to which isolationist military approaches influenced the Truman administration's military planning is explored in Sherry, *Preparing for the Next War*, pp. 49, 203–04, 229–32; Doenecke, *Not to the Swift*, p. 165; Rosenberg, "America's Atomic Strategy," p. 69; and Eden, "Capitalist Conflict," p. 253.
51. When Acheson signed the North Atlantic Treaty, he claimed that it might correct the failure of the ERP to unify Europe through the U.S. connection. See Kaplan, *The United States and NATO*, pp. 5–6; Freeland, *Origins of McCarthyism*, p. 323; LaFeber, *America, Russia, and the Cold War*, p. 84; and Joffe, "Europe's American Pacifier."
52. On British resistance to economic integration, see Hogan, *The Marshall Plan*, p. 75; and Ireland, *Entangling Alliance*, pp. 165–66. On French reluctance regarding Germany, see Schwartz, *America's Germany*, p. 38; Kaplan, *United States and NATO*, pp. 135–38; Joffe, "Europe's American Pacifier," pp. 69–70; Gaddis, *Long Peace*, p. 66; Ireland, pp. 67–71, 109, 175. On the undermining of confidence, see Hogan, pp. 310–12; and LaFeber, "NATO and the Korean War," p. 362.
53. See Kaplan, *The United States and NATO*, pp. 135–38; and Ireland, *Entangling Alliance*, p. 67.
54. Doenecke, *Not to the Swift*, p. 154. The irony that a U.S. push for a strong independent West Germany to minimize U.S. involvement in Europe had led to increased Western European demand for U.S. involvement is noted by Ireland, *Entangling Alliance*, pp. 75–76.
55. "Summary Record of a Meeting of United States Ambassadors at Paris, October 21–22," in *FRUS, 1949*, Vol. 4, p. 482.
56. See, for example, the excellent analysis of this problem in Putnam, "Diplomacy and Domestic Politics."
57. Some of the broader theoretical issues at stake in this sense of explanation are developed in Patomäki, "How to Tell Better Stories About World Politics."

58. Vandenberg, *Private Papers*, p. 479.

59. Kaplan, *Community of Interests*, p. 72. See also Hogan, *The Marshall Plan*, p. 443; and Calleo, *Beyond American Hegemony*, p. 19.

60. Buzan, "Western European Security," p. 36.

61. On Kennan's views, see Gaddis, *Long Peace*, pp. 63–64. On Dulles, see Kaplan, *The United States and NATO*, p. 185.

62. The "disguised integration" especially of the early NATO is analyzed in Stambuk, *American Forces Abroad*, pp. 167–72. See also Kaplan, *The United States and NATO*, p. 128. Hogan, *The Marshall Plan*, pp. 80, 443, points out also that the collaboration over collective security "overshadowed" but never replaced the trend toward increasing unity. There also was, of course, a slow progression of increasing security collaboration in NATO through the years, but the failure of the European Defence Community (EDC), the "withdrawal" of France, and the continued American dominance point away from integration in any meaningful sense. See also the essays in Heller and Gillingham, eds., *NATO: The Founding of the Atlantic Alliance*.

63. The role of NATO as a facilitator of further cooperation in the economic sphere is noted by Beugel, *Marshall Aid*, p. 257. Some interesting reflections on the emergence of a "liberal time" and its allocative nature is in Maier, "Politics of Time," p. 165.

64. Maier, "Making of 'Pax Americana'," pp. 42–54; and idem, "Finance and Defense," pp. 335–51. On some of the theoretical issues surrounding this link, see Gowa, "Bipolarity, Multipolarity, and Free Trade."

65. *FRUS, 1949*, Vol. 4, p. 494.

66. On this influence, see Risse-Kappen, "Long-Term Future of European Security," p. 57.

67. Acheson's comments were made in U.S. Congress, House Committee on Ways and Means, *Extension of the Reciprocal Trade Agreements Act*, p. 7. Acheson also claimed that the United States must "maintain as spacious an environment as possible in which free states might exist and flourish." Cited in Freeland, *Origins of McCarthyism*, p. 322. For a discussion of the importance of productivity, see Maier, "Politics of Productivity"; Hogan, *The Marshall Plan*, Chap. 1; and Kaplan, *Community of Interests*, p. 77.

68. Calleo, *Beyond American Hegemony*, pp. 19, 35.

69. The use of the Schuman Plan to link France and Germany is considered in Ireland, *Entangling Alliance*, pp. 168–75; Wiggershaus, "The Decision for a West German Defense Contribution," p. 199; and LaFeber, *America, Russia, and the Cold War*, p. 86.

References

Arkes, Hadley. *Bureaucracy, the Marshall Plan, and the National Interest*. Princeton: Princeton University Press, 1972.

Ambrose, Stephen. *Rise to Globalism: American Foreign Policy since 1938,* rev. 4th ed. New York: Penguin Books, 1985.

Borden, William. *The Pacific Alliance: United States Foreign Economic Policy and Japanese Trade Recovery, 1947–1955.* Madison: University of Wisconsin, 1984.

Buzan, Barry. "The Future of Western European Security." In *European Polyphony: Progress Beyond East-West Confrontation,* pp. 16–45. Edited by Ole Waever, Pierre Lamaitre, and Elzbieta Tromer. London: Macmillan, 1989.

Calleo, David. *Beyond American Hegemony: The Future of the Western Alliance.* New York: Basic Books, 1987.

Clifford, Clark. "American Relations With the Soviet Union [1946]", pp. 419–82. Reprinted in Arthur Crock, *Memoirs: Sixty Years on the Firing Line.* New York: Funk & Wagnalls, 1968.

Doenecke, Justus. *Not to the Swift: The Old Isolationists in the Cold War Era.* Lewisburg: Bucknell University Press, 1979.

Eden, Lynn. "Capitalist Conflict and the State: The Making of United States Military Policy in 1948." In *Statemaking and Social Movements: Essays in History and Theory,* pp. 233–61. Edited by Charles Bright and Susan Harding. Ann Arbor: University of Michigan Press, 1984.

Etzold, Thomas and Gaddis, John Lewis, eds. *Containment: Documents on American Policy and Strategy, 1945–1950.* New York: Columbia University Press, 1978.

Folly, Martin. "Breaking the Vicious Circle: Britain, The United States, and the Genesis of the North Atlantic Treaty." *Diplomatic History* 12 (Winter 1988): 59–77.

Freeland, Richard. *The Truman Doctrine and the Origins of McCarthyism: Foreign Policy, Domestic Politics and Internal Security, 1946–1948.* New York: Knopf, 1972.

Gaddis, John Lewis. *Strategies of Containment: A Critical Appraisal of Postwar American National Security Policy.* Oxford: Oxford University Press, 1982.

———. *The Long Peace: Inquiries into the History of the Cold War.* New York: Oxford University Press, 1987.

Gardner, Richard N. *Sterling-Dollar Diplomacy in Current Perspective: The Origins and Prospects of Our International Economic Order,* 3rd ed. New York: Columbia University Press, 1980.

Gimbel, John. *The Origins of the Marshall Plan.* Stanford: Stanford University Press, 1976.

Gowa, Joanne. "Bipolarity, Multipolarity, and Free Trade." *American Political Science Review* 83 (December 1989): 1245–56.

Haas, Ernst. "International Integration: The European and the Universal Process." *International Organization* 15 (Summer 1961): 366–92.

Heller, Francis and Gillingham, John, eds. *NATO: The Founding of the Atlantic Alliance and the Integration of Europe.* New York: St. Martin's Press, 1992.

Hogan, Michael J. *The Marshall Plan: America, Britain, and the Reconstruction of Western Europe, 1947–1952.* Cambridge: Cambridge University Press, 1987.

Ikenberry, G. John. "Rethinking the Origins of American Hegemony." *Political Science Quarterly* 104 (Fall 1989): 375–400.

Ireland, Timothy P. *Creating the Entangling Alliance: The Origins of the North Atlantic Treaty Organization.* Westport, Conn.: Greenwood Press, 1981.

Jackson, Scott. "Prologue to the Marshall Plan: The Origins of the American Commitment for a European Recovery Program." *Journal of American History* 65 (March 1979): 1043–68.

Joffe, Josef. "Europe's American Pacifier." *Foreign Policy* 54 (Spring 1984): 64–82.

Jones, Joseph Marion. *The Fifteen Weeks: February 21–June 5, 1947.* New York: Viking Press, 1955.

Kaplan, Lawrence. *A Community of Interests: NATO and the Military Assistance Program, 1948–1951.* Washington, D.C.: Office of the Secretary of Defense, 1980.

———. *The United States and NATO: The Formative Years.* Lexington: University Press of Kentucky, 1984.

Kolko, Joyce and Kolko, Gabriel. *The Limits of Power: The World and United States Foreign Policy, 1945–1954.* New York: Harper & Row, 1972.

Leffler, Melvyn. "The United States and the Strategic Dimensions of the Marshall Plan." *Diplomatic History* 12 (Summer 1988): 277–306.

———. *A Preponderance of Power: National Security, the Truman Adminis-tration, and the Cold War.* Stanford: Stanford University Press, 1992.

LaFeber, Walter. *America, Russia, and the Cold War, 1945–1984,* 5th ed. New York: Knopf, 1985.

———. "NATO and the Korean War: A Context," *Diplomatic History* 13 (Fall 1989): 461–78.

Lundestad, Geir. *The American Non-Policy Towards Eastern Europe, 1943–1947: Universalism in an Area Not of Essential Interest to the United States.* New York: Humanities, 1975.

———. "Empire by Invitation? The United States and Western Europe, 1945–1952." *Journal of Peace Research* 23 (1986): 262–78.

Maier, Charles S. "The Politics of Productivity: Foundations of American International Economic Policy after World War II." In *Between Power and Plenty: Foreign Economic Policies of Advanced Industrial States,* pp. 23–49. Edited by Peter Katzenstein. Madison: University of Wisconsin Press, 1978.

———. "Supranational Concepts and National Continuity in the Framework of the Marshall Plan." In *The Marshall Plan: A Retrospective,* pp. 29–37. Edited by Stanley Hoffmann and Charles Maier. Boulder, Co.: Westview Press, 1984.

———. "The Politics of Time: Changing Paradigms of Collective Time and Private Time in the Modern Era." In *Changing Boundaries of the Political: Essays on the Evolving Balance between State and Society, Public and Private in Europe,* pp. 151–78. Edited by Charles S. Maier. Cambridge: Cambridge University Press, 1987.

———. "The Making of 'Pax Americana': Formative Moments of United States Ascendancy, 1945–53." Paper delievered at the Diplomatic History Workshop, Harvard University, October, 1988.

———. "Empires or Nations? Territoriality and Stabilization, 1918, 1945, 1989…" Paper delievered at The New School for Social Research, March 1995.

May, Ernest. "The American Commitment to Germany, 1949–55." *Diplomatic History* 13 (Fall 1989): 431–60.

Milward, Alan S. *The Reconstruction of Western Europe, 1945–1951.* London: Methuen, 1984.

Mitrany, David. *A Working Peace System.* London: London National Peace Council, 1946.

Messer, Robert. "Paths not Taken: The United States Department of State and Alternatives to Containment." *Diplomatic History* 1 (Fall 1977): 297–320.

Pach, Jr., Chester. "Arming the Free World: The Origins of the United States Military Assistance Program." Ph.D. dissertation, Northwestern University, 1981.

Patomaki, Heikki. "How to Tell Better Stories About World Politics." *European Journal of International Relations* 2 (March 1996): 105–33.

Pollard, Robert A. *Economic Security and the Origins of the Cold War, 1945–1950.* New York: Columbia University Press, 1985.

Putnam, Robert. "Diplomacy and Domestic Politics: The Logic of Two-Level Games." *International Organization* 42 (Summer 1988): 427–60.

Rappaport, Armin. "The United States and European Integration: The First Phase." *Diplomatic History* 5 (Spring 1981): 121–49.

Risse-Kappen, Thomas. "The Long-Term Future of European Security." In *European Foreign Policy,* pp. 45–60. Edited by Walter Calsnaes and Steve Smith. London: Sage, 1994.

Rosenberg, David. "American Atomic Strategy and the Hydrogen Bomb Decision." *Journal of American History* 66 (June 1979): 62–87.

Sherry, Michael. *Preparing for the Next War: American Plans for Postwar Defense, 1941–1945.* New Haven: Yale University Press, 1977.

Smith, E. Timothy. "From Disarmament to Rearmament: The United States and the Revision of the Italian Peace Treaty of 1947." *Diplomatic History* 13 (Summer 1989): 359–82.

Ibid. *The United States, Italy and NATO, 1947–52.* New York: St. Martin's Press, 1991.

Stambuk, George. *American Military Forces Abroad: Their Impact on the Western State System.* Columbus: Ohio State University Press, 1963.

U.S. Congress. House Committee on Ways and Means. *Extension of the Reciprocal Trade Agreements Act, Hearings before a subcommittee of the House Committee on Ways and Meanson on H.R.1311,* 82nd Cong., 1951.

U.S. Department of State. *Foreign Relations of the United States, 1947.* 8 Volumes. Washington, D.C.: Government Printing Office, 1971–77.

———. *Foreign Relations of the United Sates, 1949.* 9 Volumes. Washington, D.C.: Government Printing Office, 1974–78.

Vandenberg, Arthur H. Jr. *The Private Papers of Senator Vandenberg.* Boston: Houghton Mifflin, Co. 1952.

Van Der Beugel, Ernst. *From Marshall Aid to Atlantic Partnership: European Integration as a Concern of American Foreign Policy.* Amsterdam: Elsevier, 1966.

Wiggershaus, Norbert. "The Decision for a West German Defense Contribution." In *Western Security: The Formative Years,* pp. 198–214. Edited by Olav Riste. New York: Columbia University Press, 1985.

Wilkins, Mira. *The Maturing of Multinational Enterprise: American Business Abroad from 1914 to 1970.* Cambridge: Harvard University Press, 1974.

Woods, Randall and Jones, Howard. *Dawning of the Cold War: The United States' Quest for Order.* Athens: University of Georgia Press, 1991.

PART TWO

The Others: From the Outside Looking In

CHAPTER 4

The Marshall Plan and Czechoslovak Democracy: Elements of Interdependancy

Bradley F. Abrams

This essay explores the connection between the Czechoslovak government's decision to reject participation in the Marshall Plan preliminary discussions, the ensuing assumption of total power in the state by the Communist Party of Czechoslovakia, and the United States Congress' decision to grant approval for funding the Plan. The Czechoslovak government announced on July 7, 1947, that the state would take part in the discussions slated to begin in Paris on July 12. However, on July 9, leading Czechoslovak representatives met with Stalin in Moscow and reversed their decision. Recently released documents show that, rather than being a *Diktat* on the part of Stalin, the Czechoslovaks themselves volunteered to withdraw from the Paris discussions. This episode revealed weaknesses in the Czechoslovak leaders' notions of their state's sovereignty and set a dangerous precedent for the future, (one which contributed to the ease with which the Communist Party rose to total power. The episode did not only bear mightily on Czechoslovak developments, however.) The ultimate collapse of Czechoslovak democracy, and the suicide of the Czechoslovak democracy foreign minister, Jan Masaryk, played an important role in securing support from the United States Congress for the Plan as a whole in March 1948.

Since the collapse of the communist regimes of Central and Eastern Europe, the countries of the region have begun to explore aspects of their histories formerly subjected to rigid, ideologically driven interpretations. One motivation for this is these nations' desire to portray, both to the West and to themselves, democracy and the market-oriented economy as almost culturally inherent, "traditional" attributes of their national life. In this regard, their intensive introspection is designed to ferret out a "usable past," one that will encourage the eastward expansion of Western institutions and render the hardships currently being experienced more bearable for the population. The omnipresent slogan of a "return to Europe" symbolizes the desire to view the 45 years of communist dictatorship as an aberration that threw the nations of the region from their proper historical trajectory and to which they are now returning.

As the flip side of this positively charged, and politically and psychologically practical, aspect of the Central European catharsis, the nations of the region are striving to seek out those responsible for the crimes of the communist regimes. One component of this search has involved seeking an answer to why and how their countries became Communist dictatorships, investigations that most frequently downplay domestic factors while focusing on international developments. The impulse here is to place the blame on the shoulders of outsiders and to preserve the democratic and freedom-loving pedigree of the nation in question, usually at the expense of that of the Russians. Czechoslovakia is certainly no exception in this regard, and the story of its slide into dictatorship has been the subject of much recent work by Czech and Slovak historians, as well as by a growing number of scholars from the West. Czechoslovakia represents a case of particular interest for those concerned with the history of the European Recovery Program (the Marshall Plan), for it was the only state of the region that officially and publicly announced its decision to participate in the initiative's 1947 Paris preliminary discussions. Less than a week later, however, the government retracted that declaration. Both of these governmental decisions were taken unanimously by the cabinet. This sudden volte-face, as you will shortly see, was the result of a discussion between leading Czechoslovak representatives and Stalin. The reversal has been seen as both a product of increasing tension between the wartime allies, and an illegitimate *Diktat* by Stalin that signaled the de facto end of Czechoslovak sovereignty. While the first of these is certainly true, I will argue that rather than a cruel *Diktat*, as it is usually presented in Western texts, the decision to withdraw from Marshall Plan discussions was ultimately a Czechoslovak one. The episode revealed much about the Czechoslovak democratic leadership's notions of its state's sovereignty and set a dangerous precedent for future developments in the republic.

The relationship between the Marshall Plan and Czechoslovak democracy was not a one-way street, however. The actions of the Czechoslovak government are not only interesting for what they reveal about the state of Czechoslovak democracy. The ultimate, if not predetermined, culmination of the events begun in 1945 (or perhaps even earlier[1]) and confirmed before the eyes of the world by the Marshall Plan reversal was the Communist Party's assumption of total power in February of 1948. The impact of this event, and that of the highly suspicious "suicide" of the noncommunist Czechoslovak foreign minister two weeks later, played a significant role in the United States Congress' approval of funds for the Marshall Plan. For this reason, the two sets of events can be seen as linked: The Marshall Plan revealed the weaknesses of Czechoslovak democracy, and the ultimate collapse of Czechoslovak democracy ensured the final passage of funding for the Marshall Plan. While there is no doubt the Marshall Plan did not cause Czechoslovakia to enter the Communist bloc, and the state's entry was not the sole factor in the approval of Marshall funds, this contribution aims to show that there is a connection between the two.

The Marshall Plan and the Weaknesses of Czechoslovak Democracy

First, however, a few basic facts about the structure of early postwar Czechoslovak politics are in order. The nature of the (first) end of Czechoslovakia in the wake of the 1938 Munich Accords created anomalies in postwar political arrangements. Slovakia declared its independence in March of 1939, and became a puppet state under the tutelage of Nazi Germany, at the same time as the remainder of the post-Munich Czech lands became a "protectorate" of the Third Reich. The government-in-exile, centered in London and Moscow, decided over the course of the latter stages of the war to ban parties deemed to have collaborated. This resulted in a political spectrum skewed to the left, as the conservative Agrarian Party (which had dominated the protectorate's political structures) and the conservative and clerical Slovak People's Party (which had controlled the wartime Slovak state) found themselves banned. The major parties that remained were, in the Czech lands, the Communists, the Social Democrats (internally divided over the question of how closely the party should cooperate with the Communists), the moderately left-wing National Socialists, and the Roman Catholic and centrist People's Party. In Slovakia, only two major parties existed: the largely clerical and conservative Democratic Party and the Communist

Party of Slovakia. In these circumstances, the Communist Party rode a wave of popular enthusiasm to electoral victory in 1946, capturing a plurality of 37 percent of the vote countrywide and controlling—with the votes of the Social Democrats—a slim majority in the six-party National Front government. Left-wing politics, as can be seen in the elections results, were far more popular in the Czech lands than in Slovakia, giving rise to a great deal of mutual suspicion between the political actors of the two parts of the republic.[2] Czech political actors viewed Slovakia as a hotbed of both separatist nationalism and, more importantly, reactionary political sentiment, while many Slovak political figures mistrusted both Czech social progressivism, which they saw as creeping bolshevism, and a religious indifference perceived as creeping atheism. While trying to reintegrate the state, the dominant Czech political parties played the leading role, and for this reason stood at the center of what follows. In this respect, the weaknesses in Czechoslovak politics can be seen as more "Czech" than "Slovak."

Czechoslovakia in the early summer of 1947 seemed an ideal candidate for the Marshall Plan for several interrelated reasons. Above all, the material aid from the United Nations Relief and Rehabilitation Administration (UNRRA) that had totaled some 200 million dollars had recently come to an end. In order to compensate for the loss, Czechoslovakia would have to increase imports and find the funds to pay for them, a situation rendered more problematic by the reappearance of a trade deficit in mid-1947. Overall figures suggested all was well, but there was a serious deficit in both the United States dollar and British pound accounts. Since Czechoslovakia hoped to replace a shattered Germany as supplier of heavy machinery to the industrializing lands to its east and south and to expand into the markets of the West, even greater imports from the West would be necessary, further raising the deficit. For these reasons, the Czechoslovak government had entered into negotiations aimed at securing a 50 million dollar loan from the Export-Import Bank. The announcement of the Marshall Plan must have seemed a godsend that would allow Czechoslovakia to make up for the lost UNRRA aid on the one hand, and prime the pump for export gains on the other. As a relatively highly industrialized state—the Czech lands had been the most industrialized area of the Austro-Hungarian Empire—Czechoslovakia stood to gain more from Marshall aid than the other, less-developed economies of Eastern Europe.

Quirkily, there was also a climactic factor that contributed to the need for monies to replace UNRRA aid. A long winter and a short, wet spring was followed by a serious drought across central Europe in 1947

(Hungary seems an exception). Already in June, when precipitation was two-thirds below normal, Czechoslovak officials were anticipating a decline in the harvest of some 40 percent from the average of 1934–38, and there was concern over how to raise the funds necessary to import the foodstuffs that would become necessary. Food rationing was still in effect, but by the end of the summer 43 percent of Czechoslovaks were buying food on the black market, where prices had risen to well over 200 percent of the officially determined rate. The result of the drought was that the caloric intake of the population was estimated to be 42 percent below the amount given as "optimal."[3] The potential effects of the drought were not, however, perceived by American observers prior to the Marshall Plan events.[4]

In this situation, the offer of Marshall aid was initially welcomed by both the political class and by the population at large, which was said to be "extremely anxious to participate." The non-party foreign minister, Jan Masaryk, is reported to have "immediately" accepted the invitation extended to his government by the British and French ambassadors on July 4.[5] However, the Czechoslovak government had already been busy preparing for the arrival of the expected invitation. The cabinet had met already on the June 24 to discuss participating in the preliminary discussions slated to begin on July 12 in Paris. At this meeting, a commission of ministers under the chairmanship of Foreign Minister Masaryk was created to look into the matter and report on the advisability of participation. This commission reported back on July 4, recommending that a Czechoslovak delegation be sent to Paris. The cabinet discussion on participation was, by all accounts, calm and friendly, and recommendations to accept the offer were received from as divergent sources as Roman Catholic People's Party representatives and Communist Prime Minister Klement Gottwald's economic advisor.[6] When the vote was taken, the result was unanimously in favor of accepting the invitation, and the government presidium was entrusted to work out detailed political guidelines for the Czechoslovak delegation to follow in Paris. The presidium confirmed the unanimous vote three days later, and announced it in a press release that stated: "In its Monday meeting, the Presidium of the government met concerning the invitation to the European Economic Conference. ... It was resolved to accept the invitation. ... The government will decide on its further course of action regarding the matter of Marshall's initiative on the basis of additional information about its substance that will be given at the Paris conference."[7] As we shall see, the Czechoslovak government felt it had received sufficient "additional information" already before the conference began.

Given the primacy placed by all political parties on the maintenance of Czechoslovakia's alliance with the Soviet Union and good relations with the other Slavic states, what signals was the Czechoslovak government receiving from the east? Above all, the Soviet view on Czechoslovak participation was ambiguous. As early as June 22, an article had appeared in Moscow *Pravda* calling the plan a maneuver to justify Truman's politics and Soviet Foreign Minister Molotov had stormed out of the Paris preparatory talks on 2 July.[8] However, Gottwald had received a secret telegram from the Central Committee of the Communist Party of the Soviet Union on July 5 (one day after the unanimous acceptance), recommending Czechoslovak attendance in Paris. It instructed the Czech Communist leader to attend in order to demonstrate "the unacceptability of the Anglo-French plan, prevent the adoption of a unanimous decision [on the plan], and then leave the conference, taking as many delegates of other countries as possible."[9] This was, of course, a secret communiqué, and was unknown to Masaryk when, the next day, he discussed the question with the Soviet chargé d'affairs in Prague, M. F. Bodrov, who, despite repeated questioning, claimed to have "no instructions" regarding possible Czechoslovak participation. The Soviet diplomat added his personal view that "It is not excluded that it will be necessary for you and other to go to the conference."[10] Further, already at the beginning of June top Czechoslovak ministers had been informed by Polish Prime Minister Józef Cyrankiewicz, Foreign Minister Zygmunt Modzelewski, and Minister of Trade and Industry Hilary Minc that Poland was planning on taking part in the Paris discussions. This was reiterated on July 4 by the Polish Prime Minister, who confirmed that his government would approve the sending of a delegation to Paris on July 7.[11] This news was encouraging, for it meant that Czechoslovakia would not be the sole representative from Eastern Europe in attendance.

With acceptance announced, a Czechoslovak government delegation including the Communist Prime Minister Gottwald, the non-party Foreign Minister Masaryk, and the National Socialist Minister of Justice Prokop Drtina flew to Moscow for discussions with the Soviets.[12] These were intended to discern the USSR's view of a proposed Franco-Czechoslovak mutual defense treaty and to conclude various economic and trade negotiations. Arriving on the afternoon of July 9, Gottwald apparently had an immediate and secret meeting with Stalin, from which he returned shaken, visibly disturbed by the anger the Soviet leader had displayed over the Czechoslovak decision to attend the Paris discussions. Drtina recalls Gottwald returning and pacing the room, launching into a "long, nervous and very jerky monologue" by saying "Now we're in hot water (To jsme v pěkné kaši)! Stalin is very angry that we accepted the invitation to the Marshall Plan. I have never seen him so angry! We have to figure out what we will do."[13] Gottwald must indeed have been surprised, given the telegram he had received from the very top of the Soviet power hierarchy on July 3 recommending Czechoslovak participation. However, a second telegram had been sent on July 8, which it is apparent Gottwald had not received before his departure. In this communication, Molotov urged the retraction of Czechoslovak acceptance, citing as reasons the need to preserve the economic independence and sovereignty (!) of smaller European nations and the suspicion that it represented the first step toward the establishment of "a Western bloc with the participation of Western Germany."[14] Taken aback by Gottwald's rambling tirade, Masaryk and Drtina remained silent, until Drtina responded that Stalin's views were indeed "surprising" and "unexpected," and that the ministers would have to hear his arguments and attempt to explain to him why Czechoslovakia wished and needed to participate. If they could not convince him the step was proper, however, Drtina argued that "in the long run we can always withdraw from the Paris conference if it is shown that our presence would lead us into conflict with Soviet politics." Masaryk then spoke, apparently agreeing with Drtina and making it clear to him that as a non-party minister he would leave the job of countering Gottwald to the National Socialist minister of justice.[15]

Late that evening, in keeping with Stalin's nocturnal work habits, the three ministers were summoned to meet the Soviet leader and Molotov, and the Marshall Plan had displaced the other matters at the top of the agenda. One source notes that at the outset of the meeting, Stalin had a selection of the world press on the table before him, and pointed to the headlines "Prague Losing Her Ties To Moscow" and "Breach in the Eastern Bloc."[16] After registering his displeasure at the gloating of the Western press, he launched into his opening arguments.[17] He maintained that the plan would offer poor terms of credit and was "a pretext ... [for an attempt] to form a Western bloc and isolate the Soviet Union." The Soviet leader further expressed his surprise that Czechoslovakia had agreed to participate, given that Romania, Yugoslavia, and Poland had not.[18] He then raised the stakes considerably, concluding, "We consider this matter to be a fundamental question on which our [i.e., Czechoslovak] friendship with the USSR depends. If you go to Paris, you will show that you want to cooperate in an action aimed at isolating the Soviet Union." Minister Masaryk, after noting the necessity of trade with the West and the earlier intention of the Poles to participate, concluded with what can hardly be described as a ringing defense of Czechoslovakia's chosen course:

> Minister Masaryk emphasized that all political parties are agreed that Czechoslovakia may not undertake anything which would be against the interests of the Soviet Union. The delegation will promptly notify Prague that the Soviet government considers acceptance of the Anglo-French invitation to be an act directed against it, and Minister Masaryk does not doubt in the least that the Czechoslovak government will act accordingly without delay. But Minister Masaryk here requests that the Soviet Union help us in our delicate situation. ... Perhaps the matter can be fixed in such a manner that one would go to the conference on one day and leave it on the next.

It is most remarkable that the Foreign Minister of a sovereign state makes little show of defending an action taken unanimously by his state's government, rather devoting his energy to finding a way to maintain the appearance that his state is acting with sovereignty. Stalin ignored his plea, retorting that participation in the Conference would constitute a "break in the front" that would be a success for the "Western Great Powers."

Drtina's comments showed hardly more backbone. He first assured Stalin on the part of his party—the most powerful opponents of the Communists—that it "would not participate in anything in the field of foreign policy which would appear as directed against the Soviet Union. He greatly welcome[d] this opportunity to emphasize this here. He want[ed] it to be known that Minister Drtina's party will also consistently pursue such a policy as is necessary to prevent such deals." Drtina then returned to the economic issue, arguing that the loss of the Marshall funds could result in "general impoverishment" that "would have not only serious economic consequences, but also political ones." Here he seems, incredibly, to be looking out for the electoral prospects of his greatest opponents, the Communist Party, fearing that any economic decline would be attributed to Stalin's local comrades in the parliamentary elections scheduled for the following year. Masaryk, too, chimed in, again asking Stalin if he could "facilitate our way out of the situation," and asking for forgiveness that he felt it necessary to ask for a "consolation prize."

Given this prostration, Stalin could do little else than address the ministers' concern for the potential impoverishment of the Czechoslovak population. He offered to purchase industrial products from Czechoslovakia and to ship the state two hundred thousand tons of wheat. With this, the deal seemed settled. It only remained for the Communist Gottwald to once more ask the Soviets to make Czechoslovakia's "way out of a difficult situation easier," implying that the Czechoslovak representatives had to find some way of retracting their acceptance that would allow them to save face on the international stage. Stalin's final suggestion was that the Czechoslovak government announce that "In the recent past it has become evident that the acceptance of the invitation could be interpreted as a blow against the USSR, in particular since none of the Slav or other East European states accepted the invitation." After discussion about the originally intended matters, the meeting adjourned 30 minutes after midnight on July 10.[19]

Immediately upon returning from the Kremlin, and with Stalin's final sentence obviously still in their minds, the ministers composed a telegram demanding that an emergency cabinet session be called later that day, in order to immediately reverse the decision to participate.[20] Drtina recalls that, "Even if the dispatch did not express my opinion in everything, I signed it," although he claims to have held out the hope that his fellow noncommunist cabinet members in Prague would express such disagreement that they would disobey his own instructions and order no change in policy.[21] Despite Stalin's apparent demand for a response from Prague by 11:00 in the morning (Moscow time), the Czechoslovak government could not meet early enough to conclude this. When a quorum of members convened, a rather more lively discussion than the first one ensued, interrupted by at least two telephone calls from Masaryk, two from the ill Ripka, and several from an understandably concerned Gottwald. As one American diplomat aptly noted after reading the minutes of the meeting, the debate was "reminiscent of the medieval church, where one was permitted to engage in learned disputations within an *a priori* conceptual frame of reference rather than the deliberations of a democratically constituted body in our own times."[22] In the end, the members of the Czechoslovak government again voted unanimously, this time not to send a delegation to Paris.[23] The press release came out at 9:00 in the evening of July 10, missing Stalin's deadline. It was his only disappointment, for the release contained the line, "Czechoslovak participation would be construed as an act directed against friendship with the Soviet Union and the rest of our allies. That is why the government unanimously decided that it will not take part in this conference."[24] With the desired actions carried out by the Czechoslovak government, the ministers concluded their business in Moscow and returned home. Jan Masaryk, who was so disturbed by the turn of events that he withdrew from attending an opera performance with Stalin, summed up his views even before departing the Soviet capital: "Finis Bohemiae."[25]

The withdrawal was, in the mild words of the Czechoslovak ambassador to the United States, "badly mismanaged," and was received by a shocked population.[26] The embarrassing climb down revealed many disconcerting elements of the postwar Czechoslovak political scene. Above all, it showed the tremendous weight the state placed on its relationship with the USSR. In the wake of the West's betrayal at Munich in 1938 and the liberation of Czechoslovakia by the Red Army in 1944/1945, maintaining a solid relationship with the state's perceived one true ally was the guiding star of Czechoslovak foreign policy after liberation. As Karel Kaplan has written:

> The final decision not to participate was a natural consequence of the post-war foreign policy orientation of the noncommunist parties, an orientation that collapsed, but whose main principle—alliance with the Soviet Union—was never abandoned by their leaders, because they simply lacked the courage to do so. They realized that to oppose Moscow's demands would mean repudiating the "friendship and alliance" between the two countries—something they felt would be, both internationally and domestically, risky and irresponsible.[27]

The reversal intimates that the Czechoslovak political elite was willing to sacrifice almost any initiative in order not to provoke the Kremlin. Given that we can say that, of all the Eastern European states on the road to Communist dictatorship, Czechoslovakia had the most room for political maneuver, we have to ask how its leaders *used* that space. The Soviets had rather limited means of placing direct pressure on the Czechoslovak government: it had no troops on Czechoslovak soil, and the Communist Party did not control the government. However, direct pressure was apparently unnecessary. Stalin had merely to indicate his displeasure and the Czechoslovak government was willing to immediately reverse a unanimously reached decision that held the promise of large-scale benefits for its country.

Czechoslovak noncommunist leaders who fled to the West after the Communist assumption of power in 1948 have continually bemoaned Stalin's intrusion into Czechoslovak affairs. Most frequently cited is Jan Masaryk's supposed comment that "I left for Moscow as a Czechoslovak minister, I returned as Stalin's lackey."[28] Nonetheless, from the minutes of the meeting and a wealth of other materials, it is clear that leading noncommunists rarely stopped to think what they would have concretely risked had they not fulfilled Stalin's wish. They acted far less from a political calculation that the damage to the Czechoslovak-USSR relationship from accepting the Marshall invitation would be greater than the damage to the interests of Czechoslovakia by refusing that invitation than from the fear that acting against Stalin's wishes would call out a vaguely defined catastrophe. If Czechoslovak sovereignty was damaged in any way by the Marshall episode, it was damaged by the Czechoslovak political elite itself, a fact that was not overlooked by Western representatives. As U.S. Ambassador Steinhardt ruefully noted, what had happened was that "a condition believed by the well-informed to have long existed has been removed from the realm of doubt by irrefutable evidence and publicly disclosed."[29]

One may legitimately question this criticism of the representatives of Czechoslovak democracy. What were the risks they might run by standing up to Stalin? The democratic leaders call out a number of unlikely horrors in their memoirs. Ripka raises the specter of Soviet renunciation of the alliance, but his fear that the "Soviets would have profited by it to incite the Communists to effect a *coup d'état*" was unlikely in the summer of 1947. Rather contradictorily, he then appears to blame the gullibility of the Czech and Slovak people, while cloaking his justification in the mantle of electoral calculation:

> But there was another reason [for withdrawing], still more serious. I knew that we could not win over the majority of the people for such a policy. ... Soviet propaganda was already sounding the alarm by spreading the rumor that the American capitalists were not seeking to help Europe, but that it was Germany they wanted to reconstruct first of all. This sort of argument was very dangerous, and did not fail to have an effect on a large part of our public opinion. ... All Czechs have constantly in mind the German danger which has threatened them since the Middle Ages. ... I realized that if we failed to bow to the will of Stalin the public would applaud us on the first day, only to stone us later, when the consequences of our refusal made themselves felt.[30]

For Ripka, then, the risks were of both an international and domestic character. These precluded him from recommending a rejection of Stalin's perceived ultimatum.

Drtina's reasoning is much more revealing. He, too, was worried about the ramifications for the alliance, but goes to great lengths to justify his behavior and argues against the notion that the reversal signaled the end of Czechoslovak sovereignty. He correctly points out that the Czechoslovak delegation was only to attend the Paris meetings in order to ascertain further information, and not to agree to full participation. Further, he argues that Czechoslovakia's treaty obligations required it to consult with the USSR on a matter carrying such foreign policy weight. Finally, he notes that the decision to attend was taken under the impression that the Poles would also be in attendance.[31] These are all true, but they do raise troubling questions. How did Drtina understand the notion of "consultation"? The rapidity and magnitude of the change in policy, and the notes of the meeting with Stalin all indicate that the "consultation" had less to do with consulting, and more to do with satisfying Stalin. Furthermore, Czechoslovakia may have been bound to consult with its ally on matters of international import, but Drtina elsewhere in his memoirs recalls that he regularly visited the Soviet embassy in Prague to discuss his ministerial affairs. As minister of justice, however, one is hard pressed to see how Drtina would need to "consult" with his ally, or even to change policy in order to be in conformity with Soviet desires.[32] Further, his complaint that, despite the Truman Doctrine, the United States "took no effective step against the new violation (znásilnění) of Czechoslovakia by the Soviet threat" seems rather misplaced, given Czechoslovak democrats' actions and the nature of the Marshall initiative itself. Finally, his domestic justification seems even weaker. He claims to have looked forward to the disturbance the sudden volte-face would cause among the population, and argues that his conciliatory position toward Stalin would benefit the "consolidation of parliamentary democracy" in Czechoslovakia. This would be achieved because Drtina would have ingratiated himself to Stalin, Gottwald, and the whole of the Communist Party of Czechoslovakia: "I hoped that by this [co-ordering the Czechoslovak cabinet to reverse itself] I would gain the certain, even if certainly relative, trust of Stalin and Gottwald for the possibility of the democratic continuation of the republic."[33]

One point on which this author decidedly agrees with Drtina, however, is his contention that the Marshall Plan episode did not represent the end of Czechoslovak sovereignty. What it did, in the words of the Social Democratic Minister of Food, Václav Majer, was it "smashed the *illusion* of Czechoslovak independence to smithereens."[34] Independence, after all, must be manifested to be of value. If the conduct of Czechoslovak foreign policy and, it appears from Drtina's testimony, to some extent domestic policy was profoundly influenced and largely determined by the international aims of the USSR, one must look anew at the content of terms such as "sovereign" and "independent" for Czechoslovak noncommunist elites.

If Czechoslovak democrats were understandably reluctant to contradict Stalin to his face, what other options were open to them? Three scenarios were possible for the July 10 cabinet meeting. None of these would likely have materially altered the final outcome, but would have a beneficial impact on the morale of democratic forces in Czechoslovakia and steeled the population for the struggle that lay ahead. In the first scenario, the government as a whole could have voted not to renounce its decision to participate. This would have proven impossible, as several noncommunist ministers were not in attendance.[35] Even had all ministers been in attendance, the democrats could not muster the votes: the Communists and Social Democrats (who would certainly vote with the Communists on this issue) controlled 12 of the 26 seats, and both the nonparty ministers, Ludvík Svoboda (essentially already a Communist Party member) and Masaryk (who had reached the deal with Stalin) were sure to vote for withdrawing from the Marshall discussions. The second option was for the democrats to walk out, preventing a quorum of ministers from being in attendance, but this would only delay the inevitable.[36] Although this would certainly disturb Stalin and his local representatives, the point would have been made clear to both domestic and international audiences. Finally, they could perhaps have gone even further, and tendered their resignations. Given their lack of political nerve, an act of such brinkmanship was clearly unthinkable in this case and would likely have proven foolhardy, as the democrats were to find out seven months later.

From the preceding, it seems that the end result of any democratic political maneuvering would have been the bowing to Soviet interests, a fact for which they cannot be criticized. However, they can be criticized for exhibiting a servility that could only dishearten Czechoslovak democracy's supporters both at home and abroad. If they knew that they would be outvoted, why not vote against the reversal and be on record for the benefit of their supporters? Particularly in the case of the National Socialists, the Communists' most serious electoral challenger, one must question their obsequious behavior. Not only did they vote to reverse a measure that was beneficial for the country, in line with the party's attempt to keep strong relations with the West, and greatly popular among their supporters, but thereafter they launched a strong campaign to sell the withdrawal to their manifestly disturbed members. The party convened a meeting of its presidium and parliamentary representatives, which concluded with the issuance of a communiqué intended to assuage feelings in Moscow, calm the party's members and set the party line. It read, in part: "For the National Socialist Party the alliance with the Soviet Union remains the fundamental pillar of the state's security. It was also stated that in our original acceptance of the invitation there was nothing that would be directed against this alliance."[37] In the immediate wake of this announcement, party leaders toured the land in support of the new line. Commenting on the "lively discussion" the policy change had caused, party chairman Petr Zenkl argued that "The political point of view took precedence over the economic. We are and will remain a loyal ally and will take on ourselves the advantages and disadvantages of this alliance."[38] Drtina, too, was on the hustings, telling a local party conference much the same thing. In short, Czechoslovak ministers followed a path of what can be called self-dictated appeasement from initial approval to consenting to withdrawal, to not voting against the withdrawal, to not abstaining in that vote, to attempting to drum up public support for their actions. Perhaps the height of this was reached in the confusing signal sent to the West by Foreign Minister Masaryk in an interview with the Associated Press. The resulting article was entitled "Any Talk of Ultimatum Against ÈSR [Czechoslovakia] is Silly," and in it he absolved the Soviets of even employing pressure on the delegation visiting Moscow.[39]

The Collapse of Czechoslovak Democracy and the Fate of the Marshall Plan

The failure of the Czechoslovak noncommunists to effectively utilize the political space in which they could maneuver continued after the Marshall debacle. Only months after sacrificing the anti-communist Democratic Party's power position in the leading Slovak administrative organ, noncommunist leaders embarked on an adventure that was to have fatal consequences. In February 1948, the ministers of three noncommunist parties—the National Socialist, Democratic and People's parties—resigned. In doing so, they hoped that the government would fall as a result, and that new elections, from which they hoped to bene-fit, would be forced. They took this step without fully preparing for the consequences of their actions, without securing for their plan the major-ity of ministers constitutionally necessary for the government to fall, and without informing their own party organizations of the course they intended to follow or of what steps the party memberships should be prepared to take. Further, the issue on which they chose to make their stand—the Communist packing of the middle levels of the police forces—had far less public resonance than, for example, that of the Marshall Plan.[40] The Communist Party rallied its members on the streets in the hundreds of thousands, while only a few thousand noncommunist stalwarts took part in counter-demonstrations. After five days, on February 25, 1948, the Communist victory was complete. Much as he had complied with Stalin's wishes, Jan Masaryk now complied with Klement Gottwald's, remaining as Foreign Minister until his "suicide" on March 10 after a still mystery-shrouded plummet from a Foreign Ministry window.

This is not the place for a critique of the Czechoslovak democrats' ill-fated political adventure, but rather the setting for an examination of the effect their defeat had on the fate of the Marshall Plan. Although I am not a specialist on the conduct of American policy, it seems that the fall of Czechoslovakia provided a powerful argument to those in the Truman administration and the foreign service establishment who were trying to convince recalcitrant members of Congress that Marshall aid was necessary to stop the spread of communism. The battle in the Republican-controlled Congress, and particularly in the House of Representatives, was bitterly fought. Opponents of the plan joined ranks on both President Truman's right and left. Conservatives, under the leadership of Senator Robert Taft opposed the program as financially dangerous and a strain on American resources devoted to welfare and socialistic purposes in Europe while failing to meet the greater need in China; the progressive Henry Wallace condemned the proposals as provocative and divisive.[41] Although public opinion polls in the country showed the existence of support for helping destitute, war-ravaged Europeans and opposing Communism, they also revealed that this support was vague and thin, rather than strong and reliable. Polls indicated, for example, that support for the Marshall Plan fell off considerably when it was linked to the necessity of postponing the planned tax cut or accepting increased inflation. This weak support, coupled with well-organized and disciplined congressional opposition, made the Marshall Plan questionable in its bid for passage. At the end of January, Joseph and Stewart Alsop wrote that its prognosis was "very black indeed," and Walter Lippmann forecast on February 9 that the most that could be won was interim aid.[42]

A little over two weeks after Lippmann's prediction, Czechoslovakia's Communists handed the supporters of Marshall aid a powerful political tool. Within hours of the Communist seizure of Czechoslovakia, Secretary of Defense James Forrestal met with former Secretary of State James Byrnes, and stoked his imagination with fears of the Communist menace, using the recent events in Prague and the Soviet invitation to Finland to sign a mutual assistance pact as his prime examples. Shortly thereafter, Byrnes gave a speech in which he stated that "There is nothing to justify the hope that with the complete absorption of Czechoslovakia and Finland the Soviets will be satisfied."[43] Forrestal recognized on March 2nd in his diary that the time was ripe, as he put it, "to capitalize on the present concern of the country over the events of the last week in Europe." In this, he was boosted by a well-known telegram from the American commander of the occupation forces in Germany, Lucien Clay, which read in part: "For many months, based on logical analysis, I have felt and held that war was unlikely for at least ten years. Within the last few weeks, I have felt a subtle change in Soviet attitude which I cannot define, but which now gives me a feeling that it may come with dramatic suddenness."[44] In response to this, Truman requested an assessment from the newly created Central Intelligence Agency, which reported that it did not expect war within sixty days, although it pointedly refused to predict further than that.

The war scare of early spring 1948 was a direct result of the Communist seizure of power in Czechoslovakia, and the series of events in that country fed the flames of fear in the United States. The *Washington Post* wrote on March 4 that "Until the disaster in Czechoslovakia there was a comfortable feeling here in Washington that the danger of war was something fairly remote—a matter of five to seven years. ... The comfortable assurance has vanished." The following day the paper ran a front-page map of Europe with the area under Soviet domination shaded and with the caption "Russia Moves Westward—Where next?" Arrows pointed to Italy, France, Finland and Austria. Other newspapers ran similarly dark stories.[45]

In the tense days of early March, the death of Jan Masaryk can be seen as the final catalyst in a remarkable series of events. Those who had been routinely using the fall of Czechoslovakia for political purposes, as one source puts it, "found their words suddenly informed by genuine feeling."[46] On the day of Masaryk's death, March 10, Secretary Marshall expressed his foreboding at a news conference: "The situation is very, very serious." Referring specifically to the death of the Czechoslovak foreign minister, he proclaimed that a "reign of terror" existed in that country. The following day, Truman declared his confidence in the maintenance of world peace "shaken," and proclaimed that the world was "in the midst of a great crisis," while urging the rapid approval of the Marshall Plan.[47] The president, slated to give a Saint Patrick's Day speech in New York, felt it necessary because "the grave events in Europe were moving so swiftly" to change his plans and address a joint session of Congress. In his speech, which was carried on nationwide radio,

Truman noted that "the tragic death of Czechoslovakia has sent a shock throughout the civilized world," and urged the adoption of universal military training and the rapid completion of legislative action on the Marshall Plan.[48] The congressional opposition to the latter collapsed, and a hitherto resistant House of Representatives approved Marshall aid on March 24.[49] Also in March, and under the shadow of possible war partially created by the dramatic developments in Czechoslovakia, steps leading directly to the formation of NATO were being taken.[50] Within 18 months, Western Europe had entered into a period of prosperity and security via the Marshall Plan and NATO that has lasted to this day, while Czechoslovakia slipped into the dark night of Stalinism.

Notes

1. It can be argued that the path to communist domination began in December of 1943. At that time Czechoslovak President Edvard Beneš signed a treaty of alliance between his state and the USSR that went beyond the mandate given him by the government-in-exile's cabinet. The treaty Beneš signed was both deeper than the proposal upon which the cabinet had agreed, and was to remain valid for 20 years, 15 years longer than the one the cabinet had entrusted Beneš to conclude. The duration made a particularly bad impression on both the noncommunist émigré leadership and the British Foreign Office. They considered unwise to commit to such a long-range agreement before the end of the war, while Beneš considered the treaty a great victory.

2. The 1946 election results in the Czech lands were as follows: Communists 40.17 percent, Social Democrats 15.59 percent, National Socialists 23.66 percent, and People's Party 20.23 percent. In Slovakia, the Communists received 30.48 percent and the Democrats 61.43 percent.

3. Prices for bread were 214 percent of the official price, flour 379 percent, pork 292 percent, and butter 274 percent. At the same time, the number of complaints lodged against black marketeers rose from 6,344 in August to over 10,000 in October. Josef Belda, Miroslav Bouček, Zdeněk Dezl and Miloslav Klimeš, *Na rozhraní dvou epoch*. (Praha: Svoboda, 1968), pp. 146–8. All translations, unless otherwise noted, are the author's.

4. United States Ambassador Laurence Steinhardt reported on June 19, 1947 that "There is an adequate supply of food." *Foreign Relations of the United States*. [Hereafter FRUS] 1947, Vol. IV. (Washington, DC: United States Government Printing Office, 1972), p. 213. Another observer, from the National War College in Washington, noted in late July that "Officials at the American Embassy later told me that the Czechs then had no serious food problem," and quotes Steinhardt rather undiplomatically observing that "the women of Prague had the 'largest fannies in Europe.'"

Thomas A. Bailey, *The Marshall Plan Summer. An Eyewitness Report on Europe and the Russians in 1947* (Stanford, CA: Hoover Institution Press, 1977).

5. *FRUS* 1947, Vol. III, p. 312.

6. For one report on the amity of the meeting, see Prokop Drtina, *Československo můj osud. Kniha života českého demokrata 20. Století*, Vol. Two, Book Two (Praha: Melantrich, 1992), p. 324.

7. Drtina. *Èeskoslovensko mùj osud*, p. 326.

8. Belda, et al. *Na rozhraní dvou epoch*, p. 121.

9. Scott D. Parrish, "The Turn Toward Confrontation: The Soviet Reaction to the Marshall Plan, 1947," in Scott D. Parrish and Miklhail M. Narinsky, eds., *New Evidence on the Soviet Rejection of the Marshall Plan, 1947: Two Reports*. Cold War International History Project Working Paper 9 (Washington, DC: Woodrow Wilson International Center for Scholars, 1994) p. 26.

10. Masaryk reported about Bodrov to the cabinet that *"Three times* he repeated ... that in this respect he had no instructions." Belda, et al., *Na rozhraní dvou epoch*, p. 122. Emphasis in the original. At this time, Soviet ambassador Valerian Zorin was in Geneva at a meeting of the European Economic Commission of the United Nations.

11. Hubert Ripka, *Czechoslovakia Enslaved. The Story of the Communist Coup d'État*, (London: Gollancz, 1950). Ripka's memoirs have recently been published in Czech, see Hubert Ripka, *Únorová tragédie* (Brno: Atlantis, 1995). Given the nature of this collection, English-language sources have been used wherever possible. Foreign Minister Modzelewski also informed United States Ambassador Stanton Griffiths that "although the final decision had not been made," he was "certain that [the] Polish government would accept" the invitation. See *FRUS* 1947, Vol. III, p. 313.

12. The National Socialist Minister of Trade and Industry, Hubert Ripka, had been scheduled to attend, but was replaced by Drtina at the last moment due to the former's illness.

13. He comments further that "At that moment I was convinced that Gottwald was absolutely surprised by Stalin's vehement and irate reaction, that he did not expect it at all and that it struck him the same as it did us—perhaps even worse, for it was the ire and wrath of his leader and fellow party member ... Perhaps I am wrong, but at that time I did not doubt that Gottwald was afraid of Stalin!" Prokop Drtina, *Československo můj osud*, pp. 329–30. Indeed, Gottwald must have been scared of Stalin. As one who had emerged victorious from the politically bloody Bolshevization of the Czechoslovak Communist Party, and having spent the war years in Moscow, Gottwald knew the potential penalties for error. In this case, Gottwald was in trouble up to his ears. Not only had a Czechoslovak government under his prime ministership made the wrong decision, but also it had made the decision public without consulting Moscow first.

14. Parrish. "The Turn Toward Confrontation," p. 28.

15. Drtina, *Èeskoslovensko mùj osud*, p. 331. Masaryk's position "above the parties" was the source of some concern to the United States diplomatic corps in Prague. As early as May of 1947, Ambassador Steinhardt condemned Masaryk's tactic of "trying not to antagonize the domestic supporters" of either the Communists or their opponents. The ambassador argued that the effect of this had been to "destroy his influence in Czechoslovak domestic politics and to deliver his Ministry into the hands of his Communist Under Secretary [Vladimír] Clementis." Steinhardt forecast that since "the combination of his high reputation in the West with his pliability to Communist pressure [made] him an almost ideal instrument from the Soviet viewpoint," moderate Czechoslovak politicians knew "they cannot count on him to stand up and fight on their side." *FRUS* 1947. Vol. IV, pp. 207–8.

16. Josef Josten, *Oh My Country* (London: Latimer House, 1949), p. 69. Josten was an official in the foreign ministry.

17. The minutes of the meeting were printed as Appendix IV of Drtina, *Československo mûj osud*, pp. 683–90. An English translation appears as "Stalin, Czechoslovakia, and the Marshall Plan: New Documentation from Czechoslovak Archives," introduced by Karel Kaplan, with an analysis by Vojtech Mastny, trans. by John M. Deasy, *Bohemia* 32 (1991), pp. 134–44. All citations are from this latter translation.

18. Drtina relates that he "supposes" this was the first he had heard of the Polish decision. Drtina, *Československo mûj osud*, p. 334.

19. The amenability of the Czechoslovak ministers to reverse themselves may have prevented the escalation of pressure from within the then-forming Eastern Bloc. Milovan Djilas relates the following: "a conference of East European countries was to be held in Moscow to discuss the Marshall Plan. I was designated to represent Yugoslavia. The real aim was to bring collective pressure on Czechoslovakia, whose government was not against participating in the Marshall Plan. The Soviet plane was already waiting at the Belgrade airfield, but I did not fly the next day, for a telegram arrived from Moscow stating that there was no need for the conference—the Czechoslovak government had abandoned its original line." Milovan Djilas, *Conversations with Stalin*, (New York: Harcourt, Brace and World, 1962), p. 116.

20. The telegram read, in part: "Therefore, immediately convene all available members of the government and familiarize them with the content of our discussion with Stalin and Molotov. We consider it necessary for you to decree the retraction (odvolání) of our participation in Paris and announce this such that it would be official here by four o'clock in the afternoon. In addition to this, appraise us of your decision by telephone immediately." See Zdeněk Veselý, *Československo a Marshallûv plán. Příspěvek k problematice mezinárodních souvislostí revolučího procesu v Československu v letech 1945–1948*. Acta Universitatis Carolinae. Philosophica et Historica. Monographia XCII – 1982 (Praha: Univerzita Karlova, 1985).

21. Drtina. *Československo můj osud.* 336.
22. Walter Ullmann, *The United States in Prague, 1945–1948.* East European Monographs 36 (Boulder: East European Quarterly, distributed by Columbia University Press, New York, 1978).
23. The National Socialist parliamentary representative Ota Hora recalls that his party's parliamentary delegation met to discuss the matter and also voted unanimously to withdraw. However, he claims that the representatives were insufficiently informed, and tellingly notes that he wondered to himself, "How much longer will it still be possible for the freely elected representatives of the people to express free opinions in this building [the parliament]?" If the struggle over the Marshall plan was perceived as a struggle over fundamental freedoms, why was there neither a stiffer defense nor more pressure on ministers from their party comrades below? Ota Hora, *Svědectví o puči. Z bojů proti komunizaci Československa* (Praha: Melantrich, 1991), pp. 10, 12.
24. The text of the government press release is reprinted in Ladislav Karel Feierabend. *Politické vypomínky III* (Brno: Atlantis, 1996). Note that the text Reads "would be interpreted" (byla by... vzkládána), rather than Stalin's own, less insistent "could." Ripka's English-language memoirs preserve the "could," making the Czechoslovak government's line less extreme. Interestingly, Ripka casts the fact that his proposal for the press release was accepted rather than the Communists' in a victorious light. Similarly, Ripka relates with an air of victory that Masaryk—despite commenting "You see with what arrogance, with what irony they treated us! I really had great difficulty in controlling myself"—was able to secure economic compensation from Stalin. See Ripka. *Czechoslovakia Enslaved,* pp. 61–62, 69.
25. On Masaryk's failure to attend the opera, see Drtina, *Československo můj osud,* p. 337. The quote is from the testimony of the foreign minister's general secretary, Arnošt Heidrich, who was present at the Kremlin meeting. See Feierabend, *Politické vypomínky III,* p. 467.
26. *FRUS* 1947, Vol. 4, p. 219. Optimistically, Ambassador Slavík coupled these comments with a renewed attempt to secure the 50 million dollar Export-Import Bank loan.
27. Karel Kaplan, *The Short March. The Communist Takeover in Czechoslovakia 1945–1948* (London: C. Hurst, 1987), p. 74.
28. Masaryk reportedly said this to the editor of the National Socialist Party's daily newspaper, Ivan Herben, and then repeated it to others. Herben recounts it in "Comment Staline empecha la Tchécoslovaquie de participer au plan Marchall," *Le Figaro.* August 12, 1948. Nonetheless, Drtina recalls that Herben accompanied him, not Masaryk, from the airport back to Prague, and if Masaryk had said this to Herben on the tarmac, he did not mention it to Drtina on the ride into the capital. See Drtina, *Èeskoslovensko mùj osud,* p. 347. Even if apocryphal, given Jan Masaryk's character the story rings true. The original Czech reads, "Do

Moskvy jsem jel jako československý ministr, ale vrátil jsem se jako Stalinûv pohûnek." Feierabend, *Politické vzpomínky*, p. 356. The traditional rendering is, "I left for Moscow as the foreign minister of a sovereign state, and returned as Stalin's stooge."

29. Ullmann. *The United States in Prague*, p. 81.

30. Ripka. *Czechoslovakia Enslaved*, pp. 59–60.

31. Drtina. *Československo mûj osud*, pp. 343–44, 346.

32. For just one example of this, see Drtina, *Èeskoslovensko mùj osud*, Vol. Two, Book One pp. 189–92. Here Drtina consulted with the Soviet Embassy in the matter of the sentences that would be demanded in the trial of the wartime collaborationist government. No death sentences were originally demanded, but after a Soviet diplomat demanded "at least three," Drtina's mind changed about the matter, and two were demanded. This Drtina portrays as almost a victory: "the two proposals for the highest punishment were a compromise, a partial accommodation to Soviet influence, but because there were not three it was again made clear that we did not intend to yield to great power pressure without reservations and in all matters."

33. Drtina, *Československo mûj osud*, pp. 344, 346.

34. Emphasis added. The line reads: "Rozbil napadrì iluzi o československé nezávislosti." Although Majer was in Paris at an international food conference, he sent a telegram to Prague urging the present ministers not to reverse their decision. The ministers were not informed of this message during the cabinet meeting. See his recollections in appendix 3/10 of Feierabend, *Politické vzpomínky III*, pp. 468–72.

35. The People's Party leaders Jan Šrámek and František Hála were ill, as was Ripka, Drtina was in Moscow in Ripka's place, and Majer was in Paris. Significantly, during the crisis the most powerful political figure in the land, President Beneš, was also too ill to participate. He had collapsed at a public event on July 2, and for some time thereafter his speech was impaired and it has been suggested that he could not write. However, it seems unlikely that the president would have acted in any way contrary to Stalin's wishes. See Zbyněk Zeman and Antonín Klimek, *The Life of Edvard Beneš 1884–1948: Czechoslovakia in Peace and War* (Oxford: Oxford University Press, 1997), p. 261.

36. This seems to be what Majer suggests the democrats should have done. Feierabend. *Politické vzpomínky III*, p. 470.

37. Feierabend, *Politické vzpomínky III*, p. 354.

38. From a speech in Karlovy Vary that appeared in the National Socialist newspaper, *Svobodné slovo*. Partially reprinted in Feierabend, *Politické vzpomínky III*, p. 355. On another occasion, Zenkl formulated a kind of embryonic Brezhnev Doctrine: "We know that the freedom of action of every small country is nowadays to a certain extent limited, and we know that this is doubly true about a country in our geographical position. Accepting this limitation, we do so ... in the interest of international

understanding which, as is known, demands a certain limitation of sovereignty from every state." Cited in Vladimir V. Kusin, "Czechoslovakia," in Martin McCauley, ed., *Communist Power in Europe 1944–1949* (London: MacMillan, 1977), p. 81.

39. The article was published in the official *Daily Review* of the Czechoslovak Ministry of Information and appeared in the People's Party daily, *Lidová demokracie*, on August 2. The most telling line is that Masaryk and Gottwald "did not need a lesson from Moscow to be aware that Czechoslovakia must revoke its acceptance of the invitation to the Paris meetings," but had in fact realized even before their departure that "their original decision to go to Paris must be reverted." See Ullmann, *The United States in Prague 1945–1948*, pp. 81–2 and Feierabend, *Politické vzpomínky III*, p. 356.

40. Majer notes that "It is possible that at that time [July, 1947], and perhaps only at that time, and in no way in February of 1948, tolled the fateful hour when it would perhaps still have been possible to defend Czechoslovak freedom and independence." Feierabend, *Politické vzpomínky III*, p. 471.

41. Harold F. Gosnell, *Truman's Crises: A Political Biography of Harry S. Truman*, Contributions in Political Science 33 (Westport, CT: Greenwood, 1980), p. 357.

42. Richard M. Freeland, *The Truman Doctrine and the Origins of McCarthyism: Foreign Policy, Domestic Politics and Internal Security 1946–1948*, (New York: Knopf, 1972), pp. 248, 262–63.

43. Charles L. Mee, Jr. *The Marshall Plan: The Launching of the Pax Americana*, (New York: Simon and Schuster, 1984), p. 243.

44. James Forrestal, *The Forrestal Diaries*, edited by Walter Millis with the collaboration of E. S. Duffield (New York: Viking, 1957).

45. Headlines throughout March worried, for example, that "Whispers of War Grow Loud Throughout the Capital (*Washington Times Herald*). Other headlines included "Marshall Fears War Move By Commies" (*Washington Times Herald*) and "How War Might Come" (*Washington Post*). On these and other articles see Freeland, *The Truman Doctrine and the Origins of McCarthyism*, pp. 270–4.

46. Mee, *The Marshall Plan*, p. 243.

47. Freeland, *The Truman Doctrine and the Origins of McCarthyism*, pp. 269–70.

48. Harry S. Truman, *Memoirs*, Vol. Two: Years of Trial and Hope (Garden City, New York: Doubleday, 1956), pp. 241–2.

49. Senate approval had been given on March 17.

50. The Brussels Pact between the Benelux countries, France, and Britain was signed on March 17, the same day as Truman's speech, and the talks that would lead to the eventual creation of NATO commenced on March 22. The concern here was for the security of Italy, where elections that the Communists were poised to win were slated for April 22. The United

States considered Italy vital to U.S. security. On the relationship between events in Czechoslovakia and the birth of NATO, see Mastny, Vojtech, "The February 1948 Prague Coup and the Origins of NATO," draft paper presented at the conference "The Czechoslovak 'February' 1948: Preconditions and Repercussions at Home and Abroad." (Prague, February 22–24, 1998).

References

Armitage, John A. "The View from Czechoslovakia." In: Thomas T. Hammond, ed. *Witnesses to the Origins of the Cold War.* Seattle/London: University of Washington Press, 1982.

Bailey, Thomas A. *The Marshall Plan Summer: An Eyewitness Report on Europe and the Russians in 1947.* Stanford, CA: Hoover Institution, 1977.

Belda, Josef, Miroslav Bouček, Zdeněk Deyl, and Miloslav Klimeš. *Na rozhraní dvou epoch.* [At the Dividing Line between Two Epochs.] Praha: Svoboda, 1968.

Brod, Toman. *Cesta československých komunistů k moci.* [Czechoslovak Communists' Road to Power.] Part One: Operace Velký podvod. [Operation Grand Deception.] Praha: Magnet-Press, 1990.

Milovan Djilas. *Conversations with Stalin.* New York: Harcourt, Brace and World, 1962.

Donovan, Robert J. *Conflict and Crisis: The Presidency of Harry S Truman, 1945–1948.* New York: Norton, 1977.

Drtina, Prokop. *Československo můj osud. Kniha života českého demokrata 20. století.* [Czechoslovakia My Fate. The Life of a Twentieth-Century Czechoslovak Democrat.] Volume Two, Book Two: Rok 1947–Únor 1948. [The Year 1947 through February 1948.] Praha: Melantrich, 1992.

Feierabend, Ladislav Karel. *Politické vzpomínky III.* [Political Memoirs III.] Brno: Atlantis, 1996. The relevant portions are a reprint of his *Pod vládou národní fronty.* [Under the Government of the National Front.] Washington, DC: L. K. Feierabend, 1968.

Foreign Relations of the United States. 1947–1948. Washington, DC: United States Government Printing Office, 1972, 1974.

Forrestal, James. *The Forrestal Diaries.* Edited by Walter Millis with the collaboration of E. S. Duffield. New York: Viking, 1951.

Freeland, Richard M. *The Truman Doctrine and the Origins of McCarthyism: Foreign Policy, Domestic Politics and Internal Security 1946–1948.* New York: Knopf, 1972.

Gosnell, Harold F. *Truman's Crises: A Political Biography of Harry S. Truman.* Contributions in Political Science 33. Westport, CT/London: Greenwood, 1980.

Hora, Ota. *Svědectví o puči. Z bojů proti komunizaci Československa.* [Testimony on the Putsch. From the Struggles Against the Sovietization of Czechoslovkia.] Praha: Melantrich, 1991.

Josten, Josef. *Oh My Country.* London: Latimer House, 1949.

Kaplan, Karel. *The Short March. The Communist Takeover in Czechoslovakia 1945–1948.* London: C. Hurst, 1987.

Korbel, Josef. *The Communist Subversion of Czechoslovakia 1938–1948: The Failure of Coexistence.* Princeton, NJ: Princeton University Press, 1959.

Kusin, Vladimir V. "Czechoslovakia." In: Martin McCauley, ed. *Communist Power in Europe 1944–1949.* London/Basingstoke: Macmillan and the School of Slavonic and East European Studies, University of London, 1977, 73–94.

Mastny, Vojtech. "The February 1948 Prague Coup and the Origins of NATO." Draft paper presented at the conference "The Czechoslovak 'February' 1948: Preconditions and Repercussions at Home and Abroad." Prague, 22–24 February 1998.

Mee, Charles L., Jr. *The Marshall Plan. The Launching of the Pax Americana.* New York: Simon and Schuster, 1984.

Netík, Jaromír. *Revoluce na objednávku.* [Revolution Made to Order.] Curych: Konfrontace, 1982.

Parrish, Scott D. and Mikhail M. Narinsky. "New Evidence on the Soviet Rejection of the Marshall Plan, 1947: Two Reports." Cold War International History Project Working Paper 9. Washington, DC: Woodrow Wilson International Center for Scholars, 1994.

Petruf, Pavol. *Marshallov plán.* [The Marshall Plan.] Bratislava: Slovak Academic Press, 1993.

Ripka, Hubert. *Únorová tragédie.* [The February Tragedy.] Přeložila z francouzského originálu *Le Coup de Prague: Une révolution Préfabriquée* Adriena Borovi*cková. Brno: Atlantis, 1995. Available in English as *Czechoslovakia Enslaved.* London: Victor Gollancz, 1950.

"Stalin, Czechoslovakia, and the Marshall Plan: New Documentation from Czechoslovak Archives." Introduction by Karel Kaplan. Analysis by Vojtech Mastny. *Bohemia* 32 (1991) 134–44.

Truman, Harry S. *Memoirs by Harry S. Truman.* Volume Two: Years of Hope and Trial. Garden City, New York: Doubleday, 1956.

Ullmann, Walter. *The United States in Prague, 1945–1948.* East European Monographs 36. Boulder: East European Quarterly, distributed by Columbia University Press, New York, 1978.

Veselý, Zdeněk. *Československo a Maršhallův plán. Příspěvek k problematice mezinárodních souvislostí revolučního procesu v Československu v letech 1945–1948.* [Czechoslovakia and the Marshall Plan. A Contribution on the Problem of the International Context of the Revolutionary Process in Czechoslovakia 1945–1948.] Acta Universitatis Carolinae. Philosophica et Historica. Monographia XCII—1982. Praha: Univerzita Karlova, 1985.

Zeman, Zbyněk and Antonín Klimek. *The Life of Edvard Beneš 1884–1948: Czechoslovakia in Peace and War.* Oxford: Oxford University Press, 1997.

PART THREE

The Economic Impact of the Marshall Plan

CHAPTER 5

The Marshall Plan Fifty Years Later: Three What-Ifs and a When

Roy Gardner

This paper considers the Marshall Plan from the standpoint of the theory of games and economic behavior. The paper defines the Marshall Plan in terms of its budget allocations and the strategy behind them. It then analyzed strategically four scenarios using crucial game theoretic constructs: winning coalition (failure to pass the U.S. Senate), strategic invitation (the 1947 invitation to the USSR), strategic surprise (North Korea's attack in 1950), and fiscal commitment (EU enlargement). Current plans for EU enlargement to countries not participating in the Marshall Plan constitute a fractional Marshall Plan.

The Marshall Plan, from the standpoint of 50 years later, looks on the surface like a blueprint of today's European Union (EU), together with today's European Free Trade Association (EFTA). Consider the Marshall Plan beneficiaries, shown in Figure 5.1. As you can see, the overlap with the EU and EFTA is very close.

To consider the overlap issue more closely, note that 13 current members of the EU received Marshall Plan funds. The only exceptions are Spain and Finland. Spain was excluded from funding because of the fascist Franco dictatorship—a status that also excluded it from membership in the EU until 1986. Finland was excluded from funding because of its special neutrality relationship with the USSR. In particular, Finland refused to apply for Marshall Plan funds for fear of jeopardizing

Country	Year: 48/49	Year: 49/50	Year: 50/51	Cumulative
Austria	232	166	70	488
Bel-Lux	195	222	360	777
Denmark	103	87	195	385
France	1,085	691	520	2,296
Germany	510	438	500	1,448
Greece	175	156	45	366
Iceland	6	22	15	43
Ireland	88	45		133
Italy**	594	405	205	1,204
Netherlands	471	302	355	1,128
Norway	82	90	200	372
Portugal			70	70
Sweden	39	48	260	347
Switzerland			250	250
Turkey	28	59	50	137
UK	1,316	921	1,060	3,297
Totals	49,533***	3,511	4,155	12,619

* from Wexler (1983)
**includes Trieste
***includes $11 million in commodity reserve

Figure 5.1 Marshall Plan: The Numbers 1948–50 ECA Aid Allotments, $ Millions 1950/51 EPU Quotas, $ Millions*

its status of neutrality. Three more countries now belonging to EFTA also received Marshall Plan funding: Switzerland, Iceland, and Norway. The only current EFTA member not to receive Marshall Plan funding was Liechtenstein. The only recipient of Marshall Plan funding not belonging to either the EU or EFTA is Turkey—which remains on the wait list for membership to the EU on the periphery of Europe.

The allocations to the various recipients amount to about $12.6 billion in late 1940s dollars. To convert these sums to 1998 dollars, one should multiply by a factor of 8. Thus, the $12.6 billion in 1948–51 is equivalent to about $100 billion today. In terms of Gross Domestic Product (GDP), this represented roughly 0.5 percent of the American economy annually in 1948–51. Alternatively, since the American economy is 16 times larger in terms of GDP now than it was then, another way of reckoning the total amount of spending is

(16) ($12.6 billion) = $201.6 billion

It is very unlikely that an amount of this magnitude would pass through the U.S. Congress in 1998, even on a four-year payout plan.

The Marshall Plan consisted of four objectives, two of which were fulfilled and two of which were at least partially fulfilled in the time allotted:[1]

1. *to increase production*
   Results: Between 1948–51, industrial production grew 35 percent and agricultural production grew 16 percent to levels exceeding those of 1938. This objective was fulfilled.

2. *to expand foreign trade*
   Results: Trade with Eastern Europe rises and then falls after 1949. Trade with the United States rises. There are also early attempts at a customs union. This objective was partially fulfilled. Its complete fulfillment had to await the creation of the European Economic Community (EEC), forerunner of today's EU, a decade after the Marshall Plan began.

3. *to enhance internal financial stability*
   Results: Inflation, budget deficits and unemployment were all reduced. This objective was also fulfilled. The atmosphere of macroeconomic crisis surrounding the recipient economies during 1947–48 had vanished by the expiration of Marshall Plan funding in 1951.

4. *to develop European economic cooperation*
   Results: A European Payments Union was created along with the OEEC (the forerunner of the EEC). Currencies became convertible and the phrase "European Union" was first used. This objective was partially fulfilled. Although the first use of "European Union" dates to the Marshall Plan period, the enactment of the Treaty on European Union—creating today's EU—took over 40 years after the conclusion of the Marshall Plan. To the above goals enshrined in the original legislation was added a fifth goal in September 1950.

5. *to help Western Europe rearm within the framework of an expanding economy*
   Results: NATO was created (with Germany as a member). There was a conversion of Marshall Plan aid into military assistance and a recruitment of Western European forces for U.N. duty in Korea. This late addition goal was also fulfilled, albeit soon after Marshall Plan funding expired at the end of 1951. We return to this theme when we consider the third What-if.

What If the U.S. Senate had Rejected the Economic Cooperation Act of 1948?

Although as historians such as Irwin Wall rightly point out to their students—asking counterfactual questions is dangerous—we nevertheless attempt this here. It helps that in this case the question is meaningful. Passage of the Economic Cooperation Act was hardly automatic, requiring nearly a year of coalition building. Thus, this What-if deals with coalition building.

The goal whenever one is building a coalition is to build a *winning coalition*—a coalition so big that it cannot be beat in a showdown, even if all of its opponents join forces in a counter coalition. General Marshall himself played a major role in building the coalition that ultimately prevailed in the votes of early 1948 in the U.S. Congress: labor (the AFL-CIO), business (the National Association of Manufacturers [NAM]), agriculture (through the Department of Agriculture as well as through individual Farm Bureaus), and both major political parties.

The time-honored strategy used by the coalition builders was "something for everyone." Initial projections of Marshall Plan aid requirements were driven by estimates of the dollar needs of European beneficiaries to pay for their imports from the United States. This brought American business, as represented by the NAM, quickly on board. American labor was brought on board with the promise that all Marshall Plan in-kind transfers would be carried by American ships, loaded by American dockworkers—all labor being supplied by members of the AFL-CIO. American agriculture was recruited to the coalition by the promise that farm surpluses would be used as Marshall Plan contributed food aid. In all of these cases, Marshall's lobbying the Senate was masterful.

Getting both major political parties to join the coalition behind the Marshall Plan was made much easier by the Communist takeover of Czechoslovakia at the beginning of March 1948. This made the necessity of Marshall Plan funding in Western Europe much more compelling—both to Republican partisans and to Democratic nonsupporters of President Truman.

Still, given America's isolationist tradition, even at that late moment, the possibility of rejection—although unlikely—cannot be excluded. Even if the Economic Cooperation Act (ECA) is defeated in April 1948, the big (although not yet winning) coalition is still in place. The United States continues to promote defense integration in Western Europe. The minute the USSR blockades Berlin in the summer of 1948, the big coalition becomes a winning coalition and the Senate approves the ECA.

In other counterfactuals stemming from a rejection of the ECA in April 1948, Truman is still reelected. Rejection of ECA gives him even more material with which to run against the Republican Congress. In Western Europe, France, the United Kingdom, and the Low Countries agree to the Western Union via the Treaty of Brussels even sooner—the core states of today's EU do not fall to Soviet forces, regardless of American aid. If anything, rejection of the Marshall Plan accelerates the Soviets' blockade of Berlin, triggering a Senate revote—again the ECA passes easily the second time around.

In Southern Europe, the short-run outcome is the same, regardless of passage of ECA. The Truman Doctrine, with its attendant funding, is already in place, as is American determination to defeat the Communist insurgency at any reasonable price. Thus, the Marshall Plan's $175 million of aid to Greece in 1948–49 is easily made up elsewhere in the U.S. budget.

What If the Soviets had said Yes to the Marshall Offer?

To make sense of this counterfactual, we need to establish some chronological order first. Marshall's explicit invitation to the USSR to participate was in response to a reporter's question on June 12, 1947, one week after his commencement address at Harvard. A week later, on June 17–18 in Paris, supposedly secret talks (although well monitored by KGB agents) took place in Paris between the British and French foreign ministers, Bevin and Bidault—the Two Power talks. At these talks, the United Kingdom and France agreed to respond favorably to the Marshall invitation. Ten days later, the Three Power talks commenced, also in Paris, adding Soviet foreign minister Molotov to Bevin and Bidault. Molotov, together with the enormous Soviet delegation of one hundred members (of whom many again were KGB agents), walked out of the Three Power talks at the beginning of July 1947. Finally, the Conference on European Economic Cooperation (CEEC) took place in Paris, July 12–16, 1947. Just prior to the CEEC conference, delegations from Czechoslovakia, Poland, and Hungary were recalled on direct orders from Moscow, not to participate in the conference. The main output of the conference was a coordinated European response—including the ultimate beneficiaries of Marshall Plan aid—to Marshall's offer.[2]

What I would like to argue here is that Marshall's offer is an example of a *calculated invitation*—an invitation to another party that you hope will not accept, and that you have good reason to believe will not accept.

To see the argument in its barest terms, consider the game tree shown in Figure 5.2.[3] The United States moves first, and can either invite the

USSR to participate (the branch labeled "invite" in the game tree) or not invite the USSR to participate (the branch labeled "not invite" in the game tree). If the United States does not invite the USSR to participate, the game ends—with a payoff of

$$(\text{USA payoff, USSR payoff}) = (-, +)$$

The negative payoff to the United States reflects the bad publicity of publicly not inviting its former ally in World War II, the USSR, to participate. The positive payoff to the USSR reflects the good publicity (to the USSR) of being shown disrespect publicly, and thus being able to turn this publicity into valuable propaganda worldwide.

If the United States does invite the USSR—as in fact it did—the move belongs to the USSR. The USSR can either accept the invitation (the branch labeled "accept" in the game tree) or reject the invitation (the branch labeled "reject" in the game tree). Here, the USSR, as represented by Molotov in Paris—but we now know Molotov was in close contact with Stalin in Moscow throughout the Three Powers Talks—has to decide whether to accept or reject.

Suppose the USSR accepts the Marshall Plan, and further that the U.S. Senate approves the Plan, including the USSR as a beneficiary. The Soviets get a lot of money that they need, as much as the United Kingdom does—over $3 billion in 1947 dollars, or almost $20–$25 billion in today's dollars. That's a lot of dollars—which the Soviets could

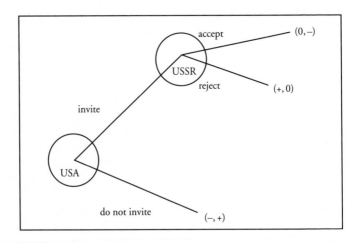

Figure 5.2 The Marshall Offer

have very much used. At the same time, the Soviets, by taking the money, also accept the following:

1. loss of control of their satellites in Eastern Europe (Poland, Czechoslovakia, and Hungary are all ready to say Yes to Marshall's offer before being directed otherwise by Moscow).
2. the rebuilding of Germany as a revanchist American ally.

Given that the principal Soviet goal in this period was preventing the rebuilding of Germany as anything but a neutral on the model of Finland, the Soviets have to attach a negative sign overall to the outcome of accepting the Marshall Plan. The Marshall funding does not offset the rebuilding of Germany.

By contrast, for the United States, Soviet acceptance of the Marshall Plan is a break-even outcome—it is just as if the United States had not issued the invitation—and warrants a zero value:

$$(\text{USA payoff, USSR payoff}) = (0, -)$$

If the USSR rejects the Marshall plan, the game tree ends in the payoffs:

$$(\text{USA payoff, USSR payoff}) = (+, 0)$$

For the United States, this is the best possible outcome of the calculated invitation—make the invitation and the unwanted guest does not accept. For the USSR, this outcome is worse than if the United States had not made the invitation in the first place. The USSR does not get a propaganda victory, and shows itself on the world stage as refusing to participate in the rebuilding of Europe. This is the payoff of 0 to the USSR shown in Figure 5.2.

According to established game theoretic principles, the solution to the strategic interaction between the United States and the USSR in Figure 5.2 is for the United States to make the invitation, and for the USSR to reject it.

This analysis nonetheless begs two strategic questions. For the United States, the strategic question is: Why make an offer that you don't want to be accepted? Here is the answer is threefold:

1. the offer is very good publicity
2. the probability of acceptance is very small $(.05)$[4]
3. even if the offer is accepted, the USA still has a safeguard, namely the U.S. Senate rejects the Marshall Plan including the USSR.

Marshall authorities are united in considering the invitation sincere.[5] However, the calculation behind the invitation, as I reconstruct it, was very calculated. Marshall made the invitation, convinced—for instance by Molotov's oft-repeated references to "dollar imperialism"—that the USSR would reject it.

Still—as was pointed out in the vigorous discussion at the conference that attended this point—the Soviets may have made a very large blunder in rejecting the invitation. If the Soviets had accepted the invitation, surely the U.S. Senate would have rejected the funding request and there would have been no plan. In this event, the rebuilding of Germany would be been put on hold for some time. Germany would have been much more prone to being "Finlandized" by the Soviet blockade of Berlin in the summer of 1948—indeed, the Soviets might have even pushed up the start date of the blockade to late Summer 1947. The Cold War would have started very differently had the Soviets accepted Marshall's invitation.

What If North Korea does not Attack South Korea in June 1950?

This What-if is an example of *strategic surprise and linkage.* The North Koreans achieved strategic surprise—American authorities were in no way prepared for what hit them, and Americans were nearly driven off the Korean peninsula in six weeks' time, left occupying only a small perimeter surrounding the coastal port of Pusan. The North Koreans also—albeit unwittingly—provided an example of strategic linkage. Here was an event half way around in the world in a remote Asian peninsula, that dramatically changed the reality on the ground in Europe, and in particular the Marshall Plan.

As far as the Marshall Plan is concerned, we can be sure that it would have wound down in any event. Funding was set to expire at the end of 1951, and the Korean War did not change that schedule. What did change was the Marshall Plan's previous focus on civilian aid. With the North Korean attack on South Korea, there was a dramatic conversion of Marshall Plan funding from economic aid to military aid. This is shown clearly in Figure 5.3, drawn from Kaplan (1980). Notice that economic aid falls at about the same rate that military aid increases during the period of the Korean War, 1950–53. Although the total remains about the same—roughly $2 billion each half year in shipments—the composition changes drastically. By the end of 1951, military aid exceeds economic aid, and the excess grows even further until the end of the Korean War. What the Korean War did was to accelerate the conversion of economic aid to military aid.

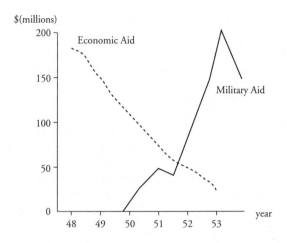

Figure 5.3 Economic and Military Aid, 1948–53*

There are two collateral events affected if North Korea does not invade South Korea in 1950. First, Eisenhower's probability of being nominated and elected president in 1952 is greatly reduced—his very effective promise "I will go to Korea" does not get made in this case. At the same time, his command of newly-formed NATO becomes much less impressive for domestic political purposes if there is no Cold War contest being fought.

Second, negotiations for the European Coal and Steel Community (which succeed) and for the West European Defense Union (which do not succeed) commence in any case. In this sense, these intra-European initiatives are not directly strategically linked to the war in Korea.

This concludes our survey of three What-ifs surrounding the Marshall Plan, and the three strategic principles exemplified by each. We now turn to one When.

When will the EU Raise the Funds for its Own European Recovery Plan for the Candidate Members in the East?

The short answer, I believe, is Never. Let's consider the commitments made at the EU Summit in Dublin, December 1997. In accordance with European Commission plans, membership offers were extended to Czech Republic, Estonia, Hungary, Poland, Slovenia, and Cyprus.[6] This commitment is limited in scope and in size. The commitment excludes the second-tier states—Romania, Bulgaria, Slovakia, Lithuania, and

Latvia—all of whom were included in the original Marshall offer. That's a limited scope. As important is the limited size of the budget backing up the membership offers. The EU budget for eastward expansion currently allocates about $5 billion/year for this purpose.

What we have here is an example of the strategic principle of *fiscal constitution*. Modern governments, in order to control their rapidly growing expenditures, adopt fiscal constitutions that have the effect of controlling those expenditures. In the case of the EU, the fiscal constitution is embodied in the rule that not more than 1.27 percent of EU GDP is to be spent in the EU budget. This spending limit has already been reached, before spending on eastward expansion of the EU is included. Given that the eastern countries are poor—they did not get to participate in the Marshall Plan 50 years ago!—their GDPs are small and so the tax base of the EU does not increase much with their inclusion. This means there is very little money available for their integration prior to membership. This budget reality is reflected in the very small (in relative terms) sum—$5 billion/year—currently allocated to eastward expansion. It's a zero-sum situation—more money allocated to poor accession states means less money allocated to existing poor EU members like Spain.

It goes without saying that this is no Marshall Plan. A Marshall-scale plan would require something like $50 billion/year of the budget to go for eastward expansion—compared to the $5 billion/year currently budgeted. The EU's plan, we can say, is a 10% Marshall Plan. And this plan is not going to change in the immediate future.[7] Any budget increase will be met with the fierce objections of Germany, which, as the largest net contributor to the EU budget, feels it is already contributing its share and more to European integration and security. The bottom line is, there is no Marshall Plan in Europe without the United States.

Conclusion

This paper has considered four principles of game theory—coalition building, calculated invitation, strategic surprise and linkage, fiscal constitution—in relation to major aspects of the Marshall Plan. I hope to have convinced you that game theory applies to major events such as this, even if the details are far more complicated than we portray them to our students. It goes without saying that the Marshall Plan was a unique episode in human history—a victor rebuilds the foes it vanquished. Nevertheless, even a unique episode can be explained within the rubric of a general theory of human decisions, rationally arrived at—the theory of games.

Notes

1. For a detailed discussion, see Wexler (1983), the definitive text on this question.
2. This sequence of events is laid out very clearly in Wrightman (1956), Chap. 2.
3. For those unfamiliar with game trees, Chap. 1 of Gardner, *Games for Business and Economics* (Wiley, 1995) will prove helpful.
4. This probability is based on hundreds of experiments conducted with human players playing games in behavior laboratories worldwide. Even in a case of very clear preferences—induced by the prospect of being paid large sums of money—the error rate (the observed frequency of picking the worse alternative) is rarely less than .05. It should be noted that at least one contemporary observer, Secretary of War Forrestal, was quoted at the time as saying, "There was no chance of Russia not joining this effort."
5. See, for instance, the exhaustive biography of Marshall by Pogue (1987).
6. The latter is a special case, hotly contested by Greece and Turkey, and not included in the Marshall offer of 1947. All the other countries on the list were included in that offer.
7. As Eichengreen (1998) points out, the funding difference in eastern Europe is being made up by private sector capital inflows, rather than EU or other governments' spending.

References

Gardner, Roy, *Games for Business and Economics* (New York: Wiley, 1995).

Kaplan, Lawrence, *A Community of Interests: NATO and the Military Assistance Program, 1948–1951* (Washington, DC: Office of the Secretary of Defense, Historical Office, U.S. Government Printing Office, 1980).

Pogue, Forest C., *George C. Marshall: Statesman, 1945-1959* (New York: Viking, 1987).

Wexler, Immanuel, *The Marshall Plan Revisited: The European Recovery Program in Economic Perspective* (Westport, CT: Greenwood Press, 1983).

Wightman, David, *Economic Co-Operation in Europe: a Study of the United Nations Economic Commission for Europe* (New York: Frederick A Praeger, Inc., 1956).

CHAPTER 6

The Market and the Marshall Plan

Barry Eichengreen

The Marshall Plan was the response of the U.S. government to two over-arching facts of economic and political life: the Cold War and the inability of private capital markets to meet the financial requirements of European reconstruction. Now both of these circumstances have been relegated to the dustbin of history, the first by the collapse of the Soviet bloc, and the second by the explosive growth of international financial transactions. This paper asks what aspects of Marshall Plan history remain relevant to a world in which the Cold War is but a distant memory and private capital markets are back with a vengeance.

D ates like the 50th anniversary of the Marshall Plan, the historic initiative announced by Secretary of State General George C. Marshall on June 5, 1947, are occasions for celebration. In this case, however, emotions are mixed, because a plan like Marshall's, however grand in retrospect, is inconceivable today. Marshall's June 5 "shot heard round the world" led to the transfer of $13 billion in U.S. government grants to promote the recovery and reconstruction of wartorn Europe.[1] Today, in contrast, most Americans see foreign aid as "welfare for foreigners"—as a cause rather than a solution of the ills of developing countries. There is little evidence that aid encourages investment or stimulates economic growth. All too often it simply subsidizes government consumption, allowing corrupt administrations to line their pockets and buy support.[2]

The Historical Context

The 1940s were different. Then there was a belief in the ability of governments to solve problems. Skepticism was reserved for the markets, which had malfunctioned famously in the Great Depression. Government was now to use administered prices, antitrust policy, and the newly discovered weapon of Keynesian stabilization policy to counter market imperfections. Its success at mobilizing resources for war had demonstrated the workability of planning, controls, and nationalized industry. Wartime and immediate postwar aid programs, like those of Lend-Lease and the United Nations Relief and Reconstruction Administration, had worked reasonably well, and there was hope that these successes would carry over.[3] There was faith that government could make a difference and fear that the unfettered market could not be trusted.

But more than just faith was needed to marshal support in the U.S. Congress for a program of such scope and ambition. The Truman Administration worked hard to gain Congressional backing: It asked leaders of the Congressional opposition like Republican Senator Arthur Vandenberg (Chair of the Senate Committee on Foreign Affairs) who they wished to see head the Marshall Plan Administration.[4] It enlisted influential opinion makers like Allan Dulles and Averell Harriman to propagandize in favor of the program.[5] That a leader with the stature of Marshall, a war hero known for his integrity, lent his name to the program gave it dignity and legitimacy. Contrast the aftermath of the 1990 Kuwait War and the Oslo Accords between Israel and the Palestinians, when calls for "a Marshall Plan for the Middle East" were not taken up. How different the outcome might have been had a military hero with the stature and reputation of a Colin Powell offered a "Powell Plan" for the region!

But more than political savvy was at work. The American economy was growing rapidly and the U.S. industrial preeminence was unrivaled, which put the American public in a generous mood. The 1940s was not an "age of diminished expectations." With incomes rising, American taxpayers did not see additional aid as a bigger slice taken from a pie of given size. That the pie was growing rapidly made them more inclined to share the wealth. And the fact that additional segments of the American economy had come to appreciate the importance of exports for their prosperity heightened the importance they attached to European recovery. Parts of California and Washington State, for example, were shifted into the internationalist camp by the wartime growth of aircraft production and shipbuilding. No aid meant no trade, and for export-oriented sectors of the U.S. economy no trade spelled disaster. It might even mean a new depression in the United States.

The one factor that most militated in favor of the Marshall Plan was the geopolitical stakes. The program was more than an attempt to stimulate economic recovery in Europe; it was the Truman Administration's response to the Cold War. By Spring 1947, the outlines of the impending U.S.–Soviet conflict were clear.[6] It was far from obvious with which camp Europe's west and east would ally. Recall that Marshall's initial offer was not limited to Western Europe but extended to all lands "west of the Urals."[7] Czechoslovakia and Poland sought to participate until Moscow vetoed their involvement.[8] The countries of Western Europe, the eastern border of which was suddenly defined by German western zones, along with Austria, Italy and Greece, were tipped into the U.S. camp.

In a sense the Marshall Plan defined the divide between East and West. It did so by defining the East-West conflict as a choice between plan and market and by tying Marshall aid to market-oriented reform.[9] Countries accepting Marshall aid had to sign bilateral agreements with the United States. They committed to decontrol prices, stabilize exchange rates, and balance budgets. In other words, they agreed to put in place the macroeconomic prerequisites for a functioning market economy.

The Marshall Plan intervened at precisely the moment when Europe was poised to decide whether to encourage or suppress the market. Communists hostile to free markets occupied key positions in the Italian and French governments in early 1947, and socialist influence was pervasive in Belgium, Sweden, and Norway, among other countries. The United States effectively made the replacement of far-left governments by centrist administrations a precondition for the disbursal of aid. Centrist politicians, for their part, could cite the loss of Marshall aid as an additional cost of opposing their programs.[10]

As a final condition for receiving Marshall aid, the recipients had to agree to liberalize their trade and commit to the goal of European integration. This last condition helped overcome French resistance to the reindustrialization of Germany.[11] With European integration locking Germany into Europe and promoting the development of institutions of transnational governance, the French government could agree to the elimination of ceilings on German industrial production. By substituting American aid, the Marshall Plan encouraged the French and other victorious powers to drop their claims to German reparations. Since

Germany was at the heart of the European economy, that heart could now beat faster. Western European stability was buttressed by the return of prosperity.

Because Europe already had most of the preconditions for economic growth in place, notably a backlog of unexploited technologies and a trained and educated labor force, all it needed was a little push to inaugurate the postwar golden age.[12] It needed well-defined property rights, private enterprise, a liberal trade regime, and a functioning price system. Marshall Plan conditionality provided just the requisite push in this direction.

The Legacy of the Plan

Some of the consequences were anticipated. Europe's decision to opt for the price system and the market economy was expected by the Marshall Planners. Price liberalization and currency stabilization drew goods back to the market, precisely as they had anticipated.[13] Once immediate postwar difficulties associated with shortages and war damage were overcome, the continent began to grow, and grow rapidly. Industrial production soared in the Marshall Plan countries, by 20 percent in 1948 alone. This was no surprise to Marshall Plan administrators, who saw growth as being held back by bottlenecks to be removed through the judicious application of foreign resources.

Other consequences were more surprising. The fact that Europe developed its own distinctive version of capitalism, namely the "mixed" or "social market" economy, was not anticipated by the Americans. But here, too, the Marshall Plan played an important role. The Marshall planners held out U.S. industrial relations as the state of the art and subsidized visits by European experts to American factories so that they might observe and emulate U.S. arrangements.[14] New Deal legislation had encouraged the development of a more corporatist form of industrial organization in the United States. By urging their European students to emulate this example, the Marshall planners fueled an already powerful strand of communitarian thought with ideological roots deep in European Christian Democracy. It encouraged governments to build on their countries' existing protocorporatist structures, such as industrial cartels and national trade union associations, whose scope exceeded anything the United States had evolved under the Roosevelt Administration. With U.S. acquiescence and encouragement, Europe moved quickly to develop the institutions to neocorporatism, the mixed economy, and the welfare state.

A final effect of the Marshall Plan was the impetus it lent European integration. The idea of a "United States of Europe," however naive, was integral to the Marshall planners' thought.[15] Americans frustrated by the fact that Europe had fought three bloody wars in three generations saw the creation of an integrated continental economy as protection against further hostilities. They made their offer of aid contingent on intra-European cooperation. It was conditional on the willingness of the recipients to establish a framework through which they could shape the decision of how to allocate the transfer. The entity they created, the Committee for European Economic Cooperation (CEEC), evolved subsequently into the OEEC and then the OECD. Early CEEC negotiations were anything but smooth; there was a tendency for the CEEC to occupy itself with drawing up "shopping lists."[16] But these meetings were the first time European governments offered one another an inside look into their balance sheets and as such represented a significant step toward transnationalism. As such, they set the stage for subsequent integrationist initiatives. The European Payments Union, itself an offspring of the Marshall Plan (started with $350 million of Marshall aid) was one of the two trans-European entities (along with the European Coal and Steel Community) that eventually evolved into the EEC. Presumably the Marshall planners would be pleased by the subsequent course of European integration. At the same time they would likely be surprised by how far the hare they loosed has run.

Accounting for the Effectiveness of the Initiative

Why was the Marshall Plan so effective when so many subsequent aid programs have failed? It is tempting to credit the structure of the program: a resident mission in each country, a central administration subordinate but not reporting or responsible to the president (as a way of minimizing political distortions), enabling legislation with "sunset provisions" to prevent administrators from building bureaucratic empires, close monitoring by the Marshall Plan administrators of the use of the each dollar, and the sequestration of counterpart funds to enhance the financial leverage of the administrators.

Accounts emphasizing such factors are too self-congratulatory; they are history written from the perspective of the rearview mirror.[17] More important surely was that European society was predisposed toward the reforms the Marshall planners had in mind. Western Europe had long experience with market-based forms of economic organization. While the disasters of the 1930s shook confidence in such arrangements, the alternative of full-fledged communism appealed only to a small (if vocal) minority. The Marshall Plan was capable of tipping the balance toward price decontrol, exchange rate stabilization, budget balance, and trade liberalization, because there already existed in Europe centuries of experience with the market and abiding support for its operation.

In the same sense, the Marshall Plan could effectively encourage European integration because there already existed in Europe a powerful strand of integrationist thought. The English Quaker William Penn had proposed a European parliament and European government. Jeremy Bentham advocated a European assembly, Jean-Jacques Rousseau a European federation, Henri Saint-Simon a European monarch and parliament. By the middle of the nineteenth century, intellectuals like Victor Hugo could speak of a United States of Europe. Between the wars, the Pan-European Union, founded by Count Richard Coudenhove-Kalergi, lobbied for a European federation. Konrad Adenauer and Georges Pompidou were both members. This was fertile ground for planting the integrationist seed. This is not to deny that the Marshall Plan mattered for the subsequent course of European integration but to suggest that it mattered only because the appropriate predispositions were in place.

The Role of Private Capital Markets

Today, politicians and publics in many developing and transition economies, reacting against the inefficiency of planning and the repression of authoritarianism, seem similarly predisposed to turn to the market and integrate into the global economy. But no Marshall Plan has been forthcoming to help them surmount their transitional difficulties. Calls were made in the late 1980s for a Marshall Plan for developing countries.[18] The collapse of the Council for Mutual Economic Assistance (CMEA) encouraged suggestions for a Marshall Plan for Eastern Europe.[19] Glasnost and the disintegration of the Soviet Union caused more than a few observers to float the idea of a Marshall Plan for Russia and the other successor states of the USSR.[20] But while some Western grants and intergovernmental loans have been forthcoming, there has been nothing like the Marshall Plan.

Or has there? Since the early 1990s, funds have been transferred to developing and transition economies by the markets at double the rate of the Marshall Plan. According to World Bank estimates, private capital flows to developing countries amounted to $62 billion in 1991, $100 billion in 1992, $154 billion in 1993, $159 billion in 1994, and

Table 6.1 Private capital flows to developing countries (gross, US $ billions)

	1991	1992	1993	1994	1995*
Foreign Direct Investment	35.0	46.6	68.3	80.1	90.3
Portfolio	7.6	14.1	45.6	34.9	22.0
Bonds	12.7	26.5	54.0	52.8	59.6
Latin America & Caribbean	8.7	12.5	26.5	19.4	24.4
East Asia & the Pacific	2.9	5.7	13.3	22.4	23.6
Eastern Europe & Central	0.8	7.4	13.6	7.5	8.3
South Asia	0.2	0	0.5	1.0	0.8
Middle East & North Africa	0	0	0	0.6	1.0
Sub-Saharan Africa	0	0.7	0	1.4	1.3
Commercial Bank Lending	2.5	13.8	−4.9	9.2	17.1
Other private flows	3.7	12.6	6.9	2.4	4.0
Total private flows	61.6	100.3	154.2	158.8	167.1

* preliminary
Source: World Debt Tables 1996.

$167 billion in 1995, and $244 billion in 1996 (see Table 6.1). Marshall Plan transfers of $3 billion a year come to $18 billion in 1995 dollars.[21] Alternatively, if we multiply this figure by 16 to adjust for the growth of the U.S. income in current dollars since 1948, $244 billion is capital transfer at nearly five times the annual rate under the Marshall Plan. Even if we multiply it by 40 to account for the growth of the global income in current dollars, $244 billion is still capital transfer at twice the rate of the Marshall Plan!

This "market-based Marshall Plan," if we may call it that, points to the most significant difference between Marshall's era and today: after World War II international capital markets were repressed and demoralized; today they are flourishing. After World War II, a Marshall Plan was necessary because the markets were unable or unwilling to lend. Today a Marshall Plan would be superfluous to all but the very poorest countries, since private capital markets stand ready to do the job.

Private lending was so limited after World War II because international bond markets had performed so poorly in the 1920s and 1930s.[22] The last defaulted debts from the 1930s were not finally cleared away until the 1950s. American investors who had lost their shirts purchasing foreign bonds in the 1920s were loath to risk a repetition of this experience after World War II. Furthermore, politicians and their constituents distrusted capital markets; they viewed them as a source of instability and as a threat to the pursuit of sound economic policies. Tight regulation of international lending went hand in hand with the tight regulation of domestic financial systems that was integral to the national economic strategies of the postwar years. Domestic regulation accounted for the reluctance of U.S. banks to enter the international lending business seriously before the 1960s.

An even more fundamental explanation for the suppression of international capital markets was real and financial disequilibria inherited from the war. European governments had issued massive quantities of debt to finance the war effort; until these debts were consolidated, deregulation and decontrol risked financial instability. Exchange rates were overvalued, Europe having little power to export. If capital controls were removed, capital flight threatened to exhaust the country's international reserves and destabilize its currency. Controls promised to bottle up these potential instabilities. But so long as controls remained in place, private capital markets could not discharge the task for which the Marshall Plan was ultimately substituted.

These arguments, which so impressed contemporaries, lose their interest in light of the recent experience of Eastern Europe and transition economies elsewhere in the world. There, too, governments inherited major real and financial disequilibria, including heavy debts, yawning deficits, overvalued currencies, and alarming trade deficits. The solution has been radical changes in relative prices. Currencies have been devalued. Wages have adjusted dramatically, sometimes falling sharply in the early stages of transition. Internal debts have been restructured through inflation or forced conversion. Very large changes in income distribution and economic structure have occurred to allow governments to make their currencies convertible and gain access to international capital markets.

This is precisely what post–World War II politicians insisted was impossible. The drastic cuts in real wages needed to improve Europe's international competitiveness, restore currency convertibility and regain access to international capital markets, they insisted, would have fomented a revolt against the market. They would have set back rather than furthered market-oriented reform. Reconciling tolerable living standards with inherited economic disequilibria required bottling up the latter with controls, which in turn required substituting the Marshall Plan for the private capital markets.[23]

Why were the governments of Western Europe after World War II so reluctant to accept changes in income distribution like those accepted by the governments of present-day transition economies? One possibility is that postwar politicians overestimated the danger of a populist backlash. Conceivably so, but there is good reason to give contemporaries the benefit of the doubt. Doing so leaves us with the following alternative interpretation. In the 1940s, there was a danger that the disaffected masses would veer away from the market in favor of state socialism because the market had been found wanting in the 1930s and an idealized vision of the alternative prevailed. The Soviet Union's impressive war effort and even more impressive official statistics on growth of industrial production encouraged contemporary observers to exaggerate the attractions of that alternative. In the 1990s, in contrast, there was less danger of a backlash because central planning had been found wanting. The radical changes in distribution needed to render currencies convertible and regain access to international capital markets may have been painful, but there existed no more attractive alternative.

A Market-Based Marshall Plan

Recently private funds have been flowing to virtually every developing country except the basket cases of Sub-Saharan Africa and the former USSR. They have been flooding into Latin America, Eastern Europe, Russia, East Asia, India, and China. In most cases, the problem is not lack of funds in response to which a program of government grants and loans like the Marshall Plan would be appropriate, but an embarrassment of riches. The issue is how to moderate the tidal wave of capital inflows to prevent them from destabilizing prices, interest rates, and domestic financial policies.

These private flows have worked to encourage reforms similar to those pushed by Marshall Plan administrators in the 1940s. Foreign investment is attracted to countries that stabilize their public finances, privatize public enterprise, decontrol prices, and liberalize trade. Governments seeking foreign finance have a strong incentive to adopt these reforms. Of course, funds can begin to flow into countries in advance of reform. Thus, foreign investment surged into Peru as early as 1990, even before the country had ended its hyperinflation. It has surged into Russia despite continued questions about the rule of law and the stability of the public finances. It has surged into India despite problems of corruption and administrative inefficiency. It has surged into China despite doubts about the security of property rights, limits on economic freedom, and an oppressive political regime.

If countries fail to follow through with the requisite reforms, the markets can be unforgiving. Not only does foreign finance dry up, as it would under the Marshall Plan had countries repudiated their bilateral agreements with the United States, but prior inflows can also be withdrawn, dealing a blow to the economic policy strategy of the offending government. The market attaches conditionality to its funds, as did the United States under the Marshall Plan.

Unfortunately, market-based conditionality can be erratic. Foreign investors see-saw between excessive enthusiasm about investment opportunities in a developing country and total despair. Their willingness to transfer funds to emerging markets can be held hostage by factors exogenous to the country itself. Central bank policy in the United States. and Europe, for example, can powerfully influence the flow of funds. When United States interest rates decline, investors are more inclined to search for yield in emerging markets.[24] Conversely, a sudden hike in U.S. rates can abruptly stem the flow of funds into emerging markets and jeopardize an otherwise sustainable restructuring program. The more diversified international investment portfolios become, the less incentive international investors have to scrutinize economic conditions in particular emerging markets. Not only do they find it more costly to gather information on the entire range of countries to which they lend, but they have less incentive to do so insofar as portfolio diversification protects them against country-specific risk.[25]

Imperfectly informed investors are prone to panic and herd. Thus, while private financial flows to emerging markets have been reasonably stable since the 1990s (even the Mexican crisis occasioned only a brief interruption), there is no guarantee that this will remain true in the future. The advantage of the Marshall Plan lay precisely in the fact that it was a multiyear program not subject to such interruptions, upon which the recipient countries could build sustainable economic policy strategies.

Hence, the role for the governments of the creditor countries today, if they seek to honor the memory of their predecessors who oversaw the Marshall Plan, is to stabilize private capital flows rather than suppress or supplement them. This means adopting sound and stable monetary policies at home and avoiding the kind of radical interest-rate increases that can destabilize the flow of funds. European governments especially must resist the temptation to close their markets to exports from low-wage developing countries as a sop to domestic political pressures. The International Monetary Fund (IMF) should be encouraged to expand its data dissemination efforts as a way of strengthening market discipline. Better data dissemination will make for better-informed investors and limit overreach by the markets.

Only the poorest countries of Sub-Saharan Africa stand to be neglected by the markets. There, infrastructure is in disrepair, debt overhangs are enormous, and even the most basic functions of government—notably economic governance—have broken down. There is a case for special measures to stimulate private capital flows to the region. Sachs (1997) has suggested deep and rapid foreign debt write-offs, temporary balance-of-payments support to aid macroeconomic stabilization, and funds for repairing and expanding key infrastructure, especially roads and telecommunications. With macroeconomic reform, the removal of debt overhangs, and the revitalization of infrastructure, private funds should begin to flow. To provide private investors the strongest possible incentive to respond to public intervention, the governments of the advanced industrial countries could also adopt corporate tax incentives to stimulate direct foreign investment in the region.

Finally, there is a role for the IMF and the Group-of-Ten countries to prevent problems in one country from spreading contagiously to others. This was a danger at the beginning of 1995, when the crisis in Mexico threatened to spill over to Argentina, Thailand, and other emerging markets. At that time the IMF, the United States, and the other Group-of-Seven countries responded with an unprecedented financial rescue of Mexico which limited foreign repercussions of its crisis. Subsequently, the Fund has streamlined its procedures for responding to such problems, tightened its surveillance of emerging markets, and augmented its financial resources. While a useful start, there is reason to think that these steps have not gone far enough.[26] There is no space here to launch into a detailed critique taken by the IMF and the G-10 countries to date, but significantly more remains to be done if the industrial countries are to succeed in developing a full-fledged financial fire brigade.

In the same way that the problem for developing and transition economies is to move from *plan* to *market,* those seeking lessons from the experience of the Economic Recovery Program have to find a way of conceptualizing the move from Marshall *Plan* to capital *market.* Now that international capital markets are flourishing again, the problem for policy is no longer that of the 1940s. The response developed by Marshall and his colleagues is no longer appropriate. But Marshall's key insight, that a market economy needs institutional and policy support to function effectively, is as timely today as 50 years ago. It just needs to be operationalized in a different way.

Notes

1. The quote is from Senator Arthur H. Vandenberg, more on whom below.
2. Perhaps the most systematic statement of this view is Boone (1996). See also Dollar and Burnside (1997). Lest the contrast be drawn too sharply, it is worth recalling that contemporary critics referred to the Marshall Plan as "Operation Rathole." See for example Beverley Smith's interview with Will Clayton (himself an early proponent of U.S. aid to Europe), in the *Saturday Evening Post* of 29 November 1947, pp. 26–27, 137–138. Clayton became so critical subsequently because he opposed allowing the recipient governments to shape the program themselves in the interest of European integration.
3. By the time the Marshall Plan began, the United States had already spent some $17 billion on foreign grants and loans (including UNRRA, aid to refugees, aid to Japan, aid to Germany, aid to China, and the 1946 Anglo-American loan). To the extent that there had been problems with earlier aid programs, these were seen as reflecting the piecemeal approach of allocating aid country by country. The solution naturally became to allocate aid in an integrated fashion to an integrated European economy.
4. The businessman Paul Hoffman was Vandenberg's choice. It is revealing of the political constraints that the speech with which Vandenberg brought the Marshall Plan bill to the full Senate lasted 15 times as long as Marshall's Harvard University commencement address.
5. As described in Wala (1993) and Wexler (1983).
6. George Kennan's famous article, "The Sources of Soviet Conduct," had already been written and was about to be published in *Foreign Affairs* under the pseudonym X. And President Truman had already taken the momentous step of offering aid to Turkey and Greece.
7. Historians question the sincerity of the U.S. offer. But extending the offer to the Soviets was critical for domestic French consumption (see Reynolds, 1997).
8. As late as July 5, Molotov still encouraged them to participate. Czechoslovakia actually accepted the invitation to attend the July 12 meeting of prospective aid recipients (and Poland privately signaled its intention of doing the same) but declined two days later when Moscow reversed course.
9. As Maier (1984, p. 29) has put it, the Marshall Plan rested on the idea "that disputes over ideology might be resolved by discussions of how best to assure economic growth. That is, issues of political power could be transformed into questions of efficiency and technique."
10. This theme is developed at greater length by Casella and Eichengreen (1993).
11. As emphasized by, among others, Gimbel (1976) and Berger and Ritschl (1995). This was important for, among other things, ensuring that the United Kingdom kept one foot in Europe while at the same time

continuing to pursue its imperial aspirations. That British Foreign Secretary Ernest Bevin took a leading role in the development of a collective response to the Marshall Plan proved critically important for this outcome. And Britain's enthusiasm for the initiative in turn prodded the French government to assume a leadership role (see Reynolds, 1997).

12. The presence of these preconditions for catch-up in postwar Europe is a theme of Abramovitz (1986).

13. As Allen Dulles put it in his tract in support of the program, "The stabilization of currencies, while it will not in itself provide enough food and cotton, fertilizer and agricultural equipment to meet the needs, will serve to bring out hidden assets and supplies of food which worthless currencies will not lure from the farmers." Dulles (1993), p. 20.

14. For a discussion of the impact on German industrial relations and industrial organization, see Berghahn (1995).

15. As John Foster Dulles saw it, it was essential to reconstruct Europe "along federal lines" and to connect to it a decentralized German confederation. Cited in Kunz (1997), p. 165.

16. Among other problems, the progress of CEEC negotiations was hindered by U.S. resistance to direct U.S. involvement, by British insistence on retaining and even strengthening the country's links with its overseas empire, by Anglo-French conflicts over leadership within Europe, and by the fact that Germany was not represented at the Paris negotiations that led to its founding.

17. Consider for example the use of counterpart funds. Governments in relatively strong financial positions could easily circumvent the efforts of Marshall Plan administrators to use them for leverage. Thus, the British government could simply set aside the domestic-currency funds sequestered into counterpart accounts, borrow the equivalent balances from the central bank, and spend the latter without American permission. In France, by contrast, a weak government and popular worries of inflation resulted in strict limits on government borrowing from the central bank and more leverage for the Marshall Plan. For discussion, see Gordon (1984) and Esposito (1994).

18. See for example, Cerami (1989).

19. See for example United Nations (1992).

20. For example, Kager and Bruckbauer (1992) and Soros (1993).

21. Normalizing by the U.S. consumer price index.

22. As documented, quantitatively, by Eichengreen and Portes (1989).

23. This is the interpretation of the Marshall Plan developed in Eichengreen and Uzan (1992). It is echoed in the discussion accompanying Cleveland (1984), in which scholars such as Charles Kindleberger (one of the junior architects of the Marshall Plan) argue that abrupt stabilization and adjustment in 1947–48 would have resulted in unemployment, political chaos, and populist reaction and question whether open societies and democratic institutions would have survived the shock.

24. See Chuhan, Classens, and Mamigni (1993) and Eichengreen and Fishlow (1996).
25. As argued by Calvo and Mendoza (1995).
26. As argued by Eichengreen and Portes (1996).

References

Abramovitz, Moses (1986), "Catching Up, Forging Ahead, Falling Behind," *Journal of Economic History*, 46, pp. 385–406.

Berghahn, Volker R. (1995), "West German Reconstruction and American Industrial Culture, 1945–1960," in Reiner Pommerin (ed.), *The American Impact on Postwar Germany*, Oxford and Providence: Berghahn Books, pp. 65–82.

Berger, Helge and Albrecht Ritschl (1995), "Germany and the Political Economy of the Marshall Plan: A Re-Revisionist View," in Barry Eichengreen (ed.), *Europe's Postwar Recovery*, Cambridge: Cambridge University Press, pp. 199–245.

Boone, Peter (1996), "Politics and the Effectiveness of Foreign Aid," *European Economic Review*, 40, pp. 289–329.

Calvo, Guillermo and Enrique G. Mendoza (1995), "Reflections on Mexico's Balance-of-Payments Crisis: A Chronicle of a Death Foretold," unpublished manuscript, University of Maryland.

Casella, Alessandra and Barry Eichengreen (1993), "Halting Inflation in Italy and France after World War II," in Michael Bordo and Forrest Capie (eds.), *Monetary Regimes in Transition*, Cambridge: Cambridge University Press, pp. 312–45.

Cerami, Charles A. (1989), *A Marshall Plan for the 1990s*, New York: Praeger.

Chuhan, Punam, Stijn Claessens, and Nlandu Mamigni (1993), "Equity and Bond Flows to Latin America and Asia: The Role of External and Domestic Factors," Policy Research Working Paper no. 1160, Washington, DC: The World Bank.

Cleveland, Harold van B. (1984), "If There Had Been No Marshall Plan . . . ," in Stanley Hoffman and Charles Maier (eds.), *The Marshall Plan: A Retrospective*, Boulder, CO: Westview, pp. 59–64.

Dollar, David and Craig Burnside (1997), "Foreign Aid and Economic Growth," unpublished manuscript, The World Bank.

Dulles, Allen W. (1993), *The Marshall Plan*, ed. Michael Wala, Oxford: Berg.

Eichengreen, Barry and Albert Fishlow (1996), "Contending with Capital Flows: What is Different about the 1990s," Council on Foreign Relations, Occasional Paper.

Eichengreen, Barry and Richard Portes (1989), "After the Deluge: Default, Negotiation and Readjustment During the Interwar Years," in Barry Eichengreen and Peter Lindert (eds.), *The International Debt Crisis in Historical Perspective*, Cambridge: MIT Press, pp. 12–47.

Eichengreen, Barry and Richard Portes (1996), "Managing the Next Mexico," in Peter B. Kenen (ed.), *From Halifax to Lyon: What Has Been Done about Crisis Management?* Princeton Essays in International Finance, no. 200 (October).

Eichengreen, Barry and Marc Uzan (1992), "The Marshall Plan: Economic Effects and Implications for Eastern Europe and the Soviet Union" *Economic Policy*, 14, pp. 13–75.

Esposito, Chiarella (1994), *America's Feeble Weapon: Funding the Marshall Plan in France and Italy, 1948–1950*, Westport, CT: Greenwood Press.

Gimbel, John (1976), *The Origins of the Marshall Plan*, Stanford: Stanford University Press.

Gordon, Lincoln (1984), "Lessons from the Marshall Plan: Successes and Limits," in Stanley Hoffman and Charles Maier (eds.), *The Marshall Plan: A Retrospective*, Boulder, CO: Westview Press, pp. 53–58.

Kager, Marianne and Stefan Bruckbauer (1992), "A Marshall Plan for the East," *East-West*, 4, pp. 32–38.

Kunz, Diane (1997), "The Marshall Plan Reconsidered," *Foreign Affairs*, 76 (May/June), pp. 162–70.

Maier, Charles S. (1984), "Supranational Concepts and National Continuity in the Framework of the Marshall Plan," in Stanley Hoffman and Charles Maier (eds.), *The Marshall Plan: A Retrospective*, Boulder, CO: Westview Press, pp. 29–37.

Reynolds, David (1997), "The European Response: Primacy of Politics," *Foreign Affairs*, 76 (May/June), pp. 171–84.

Sachs, Jeffrey (1997), "A Partnership for Growth in Africa," unpublished manuscript, Harvard Institute of International Development.

Soros, George (1993), "Needed: Hard Currency for a Social Safety Net in Russia," *International Herald Tribune* (January 5), p. 7.

United Nations, Economic Commission for Europe (1992), *Economic Survey of Europe in 1991–1992*, Geneva: United Nations.

Wala, Michael (1993), "Introduction," in Allen W. Dulles, *The Marshall Plan*, Oxford: Berg.

Wexler, Imanuel (1983), *The Marshall Plan Revisited*, Westport, CT: Greenwood Press.

CHAPTER 7

The Marshall Plan in Economic Perspective: Goals and Accomplishments

Imanuel Wexler

Although the Marshall Plan (1948–1951) was conceived as, and may properly be perceived as an instrument of American foreign policy, it was essentially an economic enterprise—an enterprise consisting of a substantial transfer of financial and technical resources from the United States to a group of West European countries for the purpose of aiding the latter to pursue specific economic tasks and reach specific economic goals within a prescribed period of time. It is shown here that only some of the goals mandated by the U.S. Congress and targeted by the European countries were actually achieved by the time the Marshall Plan ended. But it is also argued that the significance of the Marshall Plan as an economic program lies not so much in its immediate short-term economic results as in its long term impact. For what it did was to lay a firm basis from which the European nations could generate their own economic momentum and reach a point of self sustaining economic growth in the decades following the termination of the Marshall Plan itself.

Nearly 50 years after it was launched, and almost as many years after it officially ceased to exist, the European Recovery Program (popularly named the Marshall Plan) continues to provide both American and European scholars with a compelling investigative topic.

In part, this continued attention is due to the increasing availability, over time, of public records and archival collections that have enabled scholars to draw on hitherto closed material and thereby offer new insights and interpretations. But in a larger sense, the interest in the Marshall Plan may be said to stem from its close identification with U.S. foreign policy. Indeed, for a long time, historical scholarship tended to examine the Marshall Plan within the context of postwar U.S. foreign policy—most often with reference to the Cold War. The Marshall Plan, in other words, has long been perceived and treated as an instrument of early postwar U.S. foreign policy—specifically, as a major element of Cold War strategy.

The underlying theme of this paper is that although the Marshall Plan was admittedly a foreign policy measure—largely motivated by political and strategic considerations—it was couched in economic terms and presented as an economic program. Herein lies its uniqueness: Not only was the Marshall Plan the *first* large-scale U.S. foreign aid program in the post-World War II period, it was, and still is, the *only* aid program that stipulated a set of economic objectives and a specific timeframe for their fulfillment. It may, in fact, be argued that the Marshall Plan reflected, and was based on, a *mutuality* of commitments and obligations. The United States, for its part, undertook to extend a substantial amount of financial resources to a group of West European nations. And the European aid recipients committed themselves to pursue specific economic tasks and reach specific economic goals within a prescribed period of time.

Thus, in addressing the question "Did the Marshall Plan have a definite economic impact?" one may begin by asking: What exactly did the Americans—or, more precisely, the U.S. Congress—have in mind. Or, to put it more bluntly: What exactly did the Americans demand, and what did the Europeans promise to do?

In authorizing the Marshall Plan, the U.S. Congress mandated a four-year recovery program whose ultimate goal was "the achievement by the countries of Europe of a healthy economy independent of extraordinary outside assistance."[1] Such a program, Congress went on to stipulate, was to be based on four specific endeavors (or, objectives):

1. "A strong production effort"—aimed at significant and rapid increases in industrial and agricultural outputs;
2. "Expansion of foreign trade"—both among the European countries and between them and the rest of the world;
3. "Creation and maintenance of internal financial stability"—through appropriate monetary and fiscal policies designed to control inflation and maintain balanced budgets;
4. "The development of economic cooperation"—a commitment to joint and collective actions in pursuit of the recovery program

itself and to the progressive reduction and eventual elimination of trade and payment restrictions within Europe.[2]

These, then, were the specific objectives whose fulfillment—with the aid of U.S. financial assistance—was considered necessary to the restoration of a healthy and stable European economy. And, for their part, the Europeans nations formally pledged themselves to pursue these objectives by setting certain targets for productions; projecting certain levels of trade; promising to introduce fiscal and monetary reforms; and agreeing to establish a joint organization—the Organization for European Economic Cooperation (OEEC)—to coordinate their individual recovery programs and to monitor their progress.[3] The OEEC actually outlasted the Marshall Plan; it continued to function until 1961, when it was transformed into the Organization for Economic Cooperation and Development (OECD), whose members now include the leading economies of the world.

The European Recovery Plan (ERP) began in April 1948, and was administratively terminated on December 31, 1951, to be immediately succeeded by the Mutual Security Program. During that period, about $12.5 billion, mostly in the form of grants, had been allotted by the Economic Cooperation Administration (ECA) to the participating countries. The pursuit of the ERP's objectives—at least from the standpoint of U.S. policy makers—was to rest largely on three main thrusts: (1) A push to increase European productivity, through technical assistance programs aimed at introducing more efficient methods and organization of production, and improving labor/management relations; (2) a continuous campaign to persuade European governments of the need for sound fiscal and monetary policies; and (3) the promotion of effective intra-European payment-clearing mechanisms, coupled with an insistence on the progressive dismantling of trade barriers. The most visible result of these last efforts was the establishment of the European Payments Union (EPU) in 1950, and the accompanying agreement of a Code of Trade Liberalization.

And the question before us now is: What were the immediate economic results of the Marshall Plan? Or, to put it slightly differently: Was the congressionally mandated goal—namely, a viable West European economy, sufficiently strong and stable to stand on its own feet without continued American support—achieved by the time the Marshall Plan ended?

The short answer is no. Western Europe as a whole did not achieve economic viability by the beginning of 1952, though some countries did better than others. But such an answer masks several significant accomplishments which must be noted.

Thus, of the four specific endeavors stipulated by Congress and targeted by the Europeans, two—"a strong production effort" and "expansion of foreign trade"—yielded results far exceeding initial expectations and projections. Between 1947 and 1951, Western Europe's combined GNP increased by more than 30 percent—a very impressive performance. Equally impressive was the aggregate increase in *industrial* production. It had been projected to reach 30 percent above its 1938 level, but actually reached 41 percent above it.[4] Both the phenomenal growth of GNP and the rapid rise in industrial production attest to the success of the Marshall Plan in helping to rebuild Europe's productive capacity and thereby induce a sizable increase of Western Europe's total production.

A similar claim can be made with respect to foreign trade. In 1948, the OEEC had estimated that intra-European trade would not regain its prewar (1938) volume until 1952/53. The actual record shows that as early as 1950, the volume of intra-European trade was already 24 percent above its 1938 level. One year later it stood 36 percent above the prewar level; and by 1953 it had risen to 40 percent. Moreover, between 1948 and the end of 1951, the volume of intra-European trade expanded by 70 percent; and during the same period Western Europe's exports to and imports from the rest of the world increased by 66 percent and nearly 20 percent respectively.[5]

Yet, against these gains it must be noted that the increase in Europe's *agricultural* output actually fell short of the projected target and that by the end of 1951 Western Europe was still dependent on the rest of the world for about 30 percent of the food it consumed. Also, despite the significant increases in trade, Western Europe as a whole had not overcome serious balance-of-payments difficulties and shortage of foreign-exchange reserves when the Marshall Plan ended. Nor, for that matter, were the efforts to restore and maintain internal financial stability entirely successful. Despite some early progress, most West European countries found themselves plagued by renewed inflationary pressures from mid-1950 on; and by late 1951, the ground gained in tackling inflation during the first two years of the Marshall Plan had been largely lost. Finally, it must be noted that the hoped-for American ideal of European economic integration—which evolved from the initial congressional mandate stipulating economic cooperation—did not materialize during the Marshall Plan's own lifetime. It came only later, and was due largely to European rather than American initiative.

And so we come to the penultimate question: How are we to judge the overall economic impact of the Marshall Plan? In terms of its short-run economic results, the Marshall Plan was only a qualified success. But in retrospect it may be argued that the real significance of the Marshall Plan lies not so much in its immediate accomplishments as in its long-term impact. For what it did, was to lay a firm basis from which the European nations could generate their own economic momentum and reach a point of self-sustaining economic growth. This growth continued at a rapid rate throughout the 1950s and 1960s, and was accompanied by the progressive relaxation of trade and payment restrictions within Europe and the liberalization of trade with the rest of the world. By 1960, in fact, Western Europe had become the second most important industrial and trading center in the world.

Could Western Europe have recovered without the Marshall Plan? Conceivably, it could. But the process would undoubtedly have been longer and, for some countries, might have entailed such drastic sacrifices in current living standards as to pose a threat to internal political stability. Still, if European economic recovery was conceivably possible without it, was the Marshall Plan really necessary? Yes, given the American perceptions of the consequences of a West European economic collapse and its political implications for both Europe and the United States. And it is, after all, perceptions—valid or not—that dictate most foreign policy initiatives, including that of the Marshall Plan.

Notes

1. See Economic Cooperation Act of 1948, Section 102(a). Authorizing the Marshall Plan, the Economic Cooperation Act of 1948 was Title I of the Foreign Assistance Act of 1948, which was signed into law (PL 472) by President Truman on April 3, 1948.
2. See ibid.
3. For details of the European initial commitments and pledges, as well as estimated requests for American aid, see Committee of European Economic Cooperation, Vol. I, *General Report* (Paris, 1947).
4. The figure for the increase in GNP was computed from data in OEEC, *Europe—the Way Ahead: Fourth Annual Report of the OEEC* (Paris, 1952), p. 112. The figure for the aggregate increase in industrial production is an average, calculated from data in U.S. President, *First Report to Congress on the Mutual Security Program* (Washington, D.C., 1951).
5. For OEEC's trade estimates, see OEEC, *Interim Report on the European Recovery Program* (Paris, 1948). The figures for increases in trade come from the following sources: ECA, *Thirteenth Report to Congress*, p. 103; *Mutual*

Security Program for FY 1953, p. 64; and Robert Marjoliu, "The European Trade and Payments System," *Lloyds Bank Review* (January 1954), p. 2.

References

Ellwood, David W. *Rebuilding Europe: Western Europe, America, and Postwar Reconstruction*. New York: Longman Publishing, 1992.

Gimbel, John. *The Origins of the Marshall Plan*. Stanford, CA: Stanford University Press, 1976.

Hogan, Michael J. *The Marshall Plan: America, Britain, and the Reconstruction of Western Europe, 1947–1952*. New York: Cambridge University Press, 1987.

Milward, Alan S. *The Reconstruction of Western Europe, 1945–1951*. London: Methuen, 1984.

Price, Harry B. *The Marshall Plan and Its Meaning*. Ithaca, NY: Cornell University Press, 1955.

Wexler, Imanuel. *The Marshall Plan Revisited: The European Recovery Program in Economic Perspective*. Westport, CT: Greenwood Press, 1983.

CHAPTER 8

Struggle for Survival: American Aid and Greek Reconstruction

Stelios Zachariou

Although the objective of Marshall Plan aid was to stimulate economic recovery, most of the aid given to Greece was devoted to other purposes. Because Greece was engaged in a civil war, and also lacked a stable political leadership, it could only afford to devote these funds towards its basic struggle for survival. With $649 million in aid, Greece was the fourth largest recipient of Marshall Plan funds. These funds successfully supported the military campaign against communism, and also laid the foundations for future economic growth in the 1950s. Nevertheless, Greece remained economically dependent on foreign aid long after the Marshall Plan had ended.

Market economics and secure commercial frontiers was not the fundamental rationale behind Marshall Plan aid to Greece. The precarious political and socioeconomic situation in the country necessitated the immediate attention of the allies in an effort to assist the Greeks economically and militarily in the struggle for survival and security.

The Marshall Plan stimulated economic growth for many of the European states, and it secured western Europe in a cohesive and reliable alliance in a region that became one of the most heavily contested battlegrounds of the Cold War. Economic rehabilitation was a fundamental weapon in confronting both Soviet pressure and internal disenchantment. Additionally, it established the foundation for the transatlantic relationship between Europe and America that set the groundwork for future economic and defense organizations such as the European Union (EU) and the North Atlantic Treaty Organization (NATO) and would end American isolationism.

Located on the fringe of the European continent, Greece paid dearly in human lives and material resources for its contribution to the allied campaign against Nazi Germany.[1] The devastation of World War II added to the tragedy of a nation already crippled by the Balkan Wars, the First World War, and the disastrous Asia Minor Campaign of 1922 which had resulted in the influx of 1.5 million refugees into the country.[2] Greece shared in the hardships of many of the European nations overrun by the Axis powers. The occupation by Italian, Bulgarian, and German forces resulted in the loss of 7 percent of the population, the destruction of over 1,000 villages, and the sinking of approximately 90 percent of the Merchant Marine fleet.[3] Exacerbating the situation was the absence of a stable postwar government capable of subduing the Communist threat and launching an economic program to rebuild the social and financial foundations of the country. Political instability coupled with the civil unrest ensuing from the struggle for power between the Communist guerrilla group ELAS (National People's Liberation Army) and the postwar republican governments impeded the state's efforts to apply economic aid toward rehabilitation. Thus, Greece was the only European Recovery Program (ERP) recipient state engaged in a civil war and facing an imminent Communist threat while attempting to undergo a reorganization and industrialization program.

Greece was the sixth largest beneficiary of the Marshall Plan receiving $649,000,000, and the fourth largest per capita aid recipient of the Economic Recovery Program after Iceland, Norway, and Austria.[4] Additionally, Greece had received from the United States alone over half a billion dollars between the end of the war and the implementation of the Marshall Plan, making Greece one of the most heavily funded postwar recovering nations. It cannot be assumed, however, that the tremendous infusion of money funneled into the country resulted in the economic progress seen in other European nations. This is in part because Greece was late in developing industries, making it dependent on imported goods and finished products. Prior to the war Greece's main trading partner was Germany, which absorbed no less that 38 percent of Greek exports while supplying 30 percent of Greek import requirements.[5] Moreover, Greece, notwithstanding the war inflicted destruction and the loss of an important trading partner, would also have to wage a war against the Communist guerrilla movement. As a result, Greece remained economically and politically unstable throughout the first two important years of the Economic Recovery Program, during which the Congressional aid allocation for all of Europe through the Economic Recovery Program was $4.9 and $3.7 billion respectively.[6]

Two main interrelated obstacles impeded the recovery effort in Greece: (a) the Civil War, which lasted through October 16, 1949, and (b) the lack of a stable political government capable of enforcing economic policy designed to help the country regain a firm economic footing. Exacerbating the political condition was the existence of a cumbersome public administration system consisting of 23 ministries centered in Athens, which could not enforce policy due largely to the lack of local provincial government institutions.[7]

During the Civil War, funds that would otherwise have been assigned to restoration efforts were allocated to the Greek National Army. Developments in the Middle East in Fall 1946 heightened the danger of the situation in Greece. The border dispute between Iran and the Soviet Union, as well as Soviet aspirations for passage through the Dardanelles, were points of friction and tension between the respective governments. On September 12, 1946, Assistant Secretary of State William Clayton wrote to Secretary of State James Byrnes asking whether or not the United States should make changes in its overall policies "in response to the Soviet moves from the Straits to the Middle East," by helping countries "maintain their independence and develop sufficient strength to preserve law and order within their frontiers."[8] The strategic importance of Greece as a crucial geographic link to the Middle East outweighed concerns over the lack of a politically assertive Greek government. The United States was determined to follow a strong support policy in Greece despite the government's incompetence in enforcing an economic recovery program.

After the inability of the United Nations Relief & Rehabilitation Agency (UNRRA) to ameliorate the devastation in Greece, the United States decided that any additional aid would be accompanied by a mission that would advise and supervise the allocation of aid in order to avoid further misappropriation and mismanagement of funds and supplies.[9] By February 24, 1947, American administrative staff were no longer confident that any of the sequence of Greek governments were capable of responsibly administrating their own economic reconstruction program. Furthermore, the dysfunctional and, in some cases, non-existent civil service was unable to organize and enforce recuperative measures. "If this government is to provide immediate financial assistance to Greece," a State Department report would claim, "U.S. interests can be adequately served only by establishing the controls necessary to assure the effective utilization of such assistance. The Greek

Government cannot itself provide these controls in the near future."[10] The same day, the British declared their inability to financially support the Greek struggle beyond March 31, 1947.

While the British were disengaging from Greek internal affairs, the American Mission to Greece headed by Ambassador Porter was in the process of conducting a three month survey of the socioeconomic situation of the country. The mission concluded that, unless the civil war came to an end and a trustworthy conservative government was instituted, reconstruction would make no significant progress. This assessment would later be confirmed in a memorandum entitled "Suggestions for United States policy in Greece,"[11] which clearly stated that "until over-riding political problems are solved, economic theory and sound business principles cannot be controlling considerations." Thus, the establishment of the American Mission of Aid to Greece (AMAG), created for the distribution of U.S. aid under the Truman Doctrine, was the first organized and supervised effort to attempt civil relief and military support.

The Truman Doctrine gave Greece a total of $300 million allocated as $146 million in economic aid, of which only $50 million was for reconstruction, $149 million in military aid and $4.5 million for administrative costs. From appropriation to implementation there was a shift which benefited military spending. Attempts to revive the economy and apply a program of reconstruction would take second place to the communist threat and the end of the Civil War.[12] The Military program increased in 1948 from $149 million to $172 million, reducing both reconstruction by $11 million and consumption by $12 million (see Table 8.1).[13]

The importance of Greek frontier preservation to the United States was evident by the amount allocated for the Greek National Army. The geopolitical security of Greece and the suppression of the Communist guerrilla movement would take precedence over the economic rehabilitation. Emphasis on the stabilization of Greece became steadfast when in the summer of 1947 Lieutenant General James A. Van Fleet became the new chief of the Joint United States Military, Advisory, and Planning Group (JUSMAPG).[14] His appointment confirmed the significance of ending the Civil War and the importance of Greece as a Western ally.

That same summer at the Harvard University commencement Secretary of State George C. Marshall presented his idea for European rehabilitation, inviting nations to take it upon themselves to rebuild their war devastated countries. Greece responded favorably to the offer, but the Greek plan presented at the Paris conference the following month was ill-prepared, revealing the internal political disorganiza-

Table 8.1

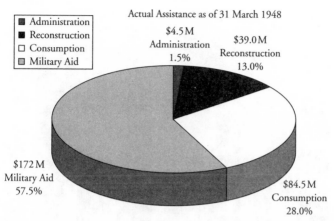

Actual Assistance as of 31 March 1948

- ■ Administration
- ■ Reconstruction
- □ Consumption
- ▨ Military Aid

$4.5 M
Administration
1.5%

$39.0 M
Reconstruction
13.0%

$172 M
Military Aid
57.5%

$84.5 M
Consumption
28.0%

Politakis G. "Greek Policies of Recovery and Reconstruction, 1944–1952". Thesis submitted for the partial fulfillment of the requirements for the degree of Doctor of Philsophy. Oxford—Trinitry 1990.

tion.[15] The Greek delegation's original request amounted to $1,467 billion ($741.4 million for reconstruction and $725.7 million for deficit reduction) for the four year program.[16] The inability of the Greek delegation to submit a realistic recovery program proposal substantiated by statistical data and information increased skepticism regarding the dependability of the government and its capacity to effectively handle the internal turmoil. Additionally, the failure of the Greek government to absorb loans, such as the $25 million Export–Import Bank loan, troubled U.S. Administration officials who became increasingly convinced that reconstruction would have to give way to the strategic defense needs of the country in order to expel the Communist element before rebuilding the infrastructure. As the war against the Greek Communist guerrillas was prolonged and global events continued to accentuate the division between the Soviet Union and the United States, the importance of reconstruction would dissipate.

When the Economic Recovery Program took effect in Greece, the precedent for economic aid had already been established by the Truman Doctrine. In the fall of 1948, even before ERP aid was dispatched to Greece, Marshall suggested that the U.S. mission stop pressing for economic reform and focus on the battle against the Communist guerrillas. "Destruction of guerrilla forces and establishment [of] internal security now have clearly assumed paramount importance as a necessary preliminary for successful American Aid to Greece. Until achieved, these

Table 8.2

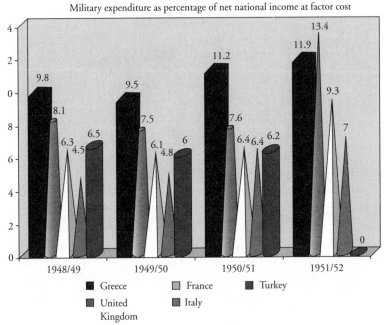

Comparative Burden of Defense

Military expenditure as percentage of net national income at factor cost

Sources: Economic Survey of Europe in 1950, U.N. Economic Commission for Europe, p. 137.

aims should henceforth take precedence over any ... program[s] which do not directly support them."[17]

The respective Greek governments were also supportive of a strong army, and pressed the Embassy and the Mission for increased military aid in their efforts to expand the Greek National Army, strongly believing that political security would best be achieved through placating the military hierarchy. It should be noted that Greece maintained the highest percentage allocation of GNP for military expenditures throughout the Marshall Plan aid period, surpassing the U.K. and France (see Table 8.2). As a result, human resources that could have contributed to the economic reconstruction process were enlisted in the armed forces in the war against the Communists.

The emphasis on defense preceded the implementation of the Marshall Plan, making Greece the only ECA/ERP member toward which U.S. policy remained consistent in geopolitical and economic terms, before and after the February 1948 Czech coup, the June Berlin blockade crisis, and finally the onset of the Korean War when U.S. foreign policy changed decisively. The assertive foreign policy which was formalized by NSC 68 and presented shortly before the outbreak of the Korean War was already in place as early as 1947 in Greece. The fear of Greece falling into the Communist sphere of influence, causing a possible domino effect throughout the Middle Eastern region, concerned policy planners in Washington, as the Western and Eastern block clashed, not on ideological principals any more, but in a struggle for preponderance of power.

The emphasis on military security, which eventually resulted in the successful conclusion of the Civil War in favor of the republic in October 1949, cannot be considered the sole reason for the difficulty in implementing the aid program. The lack of a strong Greek government with a mandate to rule resulted in a series of coalition and de facto governments which were unable to remain committed to a firm political and economic strategy. A series of weak and ineffective governments were incapable of enforcing policies in both the economic and civil areas that would result in a recuperative program for Greece. Between the end of World War II in October 1944 and the signing of the Economic Cooperation Agreement between the United States and Greece on July 2, 1948, 13 different cabinets and 9 premiers had presided in the political arena of Greece.[18] This frequent change in the leadership of the country lead to inconsistencies in the application of economic assistance and a long term strategy for a monetary stabilization policy. "Ineffectual and timorous governments have been unwilling or unable, in the absence of internal tranquillity and wholehearted cooperation of political leaders ... to institute the unpleasantly drastic reforms which both the U.S. and the U.K have counseled."[19] The weak parliamentary coalitions did not maintain a consistent economic policy of reducing the national debt, stopping the depletion of gold reserves, and enforcing an effective taxation policy that would positively effect the balance of payments gap. The diverse economic strategies frustrated foreign economic advisors and hampered the progress of reconstruction. Furthermore, political leaders strongly believed that before any significant progress could be made in terms of reconstruction, the guerrillas would have to be defeated and the borders of the nation secured.

It becomes increasingly clear from the recent research of the documents of the Ministry of Foreign Affairs that a handful of men, economists and diplomats, had great impact in securing funds for Greece while representing a country which had no effective government structure. Political parties in Athens were more interested in formulating machiavellian schemes to assume control of the reins of government than tackling the imminent dangers of hunger and communism. Thus, small groups of individuals, combined with the heavily staffed AMAG and later ERP missions, would assume responsibility for the rigorous task of helping Greece find its social and economic momentum.

Despite the hurdles, the Marshall Plan had a decisive impact on Greece. Combined with the preceding UNRRA aid, which provided Greece with a total of $347 million worth of goods,[20] and a series of loans and grants by both the United States and England in the immediate postwar period,[21] Greece managed to support the 700,000 refugees from its war-inflicted areas, overcome the Communist threat, and set the foundation for a stable political regime and for the economic and industrial development of the 1950s.[22] Greece struggled throughout the Marshall Plan years, unable to use the appropriated aid for building a sound economy and a competitive market. Unlike other ERP members, Greece lagged behind in building an industrial infrastructure mainly because the funds allocated for development supported primarily the campaign against the Communist guerrillas and the effort to implement a balance of payments system. As a result, Greece remained economically dependent on foreign aid even after the conclusion of the Marshall Plan.[23]

Over the four year period of the Marshall Plan (1949–1952) Greece received a total of $1,327.1 billion dollars in both military and economic loans and grants from the United States. This amount is $140 million less than the original amount that the Greek delegation had proposed to the Economic Cooperation Administration at the Paris conference in the summer of 1947. Of the above mentioned amount, $733.4 million was designated as economic assistance and $593.7 million for military aid.[24] Although the economic aid is representative of 55.2 percent of the total assistance, it is deceptive since the amount allocated for rehabilitation was used mostly for deficit reduction and not for infrastructure repair purposes.[25] Regional security combined with financial stability took precedent over reconstruction preventing Greece from taking full advantage of the Economic Recovery Program.

It goes without saying, however, that American aid and the Marshall Plan more specifically supported the Greek struggle for survival. It secured, more than any other European country, its Western orientation by playing an integral role in the termination of the Civil War and successfully contributing to the establishment of a stable economic foundation. Furthermore, the economic aid provided to Greece through the European Recovery Program allowed the country to engage in the proceedings for the creation of European institutions such as the European Coal & Steal Cooperation (ECSC) and the European Economic Community (EEC). This engagement allowed Greece to remain involved in the international process of European unification.[26] Greek European orientation underlay national policy making immediately after the conclusion of the Second World War and throughout the Civil War. This effort contributed significantly in the induction of Greece into the geopolitical balance designated by the Cold War strategy of containment, securing Greece as an a significant component and link to the Eastern Mediterranean region.

Notes

1. For an extensive analysis of the effect of German occupation in Greece, see Mark Mazower, *Inside Hitler's Greece The Experience of Occupation 1941–1944* (New Haven and London: Yale University Press, 1993).

2. Douglas Dakin, *The Unification of Greece, 1770–1923* (London: Ernest Benn, 1972).

3. RG 59 Class 8 International Affairs (1945–49) 868.00 Political Affairs of Greece Box 7028. General Survey of Greek Situation p. 22. Other studies include UNRRA Division of Operational Analysis, European Regional Office, Post War Public Finance in Greece, London, February 1947, p. 1 and the report presented by Constantine Doxiades on the impact of the occupation on all sections of Greek economy "Sacrifices of Greece: Requests and Reparations of the Second World War" (in Greek). For more information regarding Axis exploitation see Gabriella Etmektsoglou-Koehn "Axis Exploitation of Wartime Greece, 1941–1943" (Dissertation submitted to the Faculty of the Graduate School of Emory University, 1995).

4. Ingvar Svennilson, *Growth and Stagnation in the European Economy* (Geneva, 1954), pp. 236–37; Mutual Security Agency, Procurement Authorizations and Allotments, Division of Statistics and Reports (Data as of June 30, 1952), p. 2. Also see, Alan Milward, *The Reconstruction of Western Europe 1945–1951* (London: Methuen, 1984).

5. RG 59 Lot 24 Records of the Office of Greek, Turkish, and Iranian Affairs. Box 18 "Coombs & Coppock Economic and Financial Report" p. 6.

6. Barry Eichengreen and Marc Uzan, "The Marshall Plan: Economic Effects and implications for Eastern Europe and the former USSR" *Economic Policy* (April 1992): 44–45.

7. "The American Aid Program in Greece: A summary of the American Economic Aid Program to Greece from 1947 to the Spring of 1954". Prepared by the U.S. Operations Mission in Greece, July 1954, p. 32.

8. *Foreign Relations of the United States* (hereafter noted as *FRUS*), 1946, Vol. 2, pp. 209–12.

9. Indicative of this perspective is the statement of Undersecretary of State for Economic Affairs Clayton in a memorandum dated May 27, 1947. "...we must avoid getting into another UNRRA—The United States must run this show." *FRUS*, 1947, Vol. 3, pp. 230–32.
10. *FRUS*, 1947, Vol. 5, p. 54.
11. *FRUS*, 1947, Vol. 5, pp. 439–49.
12. William Hardy McNeill, *Greece: American Aid in Action 1946–1956* (The Twentieth Century Fund, New York, 1957) pp. 37–38. See also Diomedes D. Psilos & Richard M. Westebbe *Report No. 10 Public International Development Financing in Greece* (Columbia University School of Law, New York, September 1964).
13. Annual Report of the Bank of Greece, Presented by G. A. Mantzavinos, President of the Bank of Greece. Pg. 20.
14. *FRUS*, 1948, Vol. 4, pp. 36–37.
15. RG 59 LOT 24 "Records of the Office of Greek-Turkish and Iranian Affairs 1947–1959" Box 24 "ECA-ERP program, Marshall Plan"
16. Annual Report of the Bank of Greece, Presented by G. A. Mantzavinos, President of the Bank of Greece (For the first year the Greek delegation requested $354.5 million, $176.5 million for consumer needs, $170 million for reconstruction, and $8 million for the civil war refugees. The ECA was able to provide $106.4 million under the Economic Recovery Program, but Congress passed the Greek-Turkish aid Act of 1948, which bolstered military aid to Greece by $275 million more.)
17. *FRUS*, 1948, Vol. 4, p. 26.
18. Alkiviades Provatas, *Political History of Greece: Legislative and Executive Bodies 1821–1980* (Athens, 1980) (in Greek).
19. RG 59 Class 8 International Affairs (1945–49) 868.00 Political Affairs of Greece Box 7028. General Survey of Greek Situation p. 27.
20. Bureau of Supply Final Operational Report of UNRRA, March 1948. (Ö 2 Marshall Plan Archive, Ministry of Foreign Affairs) Greece was the fifth largest recipient of aid under UNRRA of 17 nations.
21. ECONOMIC ASSISTANCE

No.	Date	From	Agreement/Treaty	Amount
1	16/1/46	USA	Export-Import Bank	$25,000,000
2	16/5/46	USA	Foreign Liquidation Commissioner (FLC)	$10,000,000 credit for arms
3	20/9/46	USA	Credit for Maritime Equipment	$20,000,000 credit
4	25/9/46	USA	FLC	$10,000,000 credit
5	4/10/46	USA	FLC	$25,000,000 credit
6	31/12/46	UN	UNRRA (end of aid)	$342,162.0
7	1/3/47	UK	British Government	3,000,000 pounds

8	22/5/47	USA	Truman Doctrine	$300,000,000
9	31/5/47	USA	Public Law 84	$ 40 million in post-UNRRA aid
10	13/3/48	USA	ECA is passed	$649 million received in 4 years
11	3/4/48	USA	Greek-Turkish Aid Act of 1948	$275,000,000
12	6/10/49	USA	Mutual Defense Assistance Act	$211,370,000 Greece and Turkey

22. "the Greek economy grew from 1953 to 1977 at an annual rate of 6 percent only overtaken by Japan within the OECD" (Politakis, *Greek Policies and Reconstruction*, 1944–52, p. 1).

23. For additional information on American economic aid to Greece during the 1950s and Greek–American relations see Stelios Zachariou "The Road to the Garrison State: Relations Between Greece and the U.S. (1952–1963)" Presented to the University of New Orleans in partial fulfillment of the Masters degree (December 1994).

24. U.S. Agency for International Development "U.S. Overseas Loans and Grants and Assistance from International Organizations" Obligations and Loan Authorizations (July 1, 1945–September 30, 1995, Washington D.C.)

25. Letter from Chief of AMAG to Chief of Division of Greek, Turkish, and Iranian Affairs, July 22, 1949. RG 59 LOT 24 Records of the office of Greek, Turkish, and Iranian Affairs, 1947–1950 Box 16 sub file: Miscellaneous.

26. Marieta Minotou *The Prospect of European Unification after the Second World War* printed in the Greek periodical *Diachronia* 3–4, 1998, pp. 113–25 (in Greek).

PART FOUR

*The Marshall Plan and the Organization
of Political Life in Postwar Europe*

CHAPTER 9

(US, France

N14

N44

The Marshall Plan and 1456
French Politics   F35

Irwin Wall

Recent historiography on the Marshall Plan has tended to diminish its previously assumed role in the French economic takeoff following the Second World War. Instead, analysts have focused on its political effects: internally, the stabilization of democratic political regimes, and internationally, the promotion of European integration. Even in these realms, however, the effects were minimal, and the Europeans, particularly the French, were consistently able to take affairs into their own hands despite the heavy hand of American attempted interference. In part this was because the French understood that American aid was a built-in aspect of postwar development, since the reconstruction of Europe and the prevention of its fall to communism were in the American interest. The French were able to use this state of affairs very much to what they thought to be their own advantage, and in fact diverted the overwhelming part of their economic aid from 1948 to 1954 to their futile wars in Indochina, while the military aid Washington lavished upon Paris was also used in their equally useless and costly effort to hold on to Algeria. The Algerian struggle in turn brought about the fall of the Fourth Republic and the coming of de Gaulle, precisely the long-term result that the Americans, in proffering their aid in the first place, had hoped to avoid.

There was more than a little irony in the round of 50th anniversary celebrations of the Marshall Plan, for its reputation among professional historians or economists has not been as high as it once was, and does not come near to matching the image of the plan in the media, the political world, or the informed general public. In a more or less recent spate of volumes that attempted to draw lessons from the Marshall Plan for proposed aid programs for the East European and Russian economies in transition, the consensus about the uses of the Marshall Plan as a model would seem to have been negative; the Marshall Plan was not thought to have provided an example for what might or might not have been done in Eastern Europe. The conditions in the two instances were not the same: East European economies after the collapse of communism lacked market economies, functioning legal systems, and motivation to integrate politically or economically, all of which existed after the war and worked so well for the recovery of capitalist postwar Western Europe. But more seriously, in doing their analyses, economists with only a few exceptions tended to doubt the efficacy of the Marshall Plan in the first place in aiding West European construction. The recent studies indicate that in this respect it has ill-survived the Milward assault of the mid-1980s.[1] According to the contributors to Barry Eichengreen's most recent volume, which was put together in the spirit of rehabilitating the Marshall Plan, its effects were nil in England, of marginal benefit in Germany, negative in Belgium where it in fact inhibited growth, helpful in France where funds were used in conjunction with the Monnet plan, but ineffective once again in Italy.[2]

Moreover, the significance of the Marshall Plan even for its defenders is now said to have been not the transfers of currency and raw materials and foodstuffs, or even industrial product once thought to have provided the margin against Communist takeovers in the countries concerned, but rather the conditions Washington put on the disbursement of its aid: the acceptance of anti-inflation currency stabilization policies, the recreation of functioning markets, the push toward European integration coming from Washington, and the induced habits Europeans are said consequently to have developed of cooperating with one another on an international scale even to the extent of some sacrifice of national sovereignty. The prime examples of that cooperation commonly cited are the Organization of European Economic Cooperation, the European Payments Union, and the European Coal and Steel Community, otherwise known as the Schuman Plan.[3] These, it is commonly said, took shape thanks to the American impetus, and later developed into the foundations of the European Economic Community, the ancestor of today's European Union. Contemporary conclusions have thus reinforced the earlier views of French historian Pierre Melandri, who long ago stressed the importance of the Americans in the drive for the unity of postwar Europe.[4]

Economists thus have joined a few historians in concluding that if the Marshall Plan did not succeed economically, it did have significant influence politically; the economists stress moves toward European unity, however, while the historians have focused primarily on the stabilization of centrist democratic regimes in Europe that would be favorable to Washington's Cold War policies. This is the conclusion of Chiarella Esposito, whose book, *America's Feeble Weapon*, demonstrates in the case of France and Italy comparatively what my own work attempted to do for France: that counterpart funds, the control of whose release constituted the central means of economic pressure the Americans enjoyed in trying to influence French and Italian economic policies, were in fact of very limited use for that purpose.[5] In France, the Americans sought to limit the release of counterpart in order to pressure the French into tighter monetary policies to control inflation, which also meant imposing restraint on the expansionist goals of the Monnet Plan. But almost every instance in which the Americans threatened to withhold counterpart funds as a means of pressuring them, the French warned they would have recourse to advances from the Bank of France rather than restrain spending; not releasing counterpart thus would have the opposite effect of that intended, producing the inflation the Americans hoped to prevent. At the same time the Americans felt constrained to support third force coalitions against the assaults from Communists and Gaullists, which left little room for political choices unpalatable to the National Assembly's precarious majority. In Italy the political problems were the same and the economic results opposite: The Americans were committed to the de Gasperi government's survival, hence unable to influence it to depart from excessively restrictionist economic policies in the direction of the kind of investment that in France the Economic Cooperation Administration (ECA) was trying to curb. There was no equivalent of the Monnet Plan in Italy, and the Italians put monetary stabilization ahead of economic modernization, a situation that the Americans could neither prevent in Italy, nor achieve in France.

If Washington could not achieve its objectives in economic policy, did it at least achieve the political stability in France and Italy that it sought? One can argue that in the long run the Americans did not achieve political stability either: In France they ended up with de Gaulle after all, in Italy with the opening to the Left and a Mafia-ridden state; in neither country were the results entirely satisfactory. But can even these outcomes, certainly functional from Washington's point of view in terms of the Cold War, be said to have been in any respect the result of American policies? This is also highly doubtful. In most of the key instances in which the Americans were once thought to have been critically important for European developments, newer studies based on recently opened archives have tended to doubt their influence. Take, for example, the expulsion of the Communist ministers from the governments of France, Italy, and Belgium, which occurred with breathtaking simultaneity in May 1947. Historians for years have been searching for the smoking gun indicating an American order, or at least central role in these events, so important to the transition in 1947 toward the Cold War. The belief in the existence of such an order once enjoyed almost mythical status in France. But in all three cases to attribute the political outcomes to the Americans is to exaggerate their power and to minimize the anti-Communist zeal of the Europeans themselves, who had long been searching for excuses to rid themselves of their Communist allies. Abraham Boxhoorn shows that domestic policy differences best explain all three crises. In Belgium, the Communist Party decided to resign even before the Truman Doctrine, on March 10, 1947, in protest over a rise in the price of coal, apparently believing that it could strengthen its position in a successor government.[6] In France, Communist differences with the Socialists and Christian Democrats (MRP) went from foreign policy to colonial war in Indochina and Madagascar to prices and wages, with the break coming finally over a wildcat Renault strike, which the party initially opposed but in the end had no choice but to support for fear of losing its working-class base. In Italy, where participation in the government yielded little influence for the Communist Party, the personal determination of Prime Minister Alcide de Gasperi to form a homogeneous government of "technicians," without Communist participation, precipitated the break in May 1947. The PCI and its Socialist allies were unwilling to accept the same anti-inflationary budget cuts that the Americans themselves found so frustrating. However pleased Washington ultimately was with the Communist departures from the three governments, it had little to do with accomplishing them, nor were the resultant polices of the governments purged of Communist influence necessarily more to Washington's liking.

Another area in which the Marshall Plan is often held to be of great influence is in the bolstering of the noncommunist labor movements in Europe. But here again recent studies do not seem to bear this out; Dennis MacShane's work, the most thorough and convincing study to appear to date, puts my own cautious conclusions about the effects of American intervention in the French Labor Movement in broader international perspective.[7] The Trade Union splits of 1947–48, although precipitated by the Marshall Plan, emerge in MacShane's account not as consequences so much as causes of the Cold War; the history of

European Trade Unionism constitutes a powerful reminder that if the Cold War began in 1947 in terms of relationships between the Great Powers, it was present in Europe from the initial Bolshevik challenge to capitalism in 1917.

MacShane deals in sequence first with the history of international organizational efforts, specifically the World Federation of Trade Unions (Fédération Syndicale Mondiale), in which Communist trade unions had disproportionate influence, and as a specific but important example of international industrial unionism, the International Metalworkers' Federation. He then examines the national trade union federations in the United States (AFL and CIO), England (TUC), Germany (DGB), and France (CGT), in each case comparing his study of the national federation with the specific example of the metalworkers' union in each country. In each case he has exhausted the archives of the unions concerned. It will be difficult, therefore, for historians to argue with his conclusions, which differ radically with those of Ronald Radosh, Peter Weiler, Anthony Carew, and Annie Lacroix-Riz, whose emphases on the Cold War as the determining factor in union splits, and on the Americans, both the State Department and CIA on the one hand, and the AFL on the other, as the driving forces carrying out the divisions, have worked their way into more general accounts of the period.

For MacShane, the driving forces behind trade union division in the postwar era were the nationalist, indeed chauvinist, perspectives of the trade unionists concerned, who viewed international organization as vehicles for the expression of their own national perspectives, and the fragile nature of trade union unity in each country such as it was after the war. The splits between Communist and noncommunist unions occurred in 1947 and 1948, but they were incipiently present already in 1945. This can be seen on the international level in the failure of the WFTU to amalgamate with the International Federation of Metalworkers, which reconstituted itself under the leadership of the Swiss Konrad Ilg after the war. The WFTU insisted that the international secretariats of industrial unions wishing to join with it first dissolve themselves; the IMF, and other industrial unions in its wake, insisted on maintaining their organizational autonomy. Negotiations continued into 1947 but there was no bridging the differences, which in reality, MacShane shows, reflected the continuing conflict between Leninist–Stalinist norms of democratic centralism on the part of the WFTU as against the Social-Democratic values of political and organizational pluralism that dominated the perspective of the Metalworkers, and its leader, Ilg. IMF militants remembered the splitting tactics of the

Profintern, the Communist tactics of "Social Fascism," and the Nazi-Soviet pact, and they had long since lost their illusions about the nature of working class life in the USSR. Under such conditions they were unlikely to join any organization, however apolitical it momentarily seemed, in which the huge monolithic Soviet trade unions appeared to have a dominant role. Trade union splits in Europe for MacShane, as the expulsions of the Communists from the governments of Italy, France, and Belgium for Boxhoorn, appear as causes rather than consequences of the Cold War.

Historians have also seemed to have reached a consensus against the idea that the United States was the primary impulse behind the achievement of European unity. Alan Milward again has led the assault; European integration came about, he argues, for state-based reasons, rather than because of the idealism of the early "Europeans" like Monnet and Adenauer, or thanks to the push of American influence. The Europeans, Milward argues, integrated their policies only to the extent that they were enabled collectively to do what they could not individually do for themselves. Rather than the outcome being any kind of transnationalism, the result was rather the strengthening of the individual European nation-states, which since World War II have played larger roles in the lives of their citizens than at any previous time in history.[8] Milward's argument is fleshed out in the case of France by Francis M. B. Lynch, who makes a powerful argument for the effectiveness of the state in France of the Fourth Republic in both managing the economy and forging a diplomatic outcome in Europe to its liking. The Marshall Plan, for Lynch, had the primary effect of allowing France to achieve investment and growth in productivity without excessive deferral of consumption: the first impact to be felt in France was to enable the country, thanks to interim aid early in 1948, to restore the bread ration which had been reduced to 200 grams daily to 250 grams. From 1948 to 1952, Lynch estimates, counterpart aid provided 13 percent of French internal investment; the French used it to pursue their interest in becoming a leading steel producer, focusing on the rolling strip mills of the newly created steel combines Sollac and Usinor. These in turn furthered the need for German coal, which, along with the dollar crisis, propelled the French into the European Coal and Steel Community. This French proposal had the effect of giving France the leadership of Europe; France in turn then permitted the establishment of the European Payments Union, to which the Americans thoughtfully contributed, and which provided a framework for continentwide economic expansion.[9]

Lynch goes on to argue, moreover, that the French acceptance of the drive toward European unity from 1955 to 1956 was propelled by several internal policy determinants all of which owed very little if anything to Washington. There was a bitter debate in the French bureaucracy between the Ministry of Foreign affairs, which harbored proponents of traditional protectionism, and officials in the Ministry of Finance, who insisted that France could only achieve productivity by opening itself up to competition and joining an economy of scale. The balance in this debate tipped internally in France toward the advocates of competitiveness, but Europe by 1955–56 seemed to offer the French even more. Through Euratom, Paris hoped to secure European financing for an isotope separation plant deemed essential for the independent French nuclear deterrent, which the Mollet government seemed intent on building by early spring 1956. By insisting on the full inclusion of agriculture in the European Common Market, the French planned to dispose of their surpluses and rid the treasury of the onerous burden of supporting the powerful agricultural lobby. Finally, and perhaps most importantly from the present perspective, the French hoped that by forcing the inclusion of the French empire in the Common Market they could achieve joint European financing of colonial development, support in their effort to retain and develop Algeria, and the creation of an ensemble dubbed "Eurafrique," of which Paris would of necessity be the political center. Again quite paradoxically, the final push toward European integration in 1956, in both Germany and France, came as a result of negative reaction to American pressure, in the immediate aftermath of the Suez adventure, during which France and Britain, having enlisted the support of Israel, sought to regain control of the recently nationalized Suez canal. Britain capitulated to American pressure, calling a premature halt to the operation, and infuriating the French. Adenauer, who supported both the Suez campaign and the French war to retain Algeria, joined with Guy Mollet in compromising Franco-German differences over Europe in the hope of creating a counterweight that could act independently of the United States.[10]

The same or similar points are forcefully brought home in still newer studies of the period that are emerging. William Hitchcock echoes the work of John Gimbel in stressing that one of the Marshall Plan's major aims was to win French acceptance of the reconstruction of Germany.[11] But Hitchcock traces early efforts from within the Quai d'Orsay, where realism dictated the acceptance of American aims, to seek an alternative framework for German recovery than the restoration of full sovereignty, implicit both in industrial recovery, and subsequent pressure by Washington for German rearmament. France bitterly fought American plans for Germany even as it accepted the Marshall Plan and the NATO alliance, winning a seat on an International Authority for the Ruhr in the hope of maintaining a strong role in the development of the German steel industry and seeing to it that German coal became available to French steel producers. The Schuman Plan accomplished that goal; it also, Hitchcock argues, brought about a diplomatic revolution in Europe by winning American support and bringing an end to five years of postwar antagonism between Washington and Paris. This judgment seems to me much too strong; whatever brief honeymoon characterized French–American relations, it did not long survive the American push for German rearmament that followed almost immediately, in September 1950. The French reaction was first, dogmatic opposition, but when all of NATO united against Paris on the issue, the French rapidly came up with the idea for a European Defense Community, seeking a European framework for German rearmament as the ECSC provided a framework for German industrial recovery. Washington required much cajoling to go along with this idea, first correctly perceiving it to be a device by which Paris hoped to delay and perhaps kill the issue, and internal opposition within France eventually killed the EDC, of which the Americans had become much stronger supporters than the French; but Mendès France accomplished its essential aims, without the corresponding loss of French sovereignty, in the London–Paris accords of 1954–55, which kept German rearmament within the framework of the West European Union and NATO.[12]

It is not my intent in drawing upon this minimalist historical literature to adopt the largely counterfactual argument that the Marshall Plan was unnecessary, and that without it all in Europe would have turned out pretty much as it did. On the contrary, it has seemed to me that there is little profit in such counterfactual debates. It has rather seemed preferable to me to see the American intervention in postwar Europe as an inevitable part of the political landscape, given the U.S. role in World War II and the looming Cold War; the Americans were part of the political ecology of Europe and one could not extract them without fundamentally altering the entire landscape. This would seem to have been as true for the post-World War I period as the period after World War II. The point here is rather to reduce the Marshall Plan to size, for rather than symbolizing a new American interventionism, it might rather be seen as a chapter in a continuing saga of American involvement in Europe, from the Lend-Lease of the wartime coalition, to the British loan of 1946, the Blum-Byrnes loan to France of the same year, and the various stopgap loans to other countries, to the Marshall Plan itself, which held sway from 1948 to 1950. But the Marshall Plan itself was in short order succeeded by the Military Defense and Assistance Pact of 1950, the Mutual Security Act of 1951, and the flow of military aid to Europe, particularly to France, which only began to peter out by 1954 with the termination of the Indochinese war.[13] The Americans threw almost $1 billion a year without interruption into the French economy between 1944 and 1954, a total of which the Marshall Plan accounted for perhaps one-fourth; the Americans also acted not only as an ally, economic pressure group through the ECA and MSA, but also as political mentors or manipulators, opinion-molders, and finally coordinators of military policies in response to the hotter manifestations in Korea and Indochina of the Cold War. But U.S. intervention economically could not be depended upon to produce the result that was intended politically. In France, in particular, skillful politicians proved adept at manipulating American aid to their own uses and to the furtherance of their own policies. In fact, I want to argue here, that in France the Americans became, willy-nilly, accomplices, indeed mainstays, of French colonial ambitions in Indochina and paradoxically, Algeria. All this quite ironically, since their intervention in Indochina was pursued with quite different intentions than the French, and their complicity in the Algerian drama was an unwelcome outcome achieved despite themselves.

American "end item" arms flow to France began in early 1950 with passage of MDAP, and much of it was on its way to Indochina even before the Korean War began in June; Communists in France focused on the aid as destined for "la salle guerre" and campaigned to prevent dockers from unloading American ships. In fact, the American rapprochement with French policy in Indochina was accomplished by February 1950 when Washington recognized the French puppet regime of the Emperor, Bao Dai. The Russians had earlier recognized Ho Chi Minh. By the end of 1950, seven C47 transport aircraft, 26 B26 bombers, and 150 American tanks had found their way to Indochina, exclusive of financial aid.[14] In July 1950, Paul Hoffman issued the American call for European rearmament, asking for national plans to be ready in August. The ECA Mission in Paris concomitantly dropped its effort to divert French counterpart funds from domestic industrial investment to housing, expecting that it would instead be expended on the military. The first of many Franco-American misunderstandings occurred almost immediately; the French presented a military budget to Washington of

610 billion francs, plus an additional 270 billion for the Indochina war, which they wanted Washington to finance. This despite the fact that industrial production in France was already by 1950 27 percent higher than it had been in 1938, when the country had maintained an army of 110 divisions. Paris complained that it could not modernize the French economy, build an infrastructure for NATO, rearm, and fight the Indochina war all at once. The French were demanding $800 million for Indochina, which the Americans scaled down to $400 million, of which Washington expected that the first $200 million would come from Marshall Plan counterpart. The French insisted it be additional to Marshall Plan funds. And to drive the point home, the French reduced their proposed budget to 740 billion francs to reflect Washington's refusal to pick up the full tab for Indochina. It soon became clear, moreover, that neither modernization nor the Indochina war were negotiable, from Paris' point of view; reduced American funds meant reduced NATO commitment. It was in terms of the NATO "shield" in Europe that the French would give the Americans more only in proportion to what Washington was willing to pay for.[15]

By bargaining with the Americans over the general amount of their military budget and making it a function of American aid, the French were at once asking Washington directly to make up their budget deficit and inviting Washington to supervise French military expenditure. The Americans resisted the first opportunity but grasped at the second. Making up French budget deficits seemed a doubtful proposition involving French income distribution, tax policy, and the like, subjects over which the Americans habitually criticized French upper-class self-ishness, miserliness, and inefficiency, but about which they were loathe and perhaps powerless to do anything. On the other hand, it was much easier to criticize French military spending. Washington wanted Paris to give up its ambitious plans to reconstruct a modern armaments industry and buy American heavy weapons. The French would do better, in the interest of the NATO alliance as a whole, to produce light weapons, ammunition, and uniforms, for which the Americans were willing to let contracts through the "Offshore" program, an ingenious aid device which allowed the American military to do some of its procurement in Europe, or in turn to subsidize the purchases of the French military from its own French contractors. On balance, the effort to direct the nature of French arms production was no more successful than the attempt to influence how the French spent their Marshall Plan aid, and the Americans much more often ended up antagonizing the French while giving in to them. Meanwhile the French managed to make

Washington pay in large part for both the reconstruction of the French arms industry and the Indochina war.

To avoid this kind of American interference in French affairs, Paris adopted the stratagem of shifting the focus of American aid to the Indochina war, which quickly became France's largest single dollar export. In 1952, an angry President Auriol, railing against American interference in the French budgeting process, claimed that Indochina cost twice the amount France received in Marshall Plan aid. Ambassador David Bruce, unwilling publicly to contradict the French president, privately put the cost of the war at half the amount the French received in aid. Both were in a sense right, but if one understands that Auriol was talking about 1952 while Bruce was undoubtedly referring to the period of Marshall Plan aid proper from 1948 to 1951, Auriol was closer to the truth. The Indochina war cost France 568 billion francs in 1952, when American aid was $525 million or about 184 billion francs under prevailing exchange rates; Gérard Bossuat calculates this at only 30.8 percent of the cost.[16] But Marshall Plan aid proper to France from 1948 to 1951 was $2.75 billion, while the Indochina war for that entire period cost only marginally less: an estimated $2.5 billion or 900 billion francs.[17] However, Auriol was not counting end item aid or OSP contracting. Looking at Bossuat's global estimates from 1948 to 1954, the period of the Indochina war, the rough parallel between American aid and expenditure on colonial war holds; the war seems to have cost France about $7 billion while American aid to France in toto amounted to roughly $6 billion. Of the latter figure, Marshall Plan aid proper from 1948 to 1951 amounted to 2.75 billion, military aid 1951–55 to 2.1 billion, and end items to 1.2 billion dollars. This does not count about 10.7 percent of counterpart funds, which were spent in French overseas territories, including Indochina, as well. Money is fungible. Depending on how one looks at it, the United States financed a significant part of French modernization, or all of the cost of the vain attempt by France to hold on to its colonial empire. It did not do both.

Bossuat is prone to see the death of French colonialism in the American interference, because with it came implicit support for the nationalist cause in the empire, and economic penetration of France's colonial territories followed the American aid as well.[18] I would rather argue that American pressure to liberalize French rule was rather designed to maintain French influence, and that what Washington wanted was a kind of American–French condominium, with France keeping order and American capital as the motor of economic development. The Americans never intended to displace the French from the direct governance of their territories, as Paris often feared. Rather, they wanted the French to maintain order, an objective they thought best attainable by some concessions of self-government to nationalists in the colonies, and they wanted Paris to maintain an open playing field for American investment. De Gaulle himself helped conceptualize the link between decolonization and diplomacy under the Fourth Republic, the basis of the present argument. In his view, as told to Alain Peyrefitte, the Fourth Republic "nous avait fabriqué une politique étrangère docile aux mains des Américains et une politique coloniale combattue par eux" (we had devised a foreign policy that was docile in the hands of the Americans and a colonial policy that was strongly opposed by them). France was set against the countries of the Soviet bloc by the American alliance and against the countries of the Third World by its colonial policies; as it pretended to subject its colonial possessions to its eternal protection, it in turn became the protectorate of the Americans in the world arena, while Washington did not hesitate to encourage the vassals of France to rebel against it even as the United States proceeded to make of France its own vassal.[19] This, for de Gaulle, was the fateful contradiction of French foreign policy that he intended to end, ensuring that what was good for the French was decided in Paris, just as what was good for the Senegalese would be decided in Dakar. Interestingly, Peyrefitte asked de Gaulle whether the policies of the Fourth Republic were not rather coherent than contradictory: did not the subjection of France to the United States in fact enable France to maintain its protectorate over its colonies? De Gaulle left this query without a response. A significant silence, for Peyrefitte seems to have articulated the policy that de Gaulle not only inherited from the Fourth Republic but himself initially sought to continue in the earliest years of his presidency. American support was in fact the condition for the pursuit of the French war in Indochina, and in his proposal to the Americans and British for a three-power world "directorate" including France in September 1958, de Gaulle was making a bid for Anglo-American support for the French effort to keep Algeria.

Habits die hard; in October 1957, three years into the Algerian war and one year after the Suez crisis, Secretary of the Treasury George M. Humphrey noted that financially "the French are just going down the drain" and that an emergency package of aid would have to be put together for them by the end of the year. Louis Joxe, Secretary General of the Quai, confirmed to Robert Murphy that Algeria was the cause: by now it was costing Paris one billion francs per day.[20] The French government fell in October; U.S. Ambassador Amory Houghton reported that the emptiness of the treasury was the reason. France had a booming economy and full employment; there was no objective basis for the financial crisis except that escalating expenditure on the Algerian war was causing the nation to live beyond its means, and it now managed again from day to day only with United States aid.[21] In effect, the situation of 1947 was recreated ten years later: France had no domestic economic crunch or depression, but only a balance of payments deficit because of excessive imports from the dollar zone driven by rapid economic growth and heavy expenditure on colonial war. The Americans, once again desperate to keep France an active partner in NATO, stepped in to fill the breech, overlooking their repugnance at France's Algerian involvement. In October, the NSC proposed that grant aid to France be continued through 1958. It did recommend, however, that the aid package be reconsidered if the French failed to redeploy their forces from Algeria to NATO. Dulles objected, saying that he needed flexibility on this question given France's "transcendent importance" in the NATO alliance. Dulles just at that moment was in fact seeking the right to store and deploy American nuclear weapons in France and apparently feared the effect of any threat to curtail American aid. The NSC then proposed that aid be reviewed but that the policy to do so be followed but unstated. This formulation satisfied the secretary.[22]

In fact Washington helped put together a financial aid package amounting to about $650 million to stabilize the franc in late January 1958. The credit was in some respects a first, in that it tied together funds from the European Payments Union, the International Monetary Fund, and various U.S. aid agencies into a single coordinated package, designed to obtain the maximum impact on French and foreign opinion, and to underline the close cooperation of these three sources of credit.[23] It did so, so successfully that it brought a protest from the Saudi Ambassador in Washington, who was told that the package was for the purpose of stabilizing the French balance of payments and was "not related to the Algerian situation." But of course the French balance of payments crisis was a direct result of the Algerian situation. The package involved postponements of loan installments and purchase of United States agricultural surplus, Dulles said, and provided no new money to the French. The United States, the Saudis were assured, would continue to press for a fair and equitable solution to the Algerian problem.[24]

On February 8, 1958, French planes bombed the Tunisian border village of Sakiet Sidi Youssef, which they suspected of being a base for

Algerian rebels shooting at French aircraft and crossing the frontier in costly military raids. This act opened the crisis, which ended the Fourth Republic and brought de Gaulle to power. The use of American weapons in the Sakiet raid became an issue in Washington. Twenty-five planes had been used, including 11 B26 bombers, six "Corsair" fighter-bombers, and eight Mistral fighters. The B26s, Paris said, had been independently purchased by France in the United States and were not part of military aid, while the Corsairs, which were received under the aid program, were not assigned to NATO but were under French command. The Mistrals were of French manufacture. These distinctions mattered little in Washington where the only concern was that France has used weapons of American manufacture with the result of making the Americans appear to support actively French colonial policy. The French further argued that only military targets had been hit, 80 percent of these had been destroyed, and nine-tenths of the village was intact.[25] These claims were disingenuous. Reporters at the scene put the innocent civilian death total at over 70. The B26s had been clearly recycled from the Indochina war and if not these specifically, plenty of others had been received as part of MDAP military equipment aid. The Corsairs were of American manufacture and even the Mistral had been in part financed by Offshore contracting. Dulles reprimanded French Ambassador Alphand about the use of American equipment in one of the angriest Franco-American exchanges of the postwar era. To the secretary's great embarrassment, he was forced awkwardly to explain the unauthorized use of American equipment by the French at a press conference, while Senator Humphrey made a speech strongly critical of Paris for the use of American planes affected to NATO. Noting that Tunisia, where the bombardment occurred, lay outside the NATO zone of defense, Humphrey demanded that the administration request the return of the French American-built weapons that had been illicitly used. Alphand informed Paris with concern that the Americans were raising serious objections to the use of their weapons in Algeria. The Foreign Ministry instructed him to tread gingerly on the issue: privately, the French now admitted both the Corsairs and the B26s had in fact been sent to France under the title of MDAP for NATO use. MAAG and the American military attaché were aware of their use in Algeria, however, and had not raised objections. The American military was, in fact, much more sympathetic to French policy in Algeria than Eisenhower or the State Department. In view of the comprehensive attitude of MAAG with regard to the use of these weapons in Algeria, it was best not to mention in Washington that the Americans in Paris were aware; on the other hand, Alphand was authorized, if it became necessary, to say that the American military attaché knew and had chosen to say nothing.[26]

The United States did not need to finance the Algerian war for France; French economic growth from 1954-62 was sufficient to do that and provide the French increasing prosperity at the same time. But French forces in Algeria were taken from NATO deployments and weapons used in Algeria were largely of American manufacture, while Washington was there at moments of crisis to pick up temporary balance of payments deficits, even as the Americans pressured the French to come to a negotiated settlement. It is hard to escape the conclusion that American aid, both in Indochina and Algeria, while ineffective in influencing the French in directions the Americans would have liked, rather enabled France to continue its costly and futile colonial wars, which ultimately brought the Fourth Republic to its ruin. In this sense, the money spent to stabilize centrist regimes of the Fourth Republic against de Gaulle only served in the end to make his accession to power more likely. Thus does history continue to play tricks upon us all.

Notes

1. Alan Milward, *The Reconstruction of Western Europe, 1945–1951* (London: Methuen, 1984). Milward argued that European economies were enjoying a boom in 1947, rather than exhibiting the crisis American analysts perceived at the time. The Marshall Plan was, in his view, of minimal importance for the long-term growth of the European economies, and primarily represented the skill of European diplomats in convincing the Americans to help finance aspects of their industrial recovery.

2. See Barry Eichengreen, ed., *Europe's Post-War Recovery* (Cambridge: Cambridge University Press, 1995).

3. Also R. Dornbusch, W. Nölling, and R. Layard, eds., *Postwar Economic Reconstruction and Lessons for the East Today* (Cambridge, MA: MIT Press, 1993), and Barry Eichengreen and Marc Uzan, "The Marshall Plan: Economic effects and implications for Easter Europe and the former USSR," *Economic Policy*, Vol. 14 (1992), pp. 14–75.

4. Pierre Melandri, *Les Etats-Unis face à l'unification de l'Europe, 1945–1954* (Paris: A. Pedone, 1980).

5. Chiarella Esposito, *America's Feeble Weapon: Funding the Marshall Plan in France and Italy, 1948–1950* (Westport, CT: Greenwood Press, 1994); Irwin Wall, *The United States and Making of Postwar France, 1945–1954* (New York: Cambridge University Press, 1991).

6. Abraham Boxhoorn, *The Cold War and the Rift in the Governments of National Unity: Belgium, France, and Italy, a Comparison* (Amsterdam: Historisch Seminarium van de Universiteit van Amsterdam, 1993). On

the French case, see Wall, *The United States and the Making of Postwar France,* pp. 67–71.

7. Denis MacShane, *International Labor and the Origins of the Cold War* (Oxford: The Clarendon Press, 1992); Wall, *The United States and the Making of Postwar France,* pp. 96–113.

8. Alan S. Milward, *The European Rescue of the Nation State* (Berkeley: University of California Press, 1992), especially pp. 212–15; also Alan S. Milward et al., eds., *The Frontier of National Sovereignty: History and Theory 1945–1992* (London: Routledge, 1993).

9. Francis M. B. Lynch, *France and the International Economy from Vichy to the Treaty of Rome* (London: Routledge, 1997), pp. 103–10 and *passim.*

10. Irwin Wall, "Solidarité atlantique et construction européenne dans le contexte de la décolonisation," Paper presented at a conference on the United States and European Unity, University of Cergy-Pontoise, France, June 18, 1999.

11. John Gimbel, *The Origins of the Marshall Plan* (Stanford: Stanford University Press, 1976); William Hitchcock, *France Restored: Cold War Diplomacy and the Quest for Leadership in Europe 1944–1954* (Chapel Hill: University of North Carolina Press, 1998).

12. Hitchcock, p. 177 and *passim* stresses that the policy of Mendès France and of Mollet in 1956 was to anchor the construction of a small Europe of the six, excluding England, around a Franco-German partnership that it was hoped could provide the basis of a European policy independent of the Americans, after 1956 of The United States and Great Britain. One sees here the outlines of the future policies of Charles de Gaulle. This is also the conclusion of the excellent dissertation by Paul Marsh Pitman III, "France's European Choices: The Political Economy of European Integration in the 1950s" (Ph.D. dissertation, Columbia University, 1997). For a much less enthusiastic assessment of the Schuman Plan from the French point of view, however, see John Gillingham, *Coal, Steel, and the Rebirth of Europe, 1945–1955* (New York: Cambridge University Press, 1991).

13. Interestingly, one need not look to the Marshall Plan literature for the hypothesis of American hegemony and influence in Europe through aid: It was present in the literature on the British loan and the Blum-Byrnes agreements. For Britain, contrast Lloyd Gardner, *Architects of Illusion: Men and Ideas in American Foreign Policy* (Chicago: Quandrangle Books, 1970) with Peter Burnham, *The Political Economy of Postwar Reconstruction* (London: Macmillan Press, 1990). On the Blum-Byrnes agreement, Irwin Wall, "Les accords Blum-Byrnes, la modernisation de la France, et la Guerre Froide," *Vingtième Siècle,* No. 13 (Janvier-Mars 1987), pp. 45–62. Neither Britain, which received a loan of $3.75 billion in 1946, nor France, which got much less, capitulated to the United States as condition for the aid.

14. Wall, *The United States and the Making of Postwar France,* pp. 190–91; Gérard Bossuat, *La France, l'aide américaine et la construction européenne, 1944–54* (Paris: Comité pour l'histoire économique et financière de la France, 1992), Vol. 1, pp. 429–36.
15. The French also bargained their commitment to the European Defense Community in exchange for American assistance in Indochina: see the interesting thesis by Jasmine Aimaq, *For Europe or Empire? French Colonial Ambitions and the European Army Plan* (Lund, Sweden: Lund University Press, 1996).
16. Bossuat, La France, *L'aide américaine et la construction européenne,* Vol. 2, pp. 856–77.
17. American assistance in 1948 was, of course, much more than the French were spending in Indochina, which accounts for the difference. Bossuat argues that the critical importance of the Marshall Plan for France was its important infusion of funds precisely in 1948–49, before it became absorbed by colonial expenditures, when it was able to have maximum effect in achieving an economic takeoff.
18. Bossuat, Vol. 1, p. 560.
19. Roger Peyrefitte, *C'était de Gaulle* (Paris: Fayard, 1994), pp. 293–94.
20. Memorandum of Conversation, Louis Joxe and Robert Murphy, July 8, 1957, National Archives and Records Administration, Record Group 59, State Department Decimal Files, 751.00/7-557.
21. American Embassy, Paris, to Department of State, October 29, 1957, 751.00/10-2957, October 31, 1957, 10-3157, RG 59, NARA.
22. Dulles to the NSC, 2 October 1957, Eisenhower Library (Abilene, Kansas), Whitman File, NSC Series, NSC 338; Humphrey to the NSC, 7 February 1957, NSC 312.
23. See also Jacob J. Kaplan and Günther Schleiminger, *The European Payments Union* (Oxford: The Clarendon Press, 1989), p. 266.
24. U.S. Embassy, Paris, to State Department, January 25, 1958, 840.00/ 1-2558; Under-Secretary Herter to American Embassy in Paris, January 29, 1958, 840.00/1-2958; Memorandum, Near East Affairs, 840.00/2-558; RG 59.
25. "Fiche sur Sakiet Sidi Youssef," February 22, 1958, Archives du Ministère des Affaires Etrangères (Paris) [hereinafter MAE], Nations Unies, 567.
26. French Embassy, Washington, to MAE, Paris, February 18, 1958; MAE to French Embassy, Washington, February 18, 1958, MAE, Tunisie, 1958, 312.

185 - 204

(US, Europe)

N14
N44
H56
F35
F23

CHAPTER 10

A Single Path for European Recovery? American Business Debates and Conflicts over the Marshall Plan

Jacqueline McGlade

This study examines the various views of the American business and policymaking groups regarding the formation of the Marshall Plan as an impetus for European economic recovery. It notes that the fragmentated nature of U.S. goals ultimately hampered the effectiveness of Marshall aid programs intended to spark widespread business reform overseas. Also, European nations took an active role in shaping and transmitting program aid, often in favor of the recovery of traditional business practices over the introduction of reforms.

As an aid program, the Marshall Plan represented a bold break from the past for the United States. In one single act, the U.S. Congress had authorized the expenditure of $12 billion—a sum higher than the total of all previous aid extended overseas.[1] However, this embrace of state funding for the resolution of European distress seemed an abrupt, almost radical departure from laissez-faire and the traditional American preference for private investment, instead of government subsidies, as a stimulus for business recovery and economic growth.

Not surprisingly, members of the U.S. business community held decidedly mixed views over the Marshall Plan, as it symbolized the rise of government planning measures over the return of laissez-faire in the revival of the postwar world economy. As the champions of the liberalization of foreign markets, American free traders and offshore exporters eagerly supported a massive European aid package to stimulate rapid financial and business reforms and economic reinvestment overseas. Conversely, trade protectionists viewed the Marshall Plan with active suspicion and dread, as it required an unprecedented level of government involvement in world economic affairs. Small and local business owners also questioned the extension of economic aid to Western Europe, for as domestic producers, they were still struggling to reestablish their place in the postwar American economy without the benefits of government assistance. Business executives were also divided over the issue of European remilitarization and its possible achievement through the Marshall Plan. Some businessmen viewed the program as purely an economic initiative, while others believed that the Plan should aid in the revival of European military as well as economic strength.

While extremely important, the varied and often conflicted nature of American business debates have been largely overlooked by historians when studying the formation of the Marshall Plan, its aims, and its administration. In several recent studies on the Marshall Plan, the whole process of postwar U.S.–European economic policy making has been presented as a consensual event in which American government and business leaders shared common views on a path for European recovery that prevailed into the 1950s.[2]

In this study, however, political conflict, not consensus, emerges as the predominant feature of postwar U.S. foreign economic policy making as a wide variety of business and government groups engaged in a contentious struggle to establish and control American objectives for Marshall Aid and its extension into Western Europe. Ultimately, these conflicts impacted not only the administration of the Marshall Plan, but its effectiveness as a recovery measure for Western Europe. The contest over European aid also reveals, instead of a tightly knit, corporatist arrangement, a more nuanced, fractionalized picture of American government business relations during the early Cold War era. Finally, the amorphous nature of U.S. aid objectives enabled several European governments, most notably France and Italy, to forge and assert indigenous recovery programs, oftentimes over the wishes of Marshall aid administrators. For many American firms, the independent renewal of European economies fostered by U.S. aid acted to limit, not expand financial and market opportunities that had been anticipated by executives after World War II. Unlike recent accounts, then, a single path for European recovery was not obvious as American business leaders along with government officials sought measures in the late 1940s and early 1950s to alleviate distressful economic and business conditions across the Atlantic.

American Business Views and the Coming of the Marshall Plan

In 1948, the American business community found it difficult to assert one common position on the Marshall Plan, as opinions varied widely on this issue and other matters related to postwar world economic recovery. Since the end of World War II, business executives often did not speak with one voice when commenting on such matters as an appropriate path for U.S. world leadership, global economic development, and the protection of corporate interests overseas. For many, the dramatic expansion of the federal government under the New Deal and World War II posed serious concerns and questions over the further postwar expansion of state power. In 1946, former wartime production czar and GM executive Donald Nelson enthusiastically promoted the idea that close government-business planning, as achieved in wartime, would serve as a check on state power in peacetime. In his memoir, *The Arsenal of Democracy,* Nelson asserted that:

> It would be wonderful if the same sort of willing cooperation between government and business could extend beyond war into peacetime. There is an equal need ... to work together now that the last gun of World War II has been fired.[3]

The National Association of Manufacturers (NAM), one of the leading conservative forums for American executives, took a decidedly different position on maintaining a corporatist-style arrangement of government-business planning, especially in the area of foreign economic policy making and development. In a report in 1948, a NAM committee bluntly stated that "Government is not well-suited to carrying on foreign trade" and cautioned against overt state planning and involvement in the postwar recovery of world business activity and trading markets.[4]

As the president of General Electric, Philip D. Reed, however, advocated increased federal involvement and financial support for world economic development as a way to advance a rapid advance of American business interests, as well as greater social prosperity abroad. In a speech in 1945, he waxed that "Free enterprise must be understood and wanted for itself, quite apart from democracy. ... It is the cosmic

188 • Jacqueline McGlade

mechanism ... which spurs a rising standard of living ... for the peoples of the world."[5] Reflecting such views, Reed went on to serve as an important business supporter of the Marshall Plan, as well as other government aid programs aimed at foreign business reform and economic redevelopment throughout the 1950s and 1960s.

In contrast, Colgate S. Bayard, a prominent business executive and the Chairman of the NAM's International Committee, viewed foreign economic aid with a wary eye and suggested that government assume its traditional role as a promoter, not a facilitator of United States–European business recovery. However, he did admit that an enlarged peacetime role for the federal government in the area of world military security was probably inevitable as:

> United States prosperity has a direct relationship to the ... well being of the rest of the world. ... The establishment of an orderly and stable world ... is not merely an ideal of our times. It is a practical and stark necessity ... as we live in a world of long-range bombers and catastrophic military weaponry.[6]

When taken together, the statements of executives such as Nelson, Reed, and Bayard illustrate that the American business community did not hold a common, consistent set of beliefs regarding the appropriate postwar role for the American state in relationship to foreign economic policy making and recovery issues. While some like Nelson, and to a lesser extent Reed, would lend wholehearted support for a postwar expansion of federal involvement in the area of foreign economic development, others like Bayard resented overseas aid programs such as the Marshall Plan that tempered laissez-faire solutions for world recovery matters.

In many ways, the coming of the Marshall Plan in 1947–48, acted to unearth and then push wider divisions among the various factions within the business community over European recovery and the necessity of U.S. aid. In 1945, however, such signs of disruption were not immediately evident as business executives, along with Washington politicians, did not fully recognize, let alone advocate, the need to provide Western Europe with economic and industrial assistance. Despite holding hearings before the U.S. 80th Congress, State Department officials failed to convince lawmakers in January 1945 to allocate funds for the "reconstruction of [the] European economies."[7] For the next two years, it seemed that the countries of Western Europe would successfully achieve recovery without additional U.S. assistance as industrial levels approached pre-1939 levels by the end of 1946. But in 1947, steel production plunged by 40 percent as transportation and manpower shortages began to affect European coal mining and building markets. Also, agricultural yields fell by 20–30 percent due to a series of poor planting seasons and climate conditions. Exacerbated by runaway inflation and stagnated financial conditions, Europe's economic situation worsened and raised American fears.[8]

While recognizing a need to act, U.S. policy makers continued to debate over the appropriate course for a European aid program. One of the causes of political indecision on European aid in 1946–48 stemmed from the lack of strong leadership in foreign economic policy making. For over a decade, Franklin D. Roosevelt had actively fostered a shift in U.S. foreign policy away from isolationism toward internationalism.[9] Under Roosevelt, the United States amended its former protectionist trade policies in favor of liberalized foreign economic initiatives such as the Bretton Woods agreement, the negotiation of reciprocal trade agreements, and the extension of Lend-Lease aid. Upon Roosevelt's death in 1945, however, many ideological and political issues remained unresolved as to the future path of U.S. world leadership, especially on such difficult questions as European recovery aid and Soviet expansionism. Without the steadying influence of Roosevelt, American internationalists began to realign into two distinct groups by 1947. In general, influential New Deal liberals, business "progressives,"[10] and free trade advocates emerged as one faction that held supranationalist visions of a permanent world peace achieved through voluntary foreign reform and redevelopment. On the other side, vigilant anticommunists, national security pundits, and trade protectionists advocated an immediate advance of American military power and economic influence worldwide as a barrier toward Soviet expansion. As noted recently by Thomas Zeiler, liberal developmentalists in Congress and the Truman Administration often compromised the orthodoxy of free trade economics in order to "manage" protectionist attacks.[11] As a result, neither trade liberals nor protectionists held the upper hand in terms of U.S. foreign economic policy making in the immediate postwar period.

These ideological differences and schisms fragmented, then, the U.S. political scene at the very time when European distress called for swift, concerted action. By early 1948, however, liberal and conservative internationalists managed to affect a series of compromises that eventually led to the creation of the European Recovery Program (ERP). However, the absence of a direct Soviet military threat during the drafting stage of the ERP worked to the advantage of liberal internationalists, particularly business progressives, who were intent on preserving the program as a purely economic relief and reform measure.

For the next three years, business progressives would indeed dominate the shape and administration of the ERP. As business leaders, "progressive" executives stood out in contrast to their conservative colleagues as supporters of Franklin Roosevelt's New Deal and World War II administrations. To promote their ideas of closer government-business relations, "liberal" executives also formed in 1942 a new association, the Committee for Economic Development (CED), to aid in the making of U.S. economic, industrial, and social policies. As CED members, business liberals went on to attain powerful positions as government administrators and advisors after the outbreak of World War II. As wartime officials, progressive executives held key positions on the War Production Board (WPB), in the Foreign Economic Administration (FEA), and as members of the diplomatic corps.[12]

As a result, several business liberals, most notably W. Averell Harriman, Paul Hoffman of Studebaker Motorcar Company, Wall Street financier Bernard Baruch, and GE President Philip Reed, possessed a level of political privilege and access into the postwar Truman White House not held by their conservative counterparts. This influence became increasingly evident in the summer and fall of 1947 as business progressives pushed for an overseas aid program that would go beyond recovery to "reconstruct"[13] the economic and business environment of Western Europe. As members of the Harriman Committee,[14] progressive executives argued that European aid participants draft recovery plans anchored to certain economic, financial, and industrial reforms reflective of American methods and practices. According to the business progressives, lasting recovery could be achieved in Western Europe if economic growth was fostered and sustained through an expansion of consumer markets, improved business and industrial performance, liberalized trading practices, and positive state support for private capitalist ventures, enterprise, and investment.[15]

Finally, business liberals insisted that a European aid program concentrate on civilian economic recovery, not military rearmament. While concerned over the lack of anticommunist measures in the European Recovery Program (ERP), conservative internationalists eventually agreed to accept the package after an all-out push for its passage by Secretary of State George C. Marshall and the leading Republican senator, Arthur Vandenburg in March 1948. In early 1948 then, an initial consensus had been forged, but it quickly proved a fragile one as liberal and conservative internationalists began to immediately fight over the administration and direction of the ERP, or Marshall Plan as it became more commonly known.

The Marshall Plan as a Business Program

The appointment of a chief administrator served as the first contest for control of the ERP and its administration. As his initial choice, President Truman selected Dean Acheson to serve as the director of the ERP's newly formed administrative agency, the Economic Cooperation Administration (ECA). Though a Cold Warrior, Acheson, a Democrat, was unacceptable to hardline Republicans for purely political reasons, and to business progressives who wanted to insure a noticeable advance of economic reforms in Western Europe. In his rejection of the nomination, Republican Senator Arthur Vandenberg warned that, under Acheson, the ECA would employ a "Machiavellian philosophy of obstructing Soviet recovery" instead of helping "Europeans formulate and carry out a plan for ... genuine recovery."[16] When Truman tried to nominate another State Department official, former business executive Will Clayton, Vandenburg" insisted that "it was Congress desire" that the ERP Administrator come "from the outside business world with strong industrial credentials and *not* via the State Department."[17] Vandenburg's statements certainly reflected the complex, conflicted nature of United States aims for ERP administration in 1948. By failing to agree on an appropriate chief administrator, American officials demonstrated that a divide still existed between those in favor of purely economic remedies and others advocating a mixture of military and civilian aid for the relief of Western Europe.

Taking the advice of Vandenburg and Marshall, Truman finally appointed CED Chairman and car executive Paul Hoffman in April 1948 to head the ECA. While Hoffman's appointment symbolized an important victory for business liberals eager to spearhead European economic reform, it came at a heavy price. As a private business executive, Hoffman would find it difficult to gain interagency cooperation for the ECA, which sat outside of the confines of the State Department as an independent organization. As a result of its tenuous position in the U.S. government bureaucracy, the ECA floundered virtually from the start in its attempt to forge, and then implement a single, clear policy path for European recovery.

Part of the problem in the ECA's mission rested with the fact that Hoffman envisioned ERP as a kind of overseas "business advisory" agency and his job of that as "an investment banker."[18] In turn, he tended to hire private executives over political nominations, some which had been forwarded from the White House.[19] Controversy regarding the agency and its management mounted throughout 1948–49 as Hoffman and his staff proposed a distinctive, ambitious array of programs aimed at reforming European financial, industrial, and business practices. The "businesslike manner" of the ECA, however, rankled the Truman Administration, who increasingly began to question, particularly after the outbreak of the Korean War in June 1950, the agency's economic reform mission over the pressing needs of European rearmament.

Conservative executives and trade protectionists also became quite concerned over the ECA's mission to modernize as well as revive European business and industry. In particular, the goal of the ECA to "reconstruct" Western European economy as an integrated, liberalized trading environment worried American business protectionists seeking postwar overseas markets. Anticipating lucrative profits from contracts to supply equipment and materials through the ERP, frustrated business executives began to condemn the emergence of ECA policies in 1948–49 that restricted United States export and shipping opportunities overseas. ECA controls on the shipment of such American products as wood pulp and paper, aluminum, machine tools, tobacco, tuna, and livestock resulted in several protests lodged by the NAM, the National Foreign Trade Council (NFTC), and other smaller business associations. The ECA's "50–50 quota" on American–European shipping led the NAM membership to condemn such aid measures as "creating ... perma- nent barriers to an expanding world trade."[20]

Indeed, few American firms captured any real benefits from the European economic recovery programs initiated by the Economic Cooperation Administration (ECA) and later maintained by its succes- sor agency, the Foreign Operations Administration (FOA) under the Mutual Security Agency (MSA), 1953–59. Prior to such Cold War economic programs, the American business community enjoyed a $11.5 billion surplus in overseas export over import trading. While European recovery problems led to a dip in export totals from 1946 to 1947 ($16.8 billion down from $19.7 billion) it proved minor in relation to the slump ahead in 1948–49 with the enactment of ECA trade policies and restrictions. By 1950, U.S. export markets had plunged to $13.8 billion, a 33 percent decrease since 1946, with import markets (large composed of European products) rising to $12 billion or a 30 percent increase since 1945. As a result of increased imports, the annual figure in United States surplus export trading rapidly fell to only $1.8 billion and never recovered above $5.7 billion from 1950 to 1960.[21] Despite the adverse impact on U.S. trading figures, ECA officials remained committed to the spirit of the Marshall Plan legislation, creating programs to facilitate European business reform, industrial modernization, and economic self-sufficiency, not new U.S. business and export opportunities abroad. Nevertheless, American executives continued to resent the ECA and did not fully understand that the "ERP was not designed, [nor] ... administered, as a vehicle for increasing exports ... abroad."[22]

In order to alleviate the European export dip, the ECA instituted a few new programs in 1949–50, most notably the Overseas Investment Guaranties (OIG) program, and the United States Technical Assistance and Productivity (UST&P) program, in an attempt to generate American corporate reinvestment and involvement in Western Europe. While the OIG extended up to 100 percent coverage in financial guarantees, it failed to garner business interest as American private investment in recovering European firms climbed only slightly from 1948 to 1957. Overall, U.S. investment rose in this period at the unimpressive rate of only 6 percent a year from $2 billion to $4.15 billion.[23] a figure less than the top growth rates for export capital set back in the 1890s. In addition, the holdings of European companies in the United States continued to exceed those of American firms in Western Europe until 1957 when U.S. investments reached $4,151 million against $3,753 million held by European investors. By the end of 1969, the book value of American business investment in Western Europe escalated to $21,554 million while European investment in the United States proved a weak comparison at $8,510 million.[24]

Ironically, the policies that motivated U.S. private investment to take a "quantum leap forward" in Western Europe from $4.15 billion in 1957 to $24.52 billion in 1970, representing the startling increase of 600 percent, proved to be European, not American, in origin.[25] With the signing of the Treaty of Rome in 1957, American firms and investors received the guarantees they had been seeking—that European governments would actively maintain stable financial and currencies markets through convertibility, and move to lower legal and tax barriers that had previously restricted the expansion of foreign corporate interests. While the OIG had done little to inspire the export of private capital overseas, the Treaty of Rome, on the other hand, stimulated an avalanche of American financial interest across the Atlantic. By 1966, an astonishing 40 percent of all American foreign investment found its way into the European Common Market with only 17 percent in United States-owned ventures. Also, European countries began to directly solicit

U.S. investments by offering corporate subsidies and other internal incentives and financing arrangements. Buoyed up by such guarantees, the rate of new American investments in Europe grew by an average rate of 35 percent in mid-1960s. U.S. firms also actively participated in lucrative Euro-dollar and Common Market stock issues as well. Overall, 90 percent of all financial incentives for American private investment across the Atlantic by the end of the 1960s originated from European government programs, not Cold War aid programs, and with direct dollar transfers from the United States facilitating only 10 percent of the new wealth.[26]

Domestic manufacturing and trade figures also demonstrate the general reluctance of American companies to invest or expand their operations back into Western Europe prior to the 1960s. Despite the expansionist nature of Cold War foreign economic policies, the majority of the America's national income as well as business interest rested primarily in domestic versus foreign markets in the period from 1945 to 1960. As a reflection of such business protectionism, the combined total income from export–import trading rarely rose annually above 10–11 percent of the total GNP for the United States prior to 1970. Also, income from domestic business sectors accounted for 75–80 percent of the nation's wealth in the same period. As a result, these trading figures provide important evidence that Cold War foreign economic policies may have hindered, instead of assisted, the expansion of U.S. business interests and markets overseas in the early Cold War era.[27]

One program in particular, the United States Technical Assistance & Productivity Program (USTA&P), stood as a direct threat to many American business interests at home and offshore. Started in 1948 as an "exchange of persons in industry" program, the USTA&P sponsored teams of European business and labor leaders interested in viewing the operations and management of American companies and industries. While the program was first organized around the needs of British industry, by 1949–50 participation in the USTA&P had been extended to many ERP countries including France, Italy, Belgium, the Netherlands, and Norway. For the next eight years, the USTA&P built a wide array of sophisticated business reform programs such as management retraining seminars, in-plant consultancy ventures, and capital equipment purchasing programs for thousands of European firms including small artisanal and handicraft enterprises. With the rise of rearmament needs for the Korean War, the USTA&P intensified its efforts to facilitate a massive transfer of American management models and industrial techniques as a stimulus for business and production reform in Western Europe. Thus, the USTA&P became an important support program for the ECA's new "production drives" from 1950–54, which were intended to rapidly expand European manufacturing output of military equipment as well as civilian goods.[28]

For American firms, the USTA&P posed several problems. First, it supplied potential European competitors with modernized equipment, innovative practices, and management assistance through consultancy ventures and direct purchases. While the USTA&P offered to pay the salaries of American managers willing to work as business consultants overseas, very few executives or their firms participated in the program. Oftentimes, the technical aid extended through the USTA&P clashed with consultant services provided to overseas companies and clients by American firms for a fee. As a result, many of the USTA&P's overseas business consultants actually hailed from American business schools instead of companies by 1950. Citing fears over industrial sabotage and espionage, major firms such as Du Pont and General Electric also began to restrict, and in some instances, prohibit USTA&P team visits previously allowed for European business managers.[29] Finally, the attempts of the USTA&P to revive and modernize overseas industries stymied American firms looking to pursue markets and manufacturing interests in Western Europe. When taken together then, Cold War foreign aid programs as the OIG and the USTA&P created new barriers and restrictions which many American firms had never encountered in doing business across the Atlantic prior to 1948. Such data suggests then that scholars should continue to analyze U.S. foreign business interests and activities as a separate sphere apart from government plans, which at times stood in conflict with the aims of Cold War anticommunist strategies and containment geopolitics.

Conservative Backlash, 1949–50

As early as 1949 then, disgruntled business executives began to protest against ECA policies intended to foster the independent revival and modernization of European business and industry. While concerned about the disintegrating nature of business support, ECA Director Paul Hoffman resisted turning the ERP away from its economic reform agenda. Hoffman also faced mounting criticism from White House and Pentagon officials by the end of the summer of 1950 as the ECA had failed to stimulate immediate gains in European military as well as civilian production. In response, Hoffman and his aides stepped up the activities of the USTA&P and other ECA programs involved in overseas business recovery and industrial reform. By doing so, ECA officials hoped to preserve the ERP's original mission—to foster business reform and improved industry performance through European self-initiative, not American policy directives. Despite its new industry drives the ECA failed to shield the ERP from business attacks and military disfavor that rose sharply with the emerging tide of Cold War conservatism.

In many ways, business leaders led the attacks that eventually disabled the advance of economic liberalism in Europe through the ERP. Burdened by restrictive policies and slumping export markets, American protectionists criticized the liberalized economic remedies carried by the ECA under the direction of former New Dealers, progressive executives, and free trade advocates. Joined by military strategists and other "Cold Warriors," business protectionists also voiced strong concern over the lack of anti-Soviet defense measures in the ERP. Together, Cold War strategists and conservative executives began to press for an end to the economic reform agenda of the ERP even before its finish in 1952. In line with such sentiments, the Truman White House moved in late 1949 and early 1950 to oversee the passage of the Military Defense Assistance Act (MDAA), the Additional Military Production (AMP) program, and the North Atlantic Treaty Organization (NATO) charter in support of accelerating European remilitarization aid measures over that of ERP's civilian recovery mission.

With the outbreak of the Korean War in June 1950, ERP aid programs became further subsumed within the administration of European military production programs such as the MDAA and the AMP. After Hoffman's resignation in August 1950, the ECA tried to recover its business mission briefly through the efforts of its new director, William C. Foster, a former private industry executive. With the help of influential agency officials such as former MIT economics professor Richard Bissell and business executive William Batt, Foster fought hard to retain the ECA's autonomy over the planning and administration of European industrial recovery programs. In particular, Foster reorganized several of the ECA's programs, especially the USTA&P, in support of the more conservative, Cold War goal of achieving immediate gains in European military production.

Also, the ECA attempted to implement new aid restrictions outlined by the Benton-Moody Amendment in July 1950. In order to comply with provisions set by Benton-Moody, European governments faced the challenge of setting up "national productivity centers" (NPCs) to promote "free enterprise" practices and diminish radical labor activities or suffer a loss of ERP funds. In the fall of 1950, the ECA mounted an all-out campaign to aid overseas governments in creating the NPCs.

By spring 1951, it had succeeded in initiating NPCs in 11 of the 16 ERP recipient countries. Nevertheless, congressional and business critics continued to rail against the ECA as the NPCs failed to block production assistance to overseas industries that still associated with Communist and socialist unions.[30]

Along with the creation of the NPCs, the ECA also started a "pilot plants" program to showcase European companies that had adopted American-style industrial techniques and labor management practices. Reflective of the new conservatism in ERP administration, the pilot plants program along with the NPCs were managed by Pentagon as well as ECA officials serving on a newly reconstituted European Production Assistance Board (EPAB). In the past, the EPAB had been primarily staffed by European administrators who were assisted by the ECA in the letting out of ERP aid allocations and MDAA/AMP production contracts. The tightening of Cold War aims and attitudes in 1950 resulted then in a general U.S. rejection of European self-determination in favor of more hegemonic control over the administration of industrial support and production programs overseas. As a final gesture toward European remilitarization, the ECA also expanded the focus of the USTA&P management retraining programs to include firms engaged in military production as well as civilian manufacturing.

However, the efforts of the ECA to redirect the ERP closer in line with conservative Cold War aims ultimately failed with the loss of its autonomy over European aid planning and administration in late 1950. Annexed into the U.S. State Department in early 1951, the ECA ceased to function as the independent "business agency" first imagined by Hoffman and other liberal executives. Stripped of its authority over European aid, the ECA accepted an increased number of Pentagon officials on its planning boards and on industrial reform projects overseas. By the fall of 1951, the ECAs economic reform mission was essentially finished as many of the ERP business programs became slated for elimination in 1952.[31] Only a few programs survived beyond the ERP, most notably the USTA&P, which under the newly created Mutual Security Administration (MSA), continued to play an important role in fostering European military production and redevelopment until its end in 1958.

European Autonomy and Cold War Aid

While the Marshall Plan formally ended in 1952, the business and political debates over a path for U.S. assistance in European recovery did not. With the coming of the Eisenhower Administration in 1953, trade protectionists and business liberals alike anticipated a swift end to European civilian industrial aid. However, the start-up of NATO military production in many European countries had triggered serious, new economic and industrial problems.

Overall, the U.S.-led drive for European remilitarization resulted in a 30 percent decline in the manufacture and trade of civilian goods from 1950–54.[32] In the case of Great Britain, domestic production fell by 2.6 percent, particularly in such core industries as mining, metalworking, vehicles, goods, and clothing manufacturing, and civil engineering, to accommodate aircraft production output which increased at a rate of 80 percent a year from 1950–54.[33] In addition, NATO manufacturing caused drains in coal and steel supplies, sparking alarming shortages in domestic fuel, building materials, and other industrial products necessary for civilian recovery overseas.[34] By 1953, the United States added to the economic burden of Western Europe by leveling and enforcing stringent strategic trade controls, which prohibited many countries for accessing and trading in key civilian as well as military goods markets in Eastern Europe and Asia.

As a result, several European countries, led by France and Great Britain, began to insist that the United States either ease world trade restrictions as administered by the Mutual Security Administration (MSA) or maintain the extension of civilian industrial supports as well as military aid beyond the end of the ERP. While Great Britain opted for an increased level of military aid in 1953, other European countries, most notably France, West Germany and Italy, captured large subsidies for the recovery of civilian along with military industries through the MSA. On an average, European governments received $8 to $10 million annually in additional civilian manufacturing aid from 1953 to 1958.[35] Overseas firms also gained the distinct advantage when competing for lucrative NATO production contracts of receiving certain preferences by the MSA over American bidders.

The triumph of European self-determination and autonomy over U.S. directives in aid planning and decision making can also be traced on a national and transnational basis. In Norway, government officials used ERP and MSA funding to recover and expand traditional patterns of regional business and labor activity instead of adopting radical new American management methods and industrial reforms. Instead of transforming Norwegian manufacturing along the lines of U.S. mass production models, business and government officials chose to increase the existing capabilities of national firms which, in the end, resulted in higher rates of industrial performance and efficiency.[36]

Italian government officials also pushed for an independent plan for national economic and industrial recovery as a counter to the full-scale business reform mission promoted by American aid administrators. Through the "Inter-Ministerial Committee on Reconstruction" (CIR), Italian officials tempered American plans for a massive "productivity" and modernization drive into heavy industries by insisting that small manufacturing and artisan handicraft firms also receive comparable reform assistance.[37] Also, the De Gasperi government captured American aid support for substantial equipment purchases and academic exchange programs intended to revitalize Italian universities and institute scientific research and R&D laboratories in key firms such as Fiat and Olivetti.[38]

European autonomy over American hegemony in aid planning emerged transnationally as well through the activities of the Organization of European Economic Cooperation (OEEC). Starting in 1949, the OEEC had taken an active role in selecting firms as candidates for technical assistance funding and team visits as arranged through the USTA&P. With the start-up of the Korean War, the OEEC also targeted and managed communications between European defense firms chosen to receive NATO production contracts and American aid administrators. Despite its close association with U.S. agencies in aid management, the OEEC, nevertheless, succeeded by 1953 in establishing, through the auspices of its own European Productivity Agency (EPA), an independent drive for European industrial modernization, manpower development, and business reform.[39] According to historian Bent Boel, the EPA went on to play "a unique and innovative role" in building a greater transnational "network" in Europe for productivity reform and was viewed by "many member countries ... as an instrument of integration."[40] After 1953 then, the OEEC consistently supported the formation and implementation through the EPA of an indigenous plan for European transnational economic recovery and industrial reform quite apart from the aid path promoted by the United States. Even upon the end of American technical assistance funding in 1957, the OEEC chose to continue funding EPA programs intended to spark productivity reforms in European industry at an annual budget rate of $10–12 million for another three years.[41]

Conclusion

Certainly, American protectionists bitterly resented the framework of Cold War aid that evolved with the founding of the Marshall Plan and the extension of direct U.S. supports for the revival of civilian and military industries in Western Europe. After 1953, business liberals and free traders also began to question the direction taken by U.S. foreign economic policy as reshaped by the Cold War. Many free traders and business progressives joined with their conservative colleagues to heavily criticize the entrance and enforcement of strategic foreign trade controls, which had acted to bifurcate and reduce business development and trading opportunities worldwide. Confined to a single geopolitical sphere, American business executives found themselves by the end of the 1950s in competition for a limited number of Western consumer markets with European, and later Japanese, competitors strengthened by Cold War industrial supports and aid programs. Such containment measures, they would argue, not only impeded American business expansionism but also the destiny of the United States to lead an advance of democratic capitalism worldwide.

While initially committed to ending American aid supports to Western Europe, the Eisenhower Administration quickly faced overseas opposition to a radical adjustment in the framework of transatlantic aid established since 1948. As in the case of the Truman Administration, the Eisenhower White House could do little but support, in the interest of NATO solidarity and Cold War containment, the independent recovery of European economy and industry over the expansionist aims of American firms seeking lucrative export markets and trading interests across the Atlantic. After 1960, the Kennedy and Johnson administrations would also find it increasingly difficult to satisfy the demands of domestic producers for offshore business and trade opportunities, while maintaining Cold War geopolitical controls and spheres of communist containment.

For many countries in Western Europe, however, the late marriage of Marshall Plan aid with Cold War military objectives provided an unexpected period of prolonged lucrative support for their economic revival and redevelopment efforts. Along with governments, European firms, particularly large producers, directly benefited from the extension of financial capital, production contracts, and consultant services offered through American aid programs. With the help of U.S. aid and other government supports, overseas companies managed to successfully rebuild and modernize their business operations, thus recapturing, in many cases, the market advantages they had controlled prior to World War II. For some American firms, however, the renewal of European industrial strength and independence posed a daunting barrier to the expansion of export trade and business growth they had anticipated across the Atlantic after 1945. In this way then, U.S. Cold War aid policies rarely supported, and often acted to impede, the advance of American business interests and activities in the redeveloping economic environment of postwar Western Europe. Instead of meshing into a "grand strategy" then, the two postwar models of global economic leadership advanced by U.S. policy makers after 1948, liberal developmentalism and strategic containment, were, in fact, in competition and often confuted the efforts of administrators to implement a consistent, coherent set of aid programs overseas. As a result, the extension of government aid as a lever for foreign economic improvement and development remained a controversial and contentious issue that divided American business and political leaders well into the 1960s and 1970s.

Notes

1. For overview of U.S. aid spending prior to the Marshall Plan, see M. Curti, *Prelude to Point Four: American Technical Assistance Missions Overseas, 1838–1938* (Washington, DC: Government Printing Office, 1984).

2. See M. Hogan, *The Marshall Plan: America, Great Britain and the Reconstruction of Western Europe, 1947–1952* (Cambridge: Cambridge University Press, 1987) and M. Leffler, *A Preponderance of Power: National Security, the Truman Administration and the Cold War* (Stanford, CA: University of California Press, 1992).

3. D. Nelson, *The Arsenal of Democracy: The Story of American War Production* (New York: Da Capo Books, 1946), p. 347.

4. Hagley Museum and Library, Papers of the National Association of Manufacturers (hereafter NAM), Folder B, Box 26, International Committee Report, 1948, p. 1.

5. Hagley Museum and Library, Papers of Phillip D. Reed, "American Free Enterprise and the Future," February 27, 1940, pp. 1–2.

6. Hagley Museum and Library, NAM Papers, Folder B, Box 26, International Relations Report, 1942, p. 8.

7. J. Blum, *V Was for Victory: Politics and Culture during World War II* (New York: Harcourt Brace, 1976), pp. 310–12.

8. United Nations, *Survey of the Economic Situation and Prospects of Europe* (New York, 1948), p. 3 and Economic Cooperation Administration (hereafter ECA), *Third Report to Congress of the Economic Cooperation Administration* (Washington, DC: GOP, 1950). Also in M. Hogan, *The Marshall Plan: America, Great Britain and the Reconstruction of Western Europe, 1947–1952* (Cambridge: Cambridge University Press, 1987), and A. Milward, *The Reconstruction of Western Europe, 1945–1951* (Berkeley: University of California Press, 1987).

9. For additional insight into the prewar origins of U.S. internationalism, please see R. Divine, *Second Chance: The Triumph of Internationalism in America during World War II* (New York: Atheneum Press, 1971).

10. For more on the rise of business progressives and their influence in modern American politics, see K. McQuaid, *Uneasy Partners: Big Business in American Politics, 1945–1990* (Baltimore: MD: Johns Hopkins University Press, 1993), and R. Collins, *Business Response to Keynes, 1929–1964* (New York: Columbia University Press, 1981).

11. Thomas W. Zeiler, "Managing Protectionism: American Trade Policy in the Early Cold War," *Diplomatic History*, Vol. 22, No. 3 (Summer 1998), pp. 337–60.

12. On the influence of business liberals in government administration from 1941–52, see J. McGlade, "From Business Reform Programme to production drive: The Transformation of United States technical assistance to Western Europe" in M. Kipping and O. Bjarner, eds., *The Americanization of European Business: The Marshall Plan and the Transfer of United States Management Models* (London: Routledge Publishers, 1998), and also K. McQuaid, *Uneasy Partners* (Baltimore, MD: Johns Hopkins University Press, 1993), and R. Collins, *Business Response to Keynes* (New York: Columbia University Press, 1981).

13. Secretary of State George C. Marshall first applied the term "reconstruction" to describe U.S. aid objectives for a Western European aid program in his Harvard Commencement Address, June 5, 1947.

14. The Harriman Committee was formed by President Truman in Fall 1947 to examine the European relief question. It forwarded an initial set of findings and recommendations to Congress in December that acted as the basis for the drafting of a legislative aid package in Spring 1948.

15. For more on the foreign policy views of the Committee for Economic development (hereafter CED), see the Hagley Museum and Library, Papers of the CED and Papers of Phillip D. Reed. Also in M. Hogan, *The Marshall Plan* (Cambridge, 1987), pp. 95–101, and C. Maier, "The Politics of Productivity: Foundations of American International Economic Policy After World War II." *International Organization*, 31 (1977), pp. 607–33.

16. H. B. Price, *The Marshall Plan and Its Meaning* (Ithaca, NY: Cornell University Press, 1955), p. 73.

17. W. Sanford, *The American Business Community and the European Recovery Program, 1947–52* (Westport, CT: Greenwood Press, 1987), p. 102.

18. H. B. Price, *The Marshall Plan and Its Meaning* (Ithaca, NY: Cornell University Press, 1955), p. 73.

19. NARA, RG 469, ECA, OA, CLM, Box 3, 9 August 1948, H. S. Truman to P. Hoffman.

20. Hagley Museum and Library, NAM Papers, Report on International Relations 1948, Folder B, Box 26, 1948, p. 12.

21. U.S. Bureau of the Census, *Historical Statistics of the United States, Colonial Times to 1970* (Washington, DC: GOP, 1970), pp. 228–30.

22. W. Sanford, *The American Business Community and the European Recovery Program* (Westport, CT: Greenwood Press, 1987), p. 131.

23. *Survey of Current Business*, Vol. 29 (November 1949), p. 20 and ibid., Vol. 40 (September 1960), p. 20.

24. C. Tugendhat, *The Multinationals* (London: Eyre & Spottiswoode, 1971), p. 24.

25. D. Swann, *The Economics of the Common Market* (New York: Penguin, 1975), p. 73; C. F. Bergsten, T. Horst, and T. H. Moran, *American Multinationals and American Interests* (Washington, DC: The Brookings Institution Press, 1978), p. 405.

26. J. Servan-Schreiber, *The American Challenge* (New York: Atheneum, 1968), pp. 11, 14–15.

27. U.S. Bureau of the Census, *Historical Statistics of the United States, Colonial Times to 1970* (Washington, DC: GOP, 1970), pp. 228–30.

28. On the origins of the United States Technical Assistance and Productivity Program, please see A. Carew, *Labour under the Marshall Plan: The Politics of Productivity and the Marketing of Management Science* (Manchester: Manchester University Press, 1987) and J. McGlade, "The United States Technical Assistance and Productivity program and the education of Western European managers, 1948–58", in T. R. Gourvish and N. Tiratsoo, eds., *Missionaries and Managers: American Influences on European Management Education, 1945–60* (Manchester: Manchester University Press, 1998).

29. J. McGlade, "The United States Technical Assistance and Productivity program and the education of Western European managers, 1948–58," in T. R. Gourvish and N. Tiratsoo, eds., *Missionaries and Managers: American Influences on European Management Education, 1945–60* (Manchester: Manchester University Press, 1998), p. 19.

30. *Mutual Defense Assistance Program: 1950, Joint Hearings*, 81st Congress, 2nd session, 1950.

31. See J. McGlade, "The Illusion of Consensus: American Business, Cold War Aid and the Recovery of Western Europe, 1948–1958," Ph.D. dissertation (Washington, DC: The George Washington University, 1995).

32. Mutual Security Administration (hereafter MSA), *Worldwide Enforcement of Strategic Trade Controls* (Washington, DC: GOP, 1953), pp. 20–21.

33. NARA, RG 469, MSA, SR/E, PTAD, SF, Box 34, File: Defense—UK 614, Cablegram on UK 1954 Offshore Procurement Program, 30 March, 1953, pp. 4–5.

34. ECA, *Third Year Report* (Washington, DC, 1951), p.128.

35. International Cooperation Administration, *European Productivity: A Summing Up* (Paris, 1958), p.43.

36. R. P. Amdam and O. Bjarner, "Regional Business Networks and the Diffusion of American Management and Organisational Models to Norway, 1945–65," *Business History*, Vol. 39, No. 1, 1997, pp. 73–90. Also see G. Yttri, "From a Norwegian Rationalization Law to an American

Productivity Institute," *Scandinavian Journal*, Vol. 20, 1996 for a discussion of postwar Norwegian political self-determination.

37. NARA, RG 469, ECA, PTAD, OD, CSF, Box 18, File: Italy-General-Position of Miscellaneous Industries and the Craftsman Industry," 29 May, 1949, pp. 1–10.

38. Some historians has credited U.S. postwar assistance for the rise of a more "diffused" or mixed pattern of industrialization or the "Third Italy" in the northeastern region of the country. In particular, see L. Segreto, "Americanizzare o modernizzare l'economia? Progetti americani e riposte italiane negli anni Cinquanta e Sessanta," *Passato e present*, No. 37, 1996.

39. International Cooperation Administration (hereafter ICA), *European Productivity and Technical Assistance: A Summing Up, 1948–1958* (Paris, 1958), pp. 47–51.

40. B. Boel, "The European Productivity Agency: A Faithful Prophet of the American Model?" Working Paper, Conference on European Industry and the U.S. Productivity Drive, The University of Reading, UK, December 13–14, 1996, p. 13.

41. In recognition of continuing European support for the EPA, the United States also bestowed a special grant of $1 to 1.5 million annually to the program until its end in 1960. ICA, *European Productivity and Technical Assistance: A Summing Up, 1948–1958* (Paris, 1958), pp. 47–51.

CHAPTER 11

Embedded Liberalism in France? American Hegemony, the Monnet Plan, and Postwar Multilateralism

Stewart Patrick

An influential thesis in the field of international political economy attributes the form and content of the post-1945 regimes for trade and money to a "compromise of embedded liberalism." To date, evidence for this transatlantic consensus on open commerce tempered by moderate domestic intervention has rested on a single, Anglo-American case. This article, based on close examination of French archival records, expands the geographical and intellectual scope of this thesis. It demonstrates that French policymakers, influenced by new economic ideas and the lessons of the recent past, developed similar convictions about the state's role in domestic and foreign economic policy. It shows how embedded liberalism triumphed in France through ideational competition between French "neoliberals" and "structural reformers." After winning political power, the neoliberals recast France's national interests, renounced the country's historical protectionism, and committed France to an open, reciprocal, and non-discriminatory commercial order. They did so in the belief that openness would galvanize productivity, that discrimination and protection were illegitimate, and that new institutions could stabilize global markets and foster domestic welfare. This cognitive reorientation narrowed the range of disagreement during postwar Franco-American negotiations over France's recovery and reintegration into the world economy, discussions that culminated in the Blum-Byrnes Commercial and Financial Accords of May 1946. France's commitment to openness came with certain caveats: that multilateralism permit social democratic initiatives; that France's full liberalization be postponed to permit reconstruction; and that America finance a state-led program of modernization, known as the Monnet Plan. Nevertheless, these bilateral accords laid a foundation for the continent-wide recovery effort that the United States launched in June 1947.[1]

During World War II, American planners anticipated that European countries would face daunting challenges of postwar reconstruction. But they were confident that relatively modest financial and material assistance would permit Europe's rapid entry into the liberal, multilateral system of trade and payments envisioned at Bretton Woods. Indeed, winning transatlantic agreement on such an open world economy remained Washington's number one postwar foreign policy objective until 1947. In the Spring of that year, the dual specters of Soviet aggression and European economic collapse led American officials to embrace the doctrine of containment. During 15 dramatic weeks from March to June, the United States government announced the Truman Doctrine and the Marshall Plan, effectively deferring its "One World" dreams to defend a narrower "Free World" coalition. Nevertheless, multilateralism remained Washington's preferred organizing principle for postwar international commerce.

This chapter examines transatlantic bargaining over the shape of the world economy *before* the outbreak of the Cold War and the launching of the European Recovery Program. Focusing on Franco-American negotiations during and immediately after World War II, it scrutinizes a popular theory that attributes the form and content of the postwar international regimes for trade and money to a "compromise of embedded liberalism." In this view, the managed multilateral system that emerged after 1945 reflected a consensus on both sides of the Atlantic on open commerce tempered by moderate domestic intervention. This arrangement balanced the norms of liberalism, nondiscrimination, and reciprocity with safeguards permitting policies of social welfare, full employment, and nationalization. To date, evidence for this bargain has rested on a single case: the Anglo-American negotiations that culminated in the Bretton Woods Accords and the British Loan.[2] The question arises: Were these social purposes confined to the United States and Great Britain, or were they more widely shared?

This chapter broadens the geographic and intellectual scope of the embedded liberalism thesis by tracing the emergence of similar ideas in French foreign policy during and immediately after World War II. It documents a process of complex learning, whereby French decision-makers and policy experts came to share with their American counterparts certain causal and principled beliefs about the state's legitimate role in domestic and foreign economic policy. The chapter shows how French elites recast their national interests, renounced protectionism, and committed France to an open, reciprocal, and nondiscriminatory order. But it also makes clear that this engagement came with certain caveats: that multilateralism tolerate social democratic initiatives; that liberalization occur gradually to allow reconstruction; and that the United States finance a state-led program of French modernization, known as the Monnet Plan.

This commitment to embedded liberalism culminated in May 1946, when Paris and Washington signed the Blum-Byrnes Commercial and Financial Accords. Although these Franco-American negotiations have received little scholarly attention, they shaped the boundaries of transatlantic compromise over the postwar economy and paved the way for the Marshall Plan. France's intellectual reorientation also mitigated (to a degree) French discomfort with American hegemony.

Ideas, Identity, and Foreign Policy Choices

International relations theorists typically attribute the open postwar world economy to the hegemonic power and material interests of the United States.[3] But while U.S. domination was inherent in the distribution of global power in 1945, neither preponderance nor utility maximization dictated Washington's foreign policy purposes, the institutions through which it pursued these aims, or the reactions of other states. As John Ruggie has written, the postwar order owed as much to the (identity) fact of *American* hegemony as to the (material) fact of American *hegemony*.[4] What made U.S. hegemony distinctive was a commitment to *multilateralism*: an open, egalitarian, reciprocal, transparent and nondiscriminatory pattern of international relations.[5] Resonating with America's liberal-exceptionalist political culture, multilateralism emboldened U.S. officials to recast the anarchical international system in their country's image as a voluntarist and universalist community. The objective, in Anton DePorte's felicitous phrase, was to "Lockeanize a hitherto Hobbesian world."[6]

Multilateralism influenced most arenas of American postwar planning. In economic affairs, it implied that protectionism, bilateralism, and preference should yield to an open, nondiscriminatory system of trade and payments, supervised by international institutions. Purely structural and interest-based accounts do not explain why Washington embraced these norms. Nor do they explain why other countries—like France—came to share these purposes. Finally, the mainstream (neorealist and neoliberal) approaches to international relations cannot account for the qualified nature of postwar economic openness, a hybrid system that tempered commercial freedom with protections for national autonomy and social welfare.[7]

An alternative theoretical perspective known as "constructivism" can help us to address these questions by directing our attention to interest formation—and to the role of ideas and identities in shaping national purposes. Constructivist scholars remind us that shared knowledge, frameworks of meaning, and historical legacies affect the ways in which leaders and policy makers perceive their country's position and national interests within international society.[8] International regimes may arise through "complex learning," as actors redefine their interests in the light of new causal and principled understandings about past experiences and current problems. New ideas may facilitate cooperation by offering "road maps" for policy innovation or "focal points" for collective action. Once embedded in institutions, such beliefs may become *norms,* or intersubjective standards of behavior defined in terms of rights and obligations.[9]

Of course, ideas do not exert influence independent of material circumstances and conscious agents. To shape interests and institutions, new beliefs must acquire political power. They do so by offering practical and/or ethical solutions to past mistakes or current dilemmas and by demonstrating their epistemic, administrative, and political viability. To endure, new ideas must advance the agendas of ruling parties or mobilize new coalitions.[10] Dramatic external shocks and policy failures often stimulate learning by loosening elite attachment to prevailing causal beliefs and behavioral patterns. Epistemic communities may introduce new cognitive frameworks, disseminate policy-relevant knowledge, and influence state agendas. One such fluid moment followed the Great Depression and World War II. These twin disasters destroyed existing institutions, discredited past orthodoxies, and caused leaders to recast national interests, goals, and doctrines.[11]

New Thinking and French Multilateralism

This chapter attributes the rise of embedded liberalism in France to a combination of ideational and material factors. It documents how a group of French "neoliberals," responding to new economic ideas,

lessons of the recent past, and France's position within the global economy, embraced external openness compatible with domestic intervention. Redefining national interests in a context of interdependence,
these neoliberals defeated a rival group of "structural reformers"
committed to radical economic transformation and independence
behind protectionist walls.

The dynamics of policy entrepreneurship and cognitive evolution
that propelled embedded liberalism in France resemble the rise of "New
Thinking" in Soviet diplomacy during the 1980s. As in the Soviet case,
a dramatic shift in foreign policy was shaped by a group of specialists
who won over a new generation of progressive leaders, "committed to
change and receptive to new ideas for solving the country's formidable
problems."[12] Like Gorbachev's Soviet Union, France in 1945 confronted
palpable economic and geopolitical decline. In 1939, France had ranked
indisputably among the great powers, possessing a modern army, a large
empire, and a glorious political and cultural tradition. Suddenly, the
military debacle of 1940 and the meteoric rise of the superpowers
threatened to alter its global standing forever. Alongside the
"mastodons" of the postwar order, lamented one official, France would
be a "negligible quantity."[13] The country's postliberation leaders were
determined to reverse these trends.

If the context for policy change was "permissive," however, the
victory of commercial multilateralism was hardly preordained. As
Robert Herman reminds us, a state's response to any "strategic environment is indeterminate; it depends ... on how decision makers understand the world and ... interpret the frequently ambiguous lessons of
history."[14] In the French case, different factions held divergent normative and causal beliefs and offered competing prescriptions for trade
policy. Embedded liberalism triumphed only after vigorous ideational
contestation.

This process of French cognitive evolution facilitated Franco-
American convergence, narrowing the range of conceivable disagreement in bilateral negotiations over the postwar political economy.
France was not dragged into an open world; nor did it pursue multilateralism *faute de mieux*. Rather, French neoliberals, converted to
economic "new thinking," believed that France, if permitted to recover
and modernize, could flourish in an interdependent world economy.

The actual contours of Franco-American compromise emerged
through strategic bargaining during 1945–46. Material considerations,
including financial incentives and threats of coercion (or defection)
shaped the outcome of these negotiations. But France's ultimate

endorsement of multilateralism reflected a set of shared transatlantic convictions: that commercial openness would galvanize productivity, that discrimination and protection were illegitimate instruments of national policy, and that international institutions could smooth global markets and foster domestic welfare. Given France's protectionist heritage, this was a revolutionary change in French foreign policy.

This chapter marshals archival evidence to substantiate its argument that new ideas informed French commercial policy choices and under-pinned Franco-American consensus. Adopting a "process-tracing"[15] approach to causal inference, it shows how French policy élites—politicians, expert economists, and *hauts fonctionaires* (or high-level technocrats)—interpreted their situation and responded to external stimuli. Finally, the article highlights the intellectual and entrepreneur-ial skills of one individual, Jean Monnet, in forging transatlantic compromise.

Liberal Multilateralism: America's Vision for the World Economy

As U.S. wartime planners drafted blueprints for the postwar world, their immediate priority was not (yet) to contain Soviet power but rather to construct an open, rule-bound system of trade and payments. Conceived as a "regime," the new order would be based on the *principle* that liberal trade fostered global welfare and world peace; it would embody certain *norms,* particularly nondiscrimination and reciprocity; it would be governed by *rules,* including the most-favored nation convention; and it would establish *decision-making procedures* to negoti-ate reductions in tariffs and nontariff barriers. But instead of returning to the free trade of the gold-standard era, multilateralism would accom-modate new state responsibilities to stabilize the domestic and the global economy.

The beliefs underlying commercial multilateralism (like those under-lying many norms) were both "principled" and "causal."[16] On the one hand, its advocates considered protectionism and discrimination to be illegitimate devices of statecraft, being fundamentally unfair and conducive to conflict. Multilateralism thus appealed to the *logic of appropriateness.* On the other hand, idealism jibed with expediency: As the wealthiest, most productive manufacturing country, the United States stood to benefit from open and equal trade. Multilateralism thus also reflected the *logic of consequentiality.*

The most vocal advocates of liberal multilateralism were in Cordell Hull's State Department, which had engineered the Reciprocal Trade

Agreement Act of 1934 and a bilateral trade accord with Great Britain in 1938. American diplomats stressed the economic roots of military conflict and the promise of commercial openness to cut them. "Nations which act as enemies in the marketplace," declared Assistant Secretary William Clayton, "cannot long remain friends at the council table." For Hull, the lesson was simple: "When goods move, soldiers don't."[17]

This campaign for unfettered access and equal treatment targeted *all* protectionism and discrimination. This included not only Hitler's New Order and Japan's Greater East Asian Co-Prosperity Sphere but also Britain's system of Imperial Preference, which impeded legitimate U.S. trade and investment through import quotas, discriminatory tariffs, and currency restrictions. Exploiting Britain's financial vulnerability, Washington forced commercial concessions from its erstwhile ally. In return for Lend-Lease aid, the British pledged to reduce barriers to trade. Nevertheless, preoccupied with its balance of payments and intent pursuing policies of economic planning and full employment after the war, London clung to bilateralism, import controls, and imperial preference. To the State Department's chagrin, Churchill successfully diluted the open trade clause of the Atlantic Charter; Article IV called upon signatories merely "to endeavor, *with due regard for existing obligations,* to further the enjoyment by all states ... of access, on equal terms, to the trade and raw materials of the world."[18]

After Anglo-American trade talks stalled, bilateral discussions shifted to monetary issues. Here, the potential for agreement was greater. U.S. Treasury officials, skeptical of the *laissez-faire* approach of the State Department, declined to place world prosperity in invisible hands. Inspired by Keynesian ideas and the New Deal, they sought new international institutions to ameliorate postwar dislocation, enforce trade rules, ease financial crises, stabilize commodity prices, promote full employment, and encourage foreign investment and development.[19]

Indeed, on both sides of the Atlantic, depression and war had changed official and public expectations about the proper balance between the state and the market.[20] Henceforth, governments would fight unemployment and insulate the domestic economy from external shocks. London (and the European governments-in-exile) anticipated arduous postwar tasks of reconstruction and the creation of a welfare state. Since multilateralism would be predicated on domestic intervention, trading partners would need a mechanism to reconcile any disequilibria caused by competing national policies. The Bretton Woods Accords of July 1944 sought to establish a managed multilateral order by establishing an International Monetary Fund (IMF) and an

International Bank for Reconstruction and Development (IBRD). The cornerstones of the new architecture were price and exchange rate stability, currency convertibility, reduced trade barriers, and moderate domestic intervention. The IMF provided a "double screen" to cushion deficit countries from economic perturbations.[21]

"Embedded liberalism," as Ruggie terms this compromise, was a product of American power and shared social purpose. The United States exploited its structural position as a creditor and employed economic incentives during Anglo-American negotiations, but the ultimate focal point for agreement reflected the normative and technical beliefs, gleaned from contemporary economic theory and recent history, of a "loose transnational and transgovernmental 'alliance'" of expert economists and policy specialists.[22] Occupying a broad middle ground between statist intervention and free trade, embedded liberalism allowed politicians of various stripes to adopt non-discrimination while pursuing national goals and protecting social welfare. Still, Americans and Europeans did not always agree about how to balance external openness and domestic intervention or on the institutions needed to achieve these common aims. The internal and external contours of embedded liberalism emerged during painstaking negotiations.

The Culture of Commercial Policy: Competing Views of French National Interests

Whereas scholars have lavished attention on Anglo-American bargaining over postwar multilateralism, few have examined parallel Franco-American negotiations culminating in the Blum-Byrnes agreements of 1946. While less critical than Bretton Woods or the British Loan, these accords nevertheless offer insights about the compromises the American hegemon struck with important partners. They also show that "embedded liberalism" was not restricted to the United States and Great Britain.

According to Goldstein and Keohane, new ideas gain political influence by framing national interests in periods of uncertainty. Exogenous shocks—like "depressions, wars ... and the overthrow of a government"—encourage the search for new causal and principled beliefs.[23] Historically, few contexts for policy formulation have been as precarious as that confronting the Free French leadership during World War II. Having experienced depression, war, and conquest in dizzying succession, these officials regrouped in exile abroad and undercover within Vichy France. As they awaited their country's liberation, they naturally began to explore new foundations for its postwar political economy. Although marginalized from Anglo-American wartime conversations over trade and money, both the French Committee for National Liberation (CFLN) and the internal Resistance debated postwar commercial liberalization. Ultimately, the French chose a future of economic interdependence rather than economic nationalism. Given France's statist and protectionist heritage, this policy shift begs for investigation.

This article attributes the victory of embedded liberalism in France to a process of "evolutionary epistemology." Essentially, new ideas helped to redefine France's predicament, identity, and interests within the world economy. As often occurs, competition between rival epistemic communities served as the crucible for policy innovation.[24] During the war, two rival groups emerged among the Free French, championing alternative visions about the state's economic role and the value commercial openness. The victors in this battle were a group of "neoliberal" economists and policy experts, influenced by the diffusion of Keynesian ideas, who advocated a statist but multilateral future. Following France's liberation, the neoliberals defeated a rival group of "structural reformers," won over the country's political leadership, and negotiated with Washington on open trade. To consolidate their victory, they linked France's multilateral commitments to an ambitious program for recovery and modernization.

"Structural Reformers" versus "Neoliberals"

In contrast to Great Britain and the United States, France possessed a dirigiste economic tradition characterized by ambivalence toward competition and reliance on state protectionism. The Great Depression and France's 1940 collapse deepened these instincts, discrediting the liberal political economy of the Third Republic. All Resistance factions hoped to reconstruct and modernize the economy, nationalize key industries, build social democracy, and transform France's "stalemate society" (of agrarian and small business interests) into an industrial powerhouse. In March 1944, the Conseil National de La Resistance promulgated a Resistance Charter, advocating national "independence" from the economic and financial monopolies that had profited from national stagnation and social injustice.[25]

This surface unanimity cloaked important divisions among the Free French. Two prominent "subcultures"[26] emerged, differing in their political values, their assumptions about the state's economic role, and their attitude towards open commerce. The *structural reformers* sought to eliminate the capitalist oligarchy asphyxiating France and to transform the economy along socialist lines. They advocated wholesale nationalization, resistance to U.S. imperialism, and industrialization behind protectionist walls. An opposing group of *neoliberals* rejected such radical schemes. Influenced by Keynesian ideas, the Great Depression, and transatlantic contacts, they espoused a market-based future tempered by technocratic planning and accompanied by commercial openness. Their "progressive economy" would be based on free enterprise, but the state would supervise, incite and regulate market forces. Growth and productivity would reconcile social welfare aspirations with economic realities.[27]

The locus of Free French planning was a Commission on Postwar Economic, Financial and Social Problems, based in London. During 1942, as Washington pressed them to endorse the multilateral principles of the Atlantic Charter, the French debated the merits of technocratic statism versus socialist corporatism, and of multilateralism versus economic nationalism. "To what degree and at what rhythm," the Commission asked, "should France come round to the views of its allies to obtain their aid?"[28]

France's interwar economy had resembled a delicate plant in a protectionist "hothouse." Remaining there, neoliberals were certain, would mean inexorable decay. But could the French economy survive in a harsh external environment? The structural reformers, consumed by "the prospect of Anglo-American postwar economic hegemony," doubted it. In July 1942, the commission's neoliberal majority endorsed liberalized trade tempered by international coordination. However, the CFLN declined to send an opposing minority report to U.S. officials, giving Washington a misleading impression of French unity on multilateralism.[29] In fact, debates among the Free French had only just begun.

In late 1943, for example, the socialist Georges Boris warned General Charles de Gaulle that American imperialism was imminent. Washington was determined to apply its liberal "therapy" to the postwar world, and it would doubtless tempt Europe with financial credits to secure market access. France might have "no choice" than to yield to multilateralism, but this would endanger prospects for French social democracy. Having taken "certain steps ... toward a *planned economy* in the interests of the collectivity," he noted, France risked being "thrown into reverse in order to align with the United States." Washington would use financial and commercial instruments "to favor one government more than another," or "even to determine the choice of governments." In sum, Boris predicted, "Europe will not be able to elude an American hegemony which intends to orient it toward an economic organization of a capitalist and liberal type."[30]

Framing the Debate: The Courtin Report and French Policy Innovation

The divergent assumptions and causal judgments of the structural reformers and neoliberals emerge clearly in their wartime writings. The rationale for radical economic transformation was spelled out in a July 1944 report for de Gaulle. Titled *Structural Economic Reforms*, it combined progressive social policy with a "realist" view of national security. To achieve social democracy and great power status, the state must supervise economic production; divide the economy into nationalized, directed, and supervised sectors; and modernize French industry. So long as France remained "an agricultural country incapable of forging the arms needed to defend its independence," the document warned, it was "destined to be the slave of either a powerful adversary or a protecting friend" (read: the United States). Escaping imperialism implied industrializing behind a protectionist shield.[31]

The neoliberals rejected such defeatist, "Malthusian" thinking, arguing that France should welcome integration into the global economy. Pure liberalism, however, would be unwise. As Robert Marjolin (CFLN Director of Economic Affairs) recalls, the Great Depression had "shattered the optimism of classical economics" and faith in free trade. Because the crisis fragmented the world economy into discrete "case studies," neoliberal economists had been able to "test" competing hypotheses about the state's economic role. It was Keynesianism, he explains, that "furnished us with the essential conceptual tools with which to interpret economic experience." The New Deal had shown neoliberals that market failures could be tempered by "compensatory action by the state." By manipulating fiscal and monetary policy, countries could foster full employment and smooth the business cycle. In sum, "government intervention had to be limited, but it was essential."[32]

The most comprehensive distillation of neoliberal thought was the *Report on Postwar Economic Policy* (or Courtin Report) of November 1943. Evincing new understandings about the economic role of the state and the benefits of open commerce, it advocated a postwar policy of moderate social reform, planned reconstruction, and commercial multilateralism.[33]

Domestically, a managed market system could balance personal liberty and collective institutions, offering a middle way between the "frenzied individualism" of *laissez-faire* capitalism and the oppressive egalitarianism of state socialism. The postwar French state should nationalize true "economic and financial feudalities," expand social security, and institute progressive taxation. But growth, not radical redistribution, should drive social reform. Productivity, in other words, was the "precondition for all national and social goals."[34]

Externally, France must adopt multilateralism. "In neither economics nor war is it possible to shut oneself up into a purely defensive posture," René Courtin wrote in 1943. "As strong as they are, all Maginot lines end up being overrun or bypassed." The Depression had shown the futility of economic nationalism, and Vichy had deepened stagnation through its call for agrarian self-reliance. In sum, it would be "anachronistic and derisory" for France "to elaborate plans in a strictly national context."[35]

Openness, moreover, was dictated by the policies of the world's leading trading nations. Just as the Cobden-Chevalier Treaty of 1860 had brought free trade to Europe, so agreements between the United States and Great Britain would determine the future of world commerce. Washington, having "oriented itself on liberal tracks," was using its "growing authority" to advocate multilateralism. To avoid being "left behind," France needed to "renounce her isolation" and embrace "the spirit of Anglo-Saxon competition."[36]

But could France compete with other countries richer in natural resources, possessing modern industries, or demanding more from cheap labor? Many Frenchmen were "terrorized by ... the assembly lines of the factories of Detroit, by the obstinacy of the German worker, [and] by the rice bowl of the Japanese laborer." While such anxieties were natural, exposure to external competition would allow France to exploit its comparative advantages and to increase its productivity. The country should thus eliminate "all discrimination and preferential regimes" and adopt "the most favored nation clause." Of course, this transition to multilateralism would need to be gradual. After the war, France must "defend its right to reconstruction" and protect its economy temporarily from "ruinous foreign competition and the vicissitudes of world circumstances." This effort to postpone multilateralism would be difficult, since France would be a "supplicant" for U.S. credits and resources. The French would need to reassure Washington that they would "return to liberal methods as soon as their recovery is accomplished."[37]

A final concern was that the envisioned organizations to coordinate monetary and trade relations might endanger French sovereignty. Might not the United States use such multilateral institutions to impose its views on liberated Europe? It was inevitable, the Courtin Report conceded, that great powers would play a "preponderant" role in shaping world order. Fortunately, the planned international regimes would "attenuate" rather than "aggravate the pressure susceptible to be exercised on us." Being based on a "rigorous juridical equality," these multilateral forums would permit France "to explain its point of view and to participate in the management of world life." Such collective decision-making offered "incomparably greater" maneuvering room than bilateral negotiations "with the Great Powers in the silence of chancelleries." Thus, *far from constituting instruments of hegemony*," multilateral institutions would "balance the present forces and eliminate arbitrary decisions."[38]

The Courtin Report failed to persuade advocates of structural reform, who dismissed it as a warmed-over liberalism sanctioning an "American economic and financial takeover." Faced with such divisions, the CFLN leadership declined to endorse the document. Nevertheless, the report's argument (and its authors) would inform postwar French commercial policy.[39]

Other Currents of French Economic Thought

Some prominent neoliberals viewed European integration as a promising prelude to global multilateralism. CFLN officials debated such schemes for regional economic unity during 1943. Jean Monnet, the most vocal proponent of integration, argued that the requirements of economic competitiveness and international peace rendered traditional patterns of national sovereignty obsolete. Single European economies could neither satisfy their inhabitants' needs nor compete with continent-sized behemoths. The United States, the Soviet Union, and the British Empire possessed "worlds of their own into which they can temporarily withdraw," but France was "bound up in Europe. She cannot escape." At a political level, the resumption of national rivalries would mean "no peace in Europe." Attributing Franco-German antagonism to struggles over the coal of the Ruhr and the iron of Alsace-Lorraine, Monnet proposed "extract[ing] this region from the two countries," pooling France's heavy industry with its neighbors, and creating a "single free trade entity" in Europe. This economic federation would become one pillar of an open global system, competing on equal terms with the United States.[40]

General de Gaulle, the leader of the Free French, dismissed Monnet's "fanciful" scheme. Any economic federation, he reasoned, would be inconsistent with national sovereignty and destined to fall under

American tutelage. (A "United States of Europe" would assuredly become a "Europe of the United States.") Although the CFLN reached no consensus on regional economic integration, several prominent neoliberals explored projects similar to Monnet's. Alphand, who would dominate commercial policy making in postwar France, advocated a regional market "as a precondition for generalized multilateralism."[41]

Although the Free French were excluded from Anglo-American deliberations on the postwar monetary system, they drafted their own schemes for international monetary and commercial cooperation. Anticipating postwar overproduction and disequilibrium, Hervé Alphand and André Istel advocated a future regime to regulate global production and commerce. This would include an international clearing office to provide credits to deficit countries; commercial treaties to stabilize markets and redistribute global production; and bilateral monetary accords to permit the progressive resumption of convertibility. Ultimately, political weakness discouraged the Free French from advancing the Alphand-Istel Plan at Bretton Woods, where they focused instead on securing liquidity for deficit countries. The French were to be disappointed. Frustrated by the modest size of their IMF quota and their denial of a seat on the board of the World Bank, they refused to endorse the final accords.[42]

By 1944, even fascist Vichy France was reconsidering its isolation from the world economy. Vichy's first economic plan (of 1942) had recommended "normal relations with the empire," but "avoiding [foreign] trade as much as possible." As the authors bluntly wrote, "we advocate development in the direction of autarky." Vichy's second plan, the *Tranche de Démarrage* of 1944, disavowed self-reliance. Dependent on foreign markets, France would perish "under the artificial protection of trade barriers." To heal "the anemia that has reached its vital parts," it must engage in foreign trade.[43]

The Neoliberal Victory

Following France's liberation, the "structural reformers" briefly gained the upper hand in charting French economic policy. In September 1944, de Gaulle appointed Pierre Mendés-France to head a new Ministry of National Economy (MEN). Mendés-France immediately launched a three-pronged program of monetary reform, industrial restructuring, and nationalization; and he laid plans for an economy divided into "nationalized," "controlled," and "free" sectors.[44] However, his campaign against inflation, which required the populace to accept shared pain in return for future growth and national independence, collided with consumer resistance and urgent recovery needs. When the French Cabinet turned against austerity, Mendés-France resigned on April 5, 1945.

His departure was a victory for the neoliberal advocates of managed capitalism. They purged the structural reformers from the upper civil service, colonized the critical government ministries, and moved to translate their ideas into practical policy. Rejecting both socialism and liberalism, the neoliberals advocated a technocratic role for the state falling between the dirigiste *faire* ("to do") and the liberal *laissez-faire* ("to leave alone")—and that one might label *faire faire* ("to cause to be done"). As part of a broad trend in twentieth-century capitalism towards economic management, this vision called on the state to pursue full employment, moderate the business cycle, ameliorate economic dislocation, and coordinate public policy. A national economic plan would mediate an *économie concertée*: a collaboration of private firms, labor, state agencies, and the market. Productivity gains would diffuse tensions among social partners, whose distributional disputes might otherwise jeopardize economic growth. The "politics of productivity,"[45] in other words, could be found in France as in the United States.

The neoliberals viewed commercial multilateralism as inescapable, but they were confident that competition would help modernize France's economy to the level of its advanced capitalist partners. Still, they insisted that liberalization occur gradually to permit postwar recovery and that the state "control and direct the terms of interdependence," balancing open trade with social protections.[46]

The Material Context: American Aid for Multilateral Trade

Material considerations, as well as causal and principled beliefs, encouraged France to support commercial multilateralism. As Monnet reminded his colleagues, "The material support of the Anglo-Saxons— and foremost America—will be a fundamental precondition for our recovery."[47] Washington was aware of French financial dependency, and it used aid as an incentive to win French commitments to open trade. This dynamic first emerged during wartime negotiations over Lend-Lease assistance.

Although France became the third largest beneficiary of Lend-Lease (after Great Britain and the Soviet Union), it did not sign a formal Master Agreement until late in the war. Monnet engineered this accord during 1944–45 while heading the French Supply Mission in

Washington. A generation earlier, during World War I, he had helped coordinate allied war production efforts under French Minister of Commerce Étienne Clémentel. This experience convinced Monnet that the machinery for wartime collaboration could be adapted to assist postwar recovery and international economic management. In Washington during the second global conflict, Monnet cultivated prominent American contacts[48] and gathered the nucleus of his postwar economic team.

Monnet viewed Lend-Lease as a first step toward French reconstruction, since many envisioned imports would have postwar utility. Although the American Congress and the Treasury Department resisted providing such aid to France, the State Department was more sympathetic. The French Empire had constituted a protected interwar bloc, and its resumption of discrimination and preference would damage prospects for open global trade. Paris finally signed a Lend-Lease Accord on February 28, 1945. Article VII of the Master Agreement committed France to "elimina[te] ... all forms of discriminatory treatment in international commerce" and to "reduc[e] ... tariffs and other trade barriers."[49]

From "Grandeur" to "Demandeur": French Recovery Needs and Financial Dependence

On August 20, 1945—immediately after Japan's surrender—President Truman terminated Lend-Lease and reminded its recipients of their commitments to postwar multilateralism. Simultaneously, though, he alerted Congress of the "need to transform [allied] cooperation for war" into "economic cooperation for peace." Unless America took steps to ameliorate postwar dislocation and advance reconstruction, debtor countries might adopt protectionism and discrimination.[50]

The abrupt end of Lend-Lease was devastating to France, which faced immense reconstruction costs. German aggression, wartime occupation, and allied invasion had decimated the nation's productive capacities and transportation networks. Industrial production had dropped to three-fifths of its prewar level, domestic food supplies to one-third. France's budget deficit had tripled, its public debt quadrupled, and its foreign debt nearly quintupled. Worse, this destruction had followed a decade of economic decline, both relative and absolute. With no net investment during the 1930s, France's GDP had been no higher in 1938 than in 1914.[51] France needed urgent credits to pay for Lend-Lease goods still in the "pipeline." More generally, it needed a strategy to link massive imports for reconstruction and modernization with external sources of finance.

Although President de Gaulle stressed France's continued Great Power status, the tremendous burdens of recovery made the pursuit of *grandeur* untenable in 1945. French energies thus shifted to economic tasks. "Yesterday there was no national duty that had precedence over the duty to fight," de Gaulle exhorted the citizenry on May 25. "But today there is none that can take precedence over that to produce." The general was uncommitted to any particular economic philosophy, but he understood that production, planning, investment, and nationalization could influence state capabilities. Given its precarious payments position and dwindling reserves, France needed American credits to cover large imports of food, coal, raw materials, manufactures, and capital goods.[52]

For Jean Monnet, there were two challenges: first, to persuade de Gaulle that France needed a comprehensive plan for reconstruction and modernization and that only the United States could finance it; and second, to convince the government to liberalize trade. "You speak of greatness," he advised de Gaulle, "but today the French are small." Without U.S. aid, France could not regain "the first rank of industrial nations in Western Europe." In addition, Monnet believed "there was a very real danger" that the country would adopt "a protectionist shield." But he hoped that the "new, Resistance generation" would reject self-reliance and embrace competition.[53]

Fortunately, as Monnet told his superiors, Washington was willing to provide "generous aid to permit allied nations to restore world prosperity." In June 1945, Assistant Secretary of State William Clayton asked Paris to formulate a comprehensive recovery program to justify U.S. assistance. France could choose its own domestic path, so long as it supported multilateralism:

> Be liberals or *dirigistes*. Return to capitalism or head toward socialism. That's your business. ... But in either case the government must choose and not compromise between these two economies. ... If it makes the choice and demonstrates to us the seriousness of its program, we shall help your country, for its prosperity is necessary to peace.[54]

America's principal foreign economic objective remained the restoration of "multilateral trade on a private basis." Still, Washington recognized that reconstruction needs and full employment concerns abroad might require "occasional exceptions to our general principles." Paris responded with its own caveats, insisting that postwar multilateralism tolerate imperial preference and "regional economic agreements" and that the resumption of private trade be "both gradual and within strict limits."[55]

To smooth France's transition to peace, U.S. officials extended an immediate credit of $316 million in August 1945. To receive more aid, France would need to allay U.S. anxieties that it had entered a "path of autarky ... excessive customs protectionism and ... discrimination." Foreign Minister Georges Bidault assured Secretary of State James Byrnes that France would "adopt a regime of freedom," but "needed some respite and must in any case continue to protect a few of her traditional industries."[56]

Although France resumed limited private trade, it retained cumbersome commercial restrictions that annoyed U.S. officials. "We are becoming increasingly disturbed, Clayton wrote Paris, "at the evidence of the French Government's intentions to control imports and exports in contravention of the principles of relaxing trade barriers and attenuating controls."[57]

Strategic Bargaining and Issue-Linkage

During 1945–46, Franco-American negotiations over financial assistance and commercial multilateralism became deeply intertwined. Monnet understood that prospects for U.S. aid would "depend essentially on the commitments France made toward [open trade]." Washington was prepared to offer France a $550 million loan, but it insisted that Paris first lower tariffs, reduce exchange controls, and eliminate quotas. Monnet advised Paris to invert these conditions: Liberalization could "only be a consequence" of *prior* U.S. assistance to help France "change her internal conditions completely." As he warned the Americans, without "generous credits covering the entirety of [French] needs," any multilateral "negotiation on the reestablishment of commercial liberties will be in vain."[58]

Both Washington and Paris tried to exploit this connection between U.S. financial assistance and French trade policy. Secretary Byrnes, anticipating "several opportunities in the future to link policy questions with credits," instructed American diplomats to "support those in the French government ... inclined toward a liberal commercial policy." Meanwhile, Paris reminded Washington that open trade required "the concerted action of all countries relative to the resources and needs of each."[59]

Monnet predicted that France's "ultimate course" would be "closely tied" to U.S. policies over future months. To obtain significant credits, France needed to "lay her course consciously toward a policy of free and expanding commerce" by ratifying Bretton Woods. The only alternative was to "withdraw from world trade and suffer a gradual decline in its standard of living and influence in world affairs." Fortunately, Washington was willing to assist the reconstruction of any ally "committed unreservedly ... to international trade on a multilateral basis." This was a welcome change from the inter-war years, when America (abdicating its "obligations as a creditor nation") had left recovery to private capital, embraced isolationism, and adopted protectionism. U.S. officials had evidently learned that "autarky tends to produce a low standard of living and conditions that conduce toward war."[60]

Despite this common interpretation of the recent past and recognition of coincident interests, France and the United States engaged in strategic bargaining to secure the best terms for the "compromise of embedded liberalism." As Monnet told Washington, Paris refused to "discuss a future regime of international commerce without as a precondition having dealt with the *means* necessary to reconstruct and modernize her economy." Since the United States apparently accepted this reasoning, the French government planned to "make our attitude with regard to American *Proposals* on commercial policy depend on the outcome of our [envisioned bilateral] financial negotiations."[61]

Paris wanted French needs to get the same respect that Washington was currently showing Britain's request for a massive loan. The Anglo-American negotiations appeared to be opening salvo in an "extensive [U.S.] offensive in favor of free trade [and] the elimination of all discriminatory systems and all regimes of quotas." France needed to communicate its aid needs to Washington as quickly as possible, since the early announcement of a British credit (presumably linked to concessions on multilateralism) would diminish its leverage in bilateral talks. France might be forced to "withdraw into autarky or to bargain for [smaller aid] tranches."[62]

On November 8, 1945, Paris and Washington formalized the linkage between aid and trade in a pair of diplomatic notes. The first announced their "full accord" on the need for liberal commerce, the abolition of quotas and prohibitive tariffs, and a world conference to advance these goals. The second endorsed a prior bilateral meeting to discuss French financial needs. The euphoric French considered the two notes to be "an inseparable whole." Paris had won priority for national recovery, without "assuming any fundamental new engagement." Indulging in wishful thinking, Bidault claimed that France faced Washington from "a position more or less identical to that of Great Britain." Paris would hold protectionism as its trump card: If the United States declined to provide aid, France would remain outside the multilateral system. Thus, the future of world trade would "depend on the American attitude."[63]

American diplomats were pleased with France's commitments, which "involved [a] long range orientation away from self containment and toward multilateral trade with all its domestic components." For its part, Paris implored Washington to approach the upcoming talks from a "high plane" rather than engaging in a "mundane *quid pro quo*." This entreaty was disingenuous, since France was effectively threatening protectionism to secure U.S. aid. It also fell on deaf ears, since the Americans were disinclined to offer unilateral concessions. "It would, of course, be fatal," U.S. Ambassador Jefferson Caffery advised the State Department, "to give a commitment for a loan during the preliminary [financial] negotiation and as a result enter our commercial policy negotiation stripped of that bargaining power." Washington should insist that France provide an "entire list of specific [trade] benefits, actions, and concessions."[64]

American fears of renewed French protectionism increased after France's first postwar elections, held on October 21, 1945, to choose a Constituent Assembly. These confirmed that the Communist Party (PCF), with nine hundred thousand loyal working class members, was the most powerful political party in France. The communists gained several critical cabinet portfolios, and U.S. officials worried that the new, left-leaning government nurtured "closed economy aspects ... difficult to reconcile ... with [America's] broad commercial policy objectives." Such developments cast doubt on France's ability "to honor any commitments ... to free trade principles in return for a dollar loan."[65] These economic anxieties merged with strategic concerns that the PCF was a "Trojan Horse" for an increasingly confrontational Soviet Union. George Kennan worried about the party's control over organized labor, its slavish obedience to Moscow, and its "discipline, unity, and energy of leadership." Exploiting these anxieties, de Gaulle warned that without diplomatic and financial support, France might become a "Soviet Republic."[66]

The British Loan and the American "Proposals"

Although Washington declined to set a firm date for bilateral aid negotiations, the Quai d'Orsay authorized Monnet to prepare an inventory of French import needs in order to justify United States assistance. External events soon overtook these efforts. With British insolvency threatening to fragment the global economy, Washington provided London with the liquidity denied at Bretton Woods. The Anglo-American Financial Agreement of December 6, 1945, forgave Britain's Lend-Lease debts and extended a huge credit of $3.75 billion. In return, London agreed to phase out imperial preference; to end the "dollar pool;" and to dismantle remaining exchange restrictions. The two countries reiterated their "common objective of multilateral trade."[67]

Privately, Clayton boasted that Washington had loaded the British negotiations with all the conditions "the traffic could bear." But he also called attention to the self-imposed limits to American hegemony. Although Washington had insisted on *external* openness, it remained agnostic about Britain's *internal* economic structures. "To attempt to force such countries to adopt policies with respect to their domestic economies contrary to their wishes, would, in my opinion, be an unwarranted interference in their domestic affairs."[68]

Nonetheless, the loan's conditions caused consternation in Paris, which held a weaker hand than London. The British Empire—covering a quarter of the earth, possessing the world's second largest economy, and controlling an important reserve currency—was *the* key partner to America's multilateral project. Few U.S. officials placed France in the same league.[69]

To accompany the British loan, Washington released its *Proposals for Expansion of World Trade and Employment.* The document called on all countries to liberalize trade, to extend equal access to markets and raw materials, and to stimulate production and consumption. It reaffirmed that multilateralism must include safeguards for social policies, trade balances, and full employment.[70]

For over a year, Paris had temporized on ratifying the Bretton Woods accords. But as one *haut fonctionaire* warned, it was "dangerous to give the United States proofs of bad faith [when its] aid might be solicited in the near future." France's alternatives, Finance Minister René Pleven told the Constituent Assembly, were to "reconstruct herself by her own means" (accepting "unparalleled sacrifices") or to pursue rapid recovery through "international cooperation and its attendant obligations." To modernize, France must "enter resolutely into international competition." The Assembly ratified the accords on December 31, 1945.[71] Paris would now negotiate with Washington over the pace and limits of multilateralism and the means to pursue it. Once again, Jean Monnet engineered the transatlantic bargain.

The Monnet Plan: The Political Economy
of Interdependence

Despite its financial dependence and the incipient superpower rivalry, post-liberation France had clung to diplomatic nonalignment. France's "vital interest," de Gaulle declared, was "to hold ourselves strictly in balance" between East and West, "eyes open and hands free." But if France had recovered certain trappings of a great power, it lacked the finances, industry, commerce, or military to behave as one.[72] Economic revival was the precondition for all foreign policy goals.

Popular history depicts Jean Monnet as the "father of Europe." But his postwar recovery plan was designed foremost to arrest national decline and to catapult France into the front rank of industrialized countries. The key to power and prosperity was a massive program of productive investment. If the state remained passive, the economy would "crystallize at the level of mediocrity" and France would become "like Spain." Monnet, Marjolin, and Étienne Hirsch outlined France's dire situation in a December 1945 memorandum to de Gaulle. The country needed a comprehensive plan for reconstruction and modernization, supported by continual American aid. "Foreign credits" would provide the fastest and safest path to *"grandeur."*[73]

De Gaulle accepted this logic, and in January 1946 he appointed Monnet to head a new *Commissariat General du Plan* (CGP).[74] Instructed to draft a *Plan de Modernisation et d'Équipement* (PME), Monnet assembled a small but exceptionally able team of technocrats. The CGP scrambled to draft a convincing five-year recovery plan in time for bilateral talks in March.

The resulting "Monnet Plan" envisioned complementary strategies of "indicative planning" and "concertation." The state would supervise and guide the market economy by establishing sectoral priorities, directing scarce resources to concrete targets, breaking bottlenecks, and investing in critical public spheres. The government would pursue limited nationalization, subordinate consumption to investment, and embrace global interdependence.[75]

As an approach to political economy, the Plan resonated with the French state's "historic role as guide and impetus giver" and—at a deeper level—with French national identity. As Marjolin explains, "The nature of the Frenchman is that he needs to feel urged and supported by the state, to see the state give him the assurance that his individual efforts form part of an overall effort, and that if mishaps occur along the way it will intervene to get him out of difficulty."[76]

Monnet's genius was to transfer recovery and modernization from the arena of ideology into that of "crisis management," arguing that only a long-term program could end French stagnation and win U.S. aid. The Plan's unifying discourse rallied parties and the public to the banners of "growth" and "productivity;" its sectoral benchmarks permitted the French to chart national progress; and its technocratic management depoliticized economic issues, deflected ambitious social democratic objectives, and consolidated a fragile governing coalition. France became "the first Western country to be committed to economic growth as a public concept."[77]

America's own economic experience influenced the Plan's design. Monnet had been fascinated by the New Deal, particularly its private-public sector partnership, its reliance on planning, and its ideology of growth. In wartime Washington, he discovered the state's astounding capacity to mobilize domestic economic actors. After the war, the American Robert Nathan (former Chairman of the War Production Board) suggested two of the Monnet Plan's innovative elements: an inventory of France's total needs and an independent planning commission.[78]

If the Monnet Plan responded to French economic weaknesses, it was entwined with national security concerns. This explained its focus on heavy industry. Like many Frenchmen, Monnet attributed the 1940 disaster partly to industrial impotence. The PME was designed not simply to modernize France but also to give its steel industry preferential access to Ruhr coke—and thus to make France rather than Germany the industrial core of continental Europe. The Plan offered a long-term solution to France's enduring strategic dilemma.[79]

From its inception, the Plan was predicated on "continual collaboration" with the United States, the overwhelming source of essential credits and imports of food, equipment and energy. De Gaulle sanctioned this approach, provided that America's aid conditions were reasonable. Fortunately, Paris had some leverage; without sufficient credits, Monnet warned U.S. diplomats, France would modernize "slowly and necessarily within the framework of a closed economy."[80]

Monnet's remarkable connections with prominent Americans allowed him to "play a decisive part in American lending to France" during 1946. As a transatlantic intermediary, he engaged in "double-edged diplomacy" to win U.S. financing and French approval of the Plan. Abroad, he reassured U.S. officials that France would put any credits to good use and adopt open commerce following recovery. At home, he warned that deviations from multilateralism would jeopardize the Plan's U.S. funding.[81]

Monnet's prospects for achieving a significant U.S. loan were complicated by de Gaulle's sudden resignation on January 20, 1946. The general's departure opened an uneasy era of power sharing by a fragile tripartite government. The United States, hoping to thwart the most powerful Communist Party in Western Europe, would cultivate alliances with French Christian Democrats and Socialists.[82]

In broad terms, de Gaulle's departure made France more likely to follow America's lead, in commerce as well as strategic matters. As a traditional "realist," the general conceived of the international balance of power as an equilibrium of rights and obligations among great powers. If Soviet expansionism was a clear threat to this balance, so, too, in a subtler way was America's bid for hegemony within a multilateral system. Washington's "will to power" may have "cloaked itself in idealism," but this only made it more insidious. Moreover, de Gaulle's concept of national identity—his *certaine idée de la France*"—implied that "France could not be France without greatness."[83] Less consumed by *grandeur,* de Gaulle's successors reformulated the national interest for a context of *interdependence* (rather than independence) and even accepted temporary dependence as the price of recovery.

Preparing for Franco-American Negotiations

In February 1946, the new French President, Felix Gouin, announced that France would send a delegation to Washington to negotiate an aid package. But any U.S. assistance was likely to be modest: President Truman had termed the British Loan "exceptional." Judging that "an approach to Congress for a credit along lines of [the] Brit[ish] loan is not practicable," Secretary of State Byrnes suggested that France seek $500 million from the World Bank and other funds from the Export–Import Bank. Unfortunately, the former had not begun operating, and the latter's resources had dwindled to $1.9 billion (of which $1 billion was earmarked for the Soviet Union, $500 million for China).[84]

Ambassador Caffery pleaded for greater generosity. "Even though to a banker's eye France might not be considered an A-1 risk," a meager loan would eliminate "one of the last props ... to those ... who want to see France remain an independent and democratic country."[85] Such Cold War arguments would carry more weight the following year, once "containment" had begun in earnest.

French officials anticipated arduous negotiations, predicting that the Americans would oppose financing the recovery of a country that would then "compete on world markets with their own products". Moreover, a domestic American backlash against the New Deal and wartime controls was reviving "a traditionalist liberal policy of even more clearly capitalist inspiration." In this domestic climate, could Washington agree "to finance a socialist state ... that will not hesitate to use the credits to carry out a policy entirely contrary to that desired by the American people?" Indeed, American newspapers carried sardonic commentaries on this theme: "It is ironic to see with what determination the descendants of Karl Marx believe in Saint Nicholas," noted the *Wall Street Journal.*[86]

To complicate matters, the French continued to debate trade liberalization. The Finance Ministry "favor[ed] the expansion of multilateral commerce," and many Quai officials hoped "to participate in a liberal regime of international trade." But other Frenchmen doubted that France could compete. Pierre Mendes-France advocated a transition period of at least 12 years before full liberalization. Meanwhile, a Commission on Trade Policy concluded that industrialists and farmers would accept lower tariffs only if France retained quotas and cartels.[87]

Imperial and Strategic Complications

In addition, the future of imperial preference posed enormous problems. During the war, the Free French had rebuffed U.S. schemes for international trusteeship in the colonial world. After the war, France clung tenaciously to empire as an irrefutable symbol of Great Power status. In the words of Jean Chauvel, Secretary-General at the Quai, "We were still to weak ... and too poor, to detach ourselves from signs of power and glory." Although the Constitution of the Fourth Republic, under negotiation, would put relations with the empire on a more progressive footing, it was evident that the envisioned "French Union" would reassert metropolitan primacy, preserve the "franc zone," and retain imperial preference.[88]

To its champions, the French empire was "an economic solidarity prepared by nature." But imperial preference raised hackles in Washington. As Monnet observed, U.S. insistence on "equal treatment ... collides head on with the venerable imperialist colonial conception which reserves to the metropole certain economic advantages." The Ministry of Overseas France contemplated opening the empire to American loans and investment, but the Quai feared that loosening the colonies' links with France would jeopardize the country's international rank and economic prosperity.[89]

The biggest threat to France's chances for a large American loan, however, was intense disagreement over the fate of Germany. Washington, determined to unify the allied zones of occupation and to revive Germany as the economic engine of postwar Europe, was exasperated by the "French thesis" calling for Germany's dismemberment (including detachment of the Ruhr, Saar, and Rhineland). American diplomats warned Paris that its continued obstructionism would endanger its aid requests. But the French insisted on preserving their national security. "You are far away and your soldiers will not stay long in Europe," de Gaulle had told the Americans bluntly in November. "The fate of Germany is a matter of life and death for us; for you, one interesting question among many others." Although the general had departed, his successors shared his desire to restrict German revival.[90]

Such was the unpropitious setting for negotiations during which France would seek credits worth "*Four Billion dollars*" for imports of food, raw materials, and equipment. To reduce the dissonance of dependence, the Quai consoled itself that "French interests do not appear to contradict American ones."[91] But could France secure U.S. funding for a recovery plan predicated on postponing multilateralism?

On the eve of bilateral discussions in Washington, Paris instructed its negotiators to make several commitments: to accept nondiscrimination during France's transitional import program; to agree to a moderate, *ad valorem* tariff; to renounce long-term bilateral quotas; to limit current account restrictions to five years; and to end the dollar pool with French dependencies. Still, France would retain quotas until it regained current account balance and, if it failed to "obtain sufficient financial credits," continue to control foreign purchases and negotiate "discriminatory" bilateral accords. The negotiators were to rebuff all challenges to imperial preference or to the state's role in the French economy.[92]

The Blum-Byrnes Commercial and Financial Negotiations

In mid-March 1946, the eminent socialist leader Leon Blum led a large French delegation to Washington to negotiate on trade and aid. As Monnet recalls, "we arrived at the worst possible time." Congress had already begun to consider the British Loan, which Truman again called a "special case."[93]

As spokesman, Blum sought to allay U.S. fears about French discrimination and *dirigisme.* Multilateralism was no passing fancy, he assured the National Advisory Council on Postwar Economic Problems (NAC). Rather, it embodied France's "very conception of the organization a peaceful world." Nor should the state's active role in the French economy be cause for alarm, since domestic interventionism was perfectly compatible with commercial openness. In a concise statement of the "embedded liberalism" thesis, Blum made the following bold claim:

> There is no necessary connection between the internal regime of production and exchange in a given state, and … the policy practiced by that same state in its international transactions. … It is perfectly conceivable to apply principles of economic planning or collectivism at home … while in external transaction … to practice a policy of international organization based on complete freedom and equality.[94]

No U.S. officials challenged this striking assertion of principle, which became the premise of negotiations.

Blum informed his hosts that French multilateralism would "only be complete and fertile" once France gained "a position of equivalency" with the leading industrial nations. The Monnet Plan, designed to accomplish this, could only be launched only if its $11 billion funding were assured. If France failed to secure generous external financing, it would retain trade and exchange controls. Worse, it might find itself placed, by its "material misery and … moral surrender," in a perilous situation "whose evolution it would be impossible to predict." French penury, Blum hinted, might propel the Communists to power. From Paris, Bidault sharpened the warning. Without a large loan France "would almost inevitably be compelled to organize our economic policy in other directions." Moreover, a meager loan would have "political consequences," forcing Paris to turn to Moscow for help. The *New York Times* translated this message as "give us help, or else."[95]

The Blum-Byrnes negotiations lasted from March 25–May 28. The first week was devoted to a general expose of the French economic situation and the Monnet Plan. The National Advisory Council judged the latter coherent and feasible. Subsequently, work continued in three technical committees. The first examined the resolution of wartime matters, namely Lend-Lease debts, surplus American property, and Reciprocal Aid accounts. A second examined the details of the Monnet Plan, its impact on French balance of payments, and potential U.S. funding. The Plan aimed to return French industrial production to 1938 levels by the end of 1946 and to 1929 levels (25 percent higher) by 1949. To meet its investment targets, France would need a whopping $4,186 million—an amount larger than the British loan.

A third body, the Committee of Commercial Policy, considered trade issues. French negotiators reiterated that their country had "definitively renounced quotas as a protectionist measure." Nevertheless, France would maintain quantitative restrictions and "discrimination ... for strictly financial reasons" during a transition period of indefinite length. As reconstruction and modernization took hold, Paris would progressively eliminate "all measures of an autarkic character." Although pressed to discuss France's nationalization policy, the French negotiators refused to do so.

Unfortunately for the French, the U.S. Senate was at this time debating the British Loan, which Secretary of State Byrnes had repeated was "in no sense a precedent." Since half of world trade was channeled through bilateral agreements with Britain, dismantling imperial preference remained the priority for American multilateralists. Moreover, even the British Loan faced some congressional resistance. Senate Minority Leader Robert Taft, for example, wondered why America should "finance the peace just because we financed the war." When Federal Reserve Chairman Marriner Eccles pleaded that the British loan was an investment in "a peaceful and productive system of world trade and finance" (for which America had "laid down 'rules of the game'"), Taft retorted: "It's your world of multi-lateralism that doesn't exist."[96] The State Department lobbied Congress furiously, depicting the credit as an investment in a peaceful world and a bulwark for America's own liberal institutions. Its defeat, Clayton warned, would split the world into "three giant economic blocs," requiring "the complete regimentation of our external trade" and endangering America's "free" domestic economy. Its passage, Dean Acheson added, would nurture "*an economic system which is the very basis of our life*—the system of free individual enterprise."[97]

The NAC, charged with determining the scope of the credit for France, took account of certain political and strategic considerations. Frustrated by French foot-dragging on Germany, some U.S. diplomats wanted to link aid to concessions on central German agencies. Caffery warned Paris that its continued obstructionism might undermine the Blum mission. Still, most French officials doubted trading permanent control over German resources for transient economic benefits.[98]

If Paris' German policy encouraged American miserliness, the growing Communist threat in France had more ambiguous ramifications. Anticipating France's first National Assembly elections on June 2, likely to determine Paris' political alignment, Ambassador Caffery recommended a big loan to boost the electoral fortunes of French centrists: "It is in our interest to strengthen the elements with which we can work, which share our basic conceptions and which therefore make for stability." But other U.S. officials hesitated to subsidize a governing coalition including Communists. Treasury Secretary Fred Vinson advised Blum that U.S. aid would flow more freely if the PCF Ministers were expelled.[99]

The Contours of Franco-American Agreement

The pivotal decision concerning the French loan occurred at a NAC meeting of May 6, 1946. Clayton advocated an Export-Import Bank loan of $750 million, arguing that a smaller amount would be a "catastrophe" for French democracy. But Federal Reserve Chairman Marriner Eccles, who disapproved of politically motivated loans, feared that the United States would be "accused of undertaking to buy a foreign election." Washington's objective was "getting countries back on their feet," he noted, irrespective of "whether the government is socialistic, communistic, or [a] capitalist democracy." On this point Clayton demurred, confessing "great difficulty in separating political from economic considerations in thinking about Europe." France and Great Britain were the "bulwarks" of European democracy, and their recovery would provide "a good chance of saving Western Europe from a collapse and social chaos."[100] By a 3–2 vote, the NAC approved a loan of $650 million—far less than the French had sought.

The *New York Times* placed the loan in the context of an emerging Cold War, calling it "an investment in democracy" and "in a system of government and a way of life."[101] But it would be incorrect to describe the Export-Import Bank credit as a purely "political" loan. The United States had not yet declared the Cold War, much less chosen the instruments to wage it. (Indeed, Washington was still considering a $1 billion credit to assist Soviet recovery.)

Blum and Byrnes signed the Washington Commercial and Financial Accords on May 28, 1946. Declaring its "complete agreement on the principles" of the American *Proposals,* France pledged to abandon protectionist import quotas; to confine all discrimination to its period of "convalescence;" to adopt a reasonable *ad valorem* tariffs; to reduce its import program; to terminate the French Supply Council following reconstruction; to restore private channels of trade; and to limit nationalization. "On commercial policy," Ambassador Caffery exulted, "we have secured France's articulate support to our views as well as the removal of certain practices adverse to our business interests."[102]

The final Lend-Lease settlement wrote off approximately $2.25 billion in wartime aid to France and provided a low-interest loan to cover its consolidated debt. More importantly, the $650 million credit from the Export–Import Bank would permit France to purchase essential capital goods, food, and raw materials. Still, Paris was disappointed. The new money seemed paltry compared to the $3.75 billion British loan. France received only one-sixth of the $4 billion dollars it had sought. "Definitely," Alphand lamented, "there is no comparison."[103]

Paris accepted several nettlesome conditions in return for the Eximbank loan, but these obligations were not particularly onerous.[104] Although some "revisionist" historians have depicted the Blum-Byrnes Accords as a battering ram in America's "Open Door" policy, France made few concessions it had not already offered in principle. Moreover, the French held firm both on the need to control imports for the duration of the Monnet Plan and on the commercial and monetary unity of the French Union; unlike Great Britain, France was not required to eliminate imperial preference. Finally, many neoliberal French officials welcomed the linkage between aid and multilateralism; they were confident that foreign competition would catalyze productivity and that America's "external constraint" would permit them to deflect the more radical reforms espoused by French structural reformers.[105]

Winning Domestic Approval for Embedded Liberalism

Upon return to France, the Blum delegation still had to persuade the Constituent Assembly to ratify the accords. This effort was complicated by domestic suspicions (fueled by the Communists and their fellow travelers) that France had capitulated to American imperialism. Leon Blum denied such allegations, insisting that the accords had involved "neither explicitly nor implicitly, neither directly nor indirectly, any precondition of any type, [whether] civil, military, political, or diplomatic." Rather they reflected the "complete agreement" of the two governments on "general principles of commercial policy" and a shared belief that world peace required nations to be "conscious of their interdependence and ... solidarity." Moreover, Washington had conceded that multilateralism could coexist with a "regime within France of economic direction and nationalization of parts of its means of production."[106]

Denying that they had exchanged a trade *quid* for an aid *quo,* the negotiators insisted that the "*renunciation of restrictive foreign trade measures was neither formally nor implicitly a condition of the Franco-American Accords.*" Since France had earlier adopted multilateralism, the negotiations had focused on "*provid[ing] the means for a freely decided policy for the expansion of such trade.*" (The consensual nature of these negotiations "differed utterly" from the British talks, during which

Washington had "imposed" the "abandonment of bilateralism and discrimination"). Moreover, the broad support for multilateralism within France's governing coalition demonstrated that "*the repudiation of autarky for France proceeds not from political considerations, but responds well and truly to an economic and social imperative.*" Finally, multilateralism had normative and cultural justification. Simply put, "*autarky is repugnant to the French genius. Economic separation from other countries leads to moral isolation, whereas our civilization is by essence and tradition universal.*"[107]

President Gouin repeated these points when introducing the accords for Assembly ratification. "Very far from this policy being imposed on us," he declared, "... we have been the promoters of it because we will be its beneficiaries." Although the size and terms of the aid were "far from perfect," the accords would place "Franco-American cooperation in the context of global economic reconstruction" and discourage the world's division "into autarkic blocs." They also "safeguard[ed] [France's] liberty of action" by linking the pace of liberalization to the nation's productivity and current account balance.[108]

American officials predicted that the French Communists would try to thwart an "Occidental orientation of France's national economy" and "the reestablishment ... of democracy and freedom of commerce in the American understanding of these expressions." Indeed, PCF leader Jacques Duclos disparaged the "seductive ideal" of free trade. It was not "progress" that governed capitalism, he reminded the Assembly, but "the law of the jungle." Integration into global markets would expose France to "brutal foreign competition," restructuring its economy according to external dynamics rather than internal desires. He advocated instead a national production strategy protected by high tariffs.[109] Ultimately, the PCF abstained from voting to preserve their role in the governing coalition. The remaining deputies ratified the accords unanimously on August 1, 1946.

A relieved Leon Blum believed that American financing would permit France to "execut[e] ... the plan of repair and modernization with greater confidence."[110] In reality, Paris' failure to secure a British-size loan meant that launching the Monnet Plan would require a leap of faith. Monnet claims to have known there was "no hope of obtaining massive credits in one lump." The modest loan would imply annual pilgrimages to Washington, where French officials would need to "prove what efforts we were making." Nevertheless, Monnet was confident that the Plan's momentum would generate future American aid: Just as "[t]he Plan permitted the conclusion of the accords, [so] the accords will permit the execution of the Plan." Washington had committed itself practically and morally to the PME, providing a "guarantee that we could embark on the Plan without fear of having to stop halfway."[111]

Monnet anticipated that France would face a financial crisis in 1947, but he was sure that Washington would pursue enlightened self-interest by devoting massive resources European reconstruction. After all, denying such credits would destroy prospects for multilateralism. The Marshall Plan of June 1947 vindicated this wager. In retrospect, as Marjolin contends, the Blum-Byrnes Accords bought France time "to wait for an American initiative on the grand scale."[112]

Conclusion

This chapter has shown how French and American decision-makers negotiated a broad consensus on the form and content of the postwar trading regime through a "compromise of embedded liberalism." As in the more famous British Loan negotiations, so in the French case transatlantic agreement was mediated by influential economists and technocrats sharing policy-relevant causal and principled beliefs. French neoliberals, armed with new knowledge of economic management, became convinced that France must abandon futile inward-looking policies in favor of openness, nondiscrimination, and reciprocity. By integrating into world markets, France could avoid repeating its painful interwar experiences, gain American credits for national recovery, and modernize its antiquated economy. This initial consensus narrowed the range of conceivable conflict during the Franco-American commercial and financial negotiations of Spring 1946. As the final report of the Blum mission explains, "previous agreements between the two governments delimited the scope in which the Washington negotiations took place."[113]

John Ruggie contends that "history seemed not to require any special agent" to achieve the compromise of embedded liberalism.[114] This may have been true during the Anglo-American negotiations. In contrast, the emergence of embedded liberalism in France relied heavily on the contributions of a single individual, Jean Monnet. Helping to reformulate French national interests for a context of interdependence, Monnet won domestic and American support for a comprehensive plan of reconstruction and modernization and persuaded both Paris and Washington to accept France's gradual reinsertion into the global economy.

Within the boundaries of normative agreement that Monnet helped to establish, Washington and Paris debated the terms of (and limits to) French multilateralism. It was in these negotiations that strategic bargaining played a role. The United States exploited its structural power as a creditor nation, manipulating financial incentives to secure France's prompt liberalization. Likewise, France threatened to defect from Washington's open world scheme in order to procure American aid. But Franco-American bargaining also included appeals to common standards, shared values, and accepted solutions. Possessing overlapping but not identical understandings of the world economy and their national interests within it, each side used persuasive arguments and appeals to empathy to modify the other's policy preferences and to forge a particular consensus on the practical application of norms of state conduct.[115] Thus, to postpone multilateralism, France invoked new causal and principled understandings that Washington recognized as legitimate, including the state's duty to assure employment and stability.

In the end, France committed itself to multilateralism, with several caveats: that openness occur slowly to permit reconstruction; that it accommodate domestic intervention; that it protect France's imperial arrangements; and that it strengthen French claims on German resources. Although the French were disappointed not to receive more aid, they consoled themselves that Washington was committed to French recovery. Support for multilateralism and trust in American intentions reduced their worries about temporary dependence.

France's embrace of embedded liberalism reflected a process of *cognitive evolution* rather than of "hegemonic socialization." According to proponents of the latter hypothesis, the United States created an open postwar economy by "embedd[ing] norms among European elites." The shortcoming of that perspective is that it depicts America's junior partners as passive entities who merely internalized Washington's postwar vision. As this chapter shows, America's erstwhile "followers" were strong-willed actors who debated the terms and pace of global integration, forced Washington to modify its open world blueprint, and forged transatlantic coalitions behind a multilateral future.[116]

For the United States, the Blum-Byrnes Accords were consistent with a consensual style of hegemonic leadership willing to tolerate (at least in Europe) domestic economic systems that differed considerably from its own. More preoccupied with encouraging multilateralism than with defeating socialism, Washington accepted political and economic diversity among its partners and collaborated with the democratic left. Finally, if West European governments were initially wary of multilateralism as a threat to social democracy, imperial preference, or regionalism, most eventually concluded that nationally based strategies were not viable alternatives to an open world economy.[117]

Washington reiterated its commitment to embedded liberalism in September 1946, releasing a *Suggested Charter for an International Trade Organization of the United Nations*. This declared that "stabilization and trade policies should be consistent," and if they clashed, "they must be *compromised*." Countries could adopt any mixture of entrepreneurship, technocratic planning, or public ownership, provided that this diversity did not fragment the world into "exclusive trading blocs."[118]

As it happened, Washington's hopes for rapid movement to global multilateral trade and monetary regimes soon collided with Cold War conflict and European economic dislocation. To restore economic health and political stability to Western Europe, the United States announced the Marshall Plan in June 1947. The open, reciprocal, and nondiscriminatory order envisioned at Bretton Woods would emerge slowly and incompletely over the next decade.

Nevertheless, the Blum-Byrnes accords were an important "first step in the difficult elaboration of a liberal Atlantic consensus" on multilateralism.[119] Indeed, Franco-American agreement on the Monnet Plan and on a gradual transition to open commerce laid an intellectual foundation for European Recovery Program. The Monnet Plan's approach, including the definition of total dollar needs and the identification of economic targets, provided Washington with a small-scale model for a coordinated, continentwide scheme for recovery and modernization that became known as the Marshall Plan.

As for France, it would find no long-term escape from the dilemma confronting it at the end of World War II: How could the country balance integration into the global economy with the pursuit of domestic social welfare? Trapped between the anxiety of being left behind and fears of competition in a world of untamed capitalism, Paris would seek during the next half century to benefit from multilateral commerce while controlling the terms of interdependence. This rearguard action would grow more complicated as globalization undermined the fragile compact between liberal multilateralism and the welfare state.[120]

Notes

1. Stewart Patrick is Research Associate at New York University's Center on International Cooperation. He is grateful for comments from Rosemary Foot, Andrew Hurrell, Peter Johnson, Irwin Wall, and Andrew Walter, and for research assistance from the Fondation Jean Monnet pour l'Europe (Lausanne) and the Archives Nationales and Archives du Quai d'Orsay (Paris). For generous research support, the author thanks the Norwegian Nobel Institute and the Brookings Institution.

2. John Gerard Ruggie, "International Regimes, Transactions, and Change: Embedded Liberalism in the Postwar Economic Order," *International Organization* 36 (Spring 1982). G. John Ikenberry, "Creating Yesterday's New World Order: Keynesian 'New Thinking' and the Anglo-American Postwar Settlement," in Robert O. Keohane and Judith Goldstein, eds., *Ideas and Foreign Policy: Beliefs, Institutions, and Political Change* (Ithaca, NY: Cornell University Press, 1993).

3. Robert O. Keohane, *After Hegemony: Cooperation and Discord in the World Political Economy* (Princeton: Princeton University Press, 1984). Robert Gilpin, *Political Economy of International Relations* (Princeton: Princeton University Press, 1987), p. 76.

4. John Gerard Ruggie, "Multilateralism: The Anatomy of an Institution," in Ruggie, ed., *Multilateralism Matters: The Theory and Praxis of an Institutional Form* (New York: Columbia University Press, 1993). Charles S. Maier, "Alliance and Autonomy: European Identity and United States Foreign Policy Objectives in the Truman Years," in Michael J. Lacey, ed., *The Truman Presidency* (Cambridge: Cambridge University Press, 1989).

5 James A. Caporaso, "International Relations Theory and Multilateralism: The Search for Foundations," in Ruggie, ed. (fn. 3).

6. Anton DePorte, *Europe between the Superpowers: The Enduring Balance* (New Haven: Yale University Press, 1986), p. 80. Louis Hartz, *The Liberal Tradition in America: An Interpretation of American Political Thought since the Revolution* (New York: Harcourt, Brace, 1955). Edward Weisband, *The Ideology of American Foreign Policy: A Paradigm of Lockian Liberalism* (Beverly Hills, CA: Sage, 1973).

7. Ruggie (fn. 3). Ruggie (fn. 1).

8. Alexander Wendt, "Anarchy is what States Make of It," *International Organization,* 46 (Spring 1992). Peter Katzenstein, ed., *The Culture of National Security: Norms and Identity in World Politics* (New York: Columbia University Press, 1996).

9. Andreas Hasenclever, Peter Mayer, and Volker Rittberger, *Theories of International Regimes* (Cambridge: Cambridge University Press, 1997), pp. 136–210. Judith Goldstein and Robert O. Keohane, "Ideas and Foreign Policy: An Analytical Framework," in Goldstein and Keohane, eds. (fn. 1).

10. Peter A. Hall, ed., *The Political Power of Economic Ideas: Keynesianism across Nations* (Princeton: Princeton University Press, 1989).

11. Peter M. Haas, "Introduction: Epistemic Communities and International Policy Coordination," *International Organization,* 46 (Winter 1992), p. 3.

12. Robert G. Herman, 'Identity, Norms, and National Security: The Soviet Foreign Policy Revolution and the End of the Cold War,' in Katzenstein (fn. 8), pp. 273–77.

13. Hervé Alphand, *L'Étonnement de l'Etre: Journal 1939–1973* (Paris: Fayard, 1977), pp. 171, 184.

14. Herman (fn. 12), pp. 273–77.

15. Alexander L. George and Timothy J. McKeown, "Case Studies and Theories of Organizational Decision Making," *Advances in Information Processing in Organizations* (1985), pp. 21–58.

16. Contrast Goldstein and Keohane (fn. 9), pp. 9–10, who make a firm distinction between "causal" and "principled" beliefs.

17. Robert A. Pollard, *Economic Security and the Origins of the Cold War, 1945–1950* (New York: Columbia University Press, 1985), p. 2. Cordell Hull, *Memoirs* (New York: Macmillan, 1948), p. 81.

18. *State Department Bulletin* (henceforth *Bulletin*), August 16, 1941, pp. 125–26 (emphasis added).

19. Anne-Marie Burley, "Regulating the World: Multilateralism, International Law, and the Projection of the New Deal Regulatory State," in Ruggie, ed. (fn. 3).

20. Ruggie, ed. (fn. 1).

21. Richard Cooper, "Prolegomena to the Choice of an International Monetary System," *International Organization,* 29, pp. 63–98. Richard N. Gardner, *Sterling-Dollar Diplomacy: Anglo-American Collaboration in the Reconstruction of Multilateral Trade* (Oxford: Clarendon Press, 1956).

22. G. John Ikenberry, "A World Economy Restored: Expert Consensus and the Anglo-American Postwar Settlement," *International Organization,* 46 (Winter 1992). Ruggie, ed. (fn. 1).

23. Goldstein and Keohane (fn. 9), pp. 16–17.

24. To understand the content of any policy innovation, wrote Hasenclever, Mayer, and Rittberger (fn. 9), p. 153, "we need to know more about the selection process in the course of which a particular epistemic community prevails over its competitors." Emanuel Adler, "Cognitive Evolution: A Dynamic Approach for the Study of International Relations and their Progress," in Emanuel Adler and Beverley Crawford, eds., *Progress in Postwar International Relations* (New York: Columbia University Press, 1991).

25. Richard F. Kuisel, *Capitalism and the State in Modern France: Renovation and Economic Management in the Twentieth Century* (Cambridge: Cambridge University Press, 1981), pp. 275, 185.

26. Elizabeth Kier discusses the concept of "political-military subcultures" in "Culture and French Military Doctrine before World War II," in Katzenstein (fn. 8).

27. Prominent structural reformers included André Philip, Georges Boris, Jules Moch, Félix Gouin, and Pierre Mendés-France. Their neoliberal counterparts included Hervé Alphand, René Pleven, Guillaume Guindey, Étienne Hirsch, René Courtin, Henri Teitgen, Alexandre Parodi, and Jean Monnet. General de Gaulle and the Communists remained aloof from these policy debates. Kuisel (fn. 25), pp. 157–71.

28. François Bloch-Lainé and Jean Bouvier, *La France Restaurée 1944–1954: Dialogue sur les Choix d'Une Modernisation* (Paris: Fayard, 1986), p. 90.

29. John Zysman, "The French State in the International Economy," *International Organization*, 31 (1977), p. 845. Kuisel (fn. 25), pp. 162–63.
30. Bloch-Lainé and Bouvier (fn. 28), pp. 91–93 (italics added).
31. Bloch-Lainé and Bouvier (fn. 28), p. 91. Kuisel (fn. 5), pp. 177–8.
32. Robert Marjolin, *Architect of European Unity: Memoirs 1911–1986* (London: Weidenfeld and Nicolson, 1989), pp. 143, 120–22, 61–62.
33. Comité National d'Études, *Rapport sur la Politique Économique d'Après-Guerre* (henceforth Courtin Report) (Alger: Éditions 'Combat', 1944), pp. 9–12.
34. Marjolin (fn. 32), pp. 72, 123, 155.
35. Kuisel (fn. 25), p. 171. According to Guillaume Guindey, postwar Director of External Finance, neoliberals were guided "by the idea that trade liberalization [and] competition … was indispensable for the 'aeration' of the too-long suffocated French economy." Bloch-Lainé and Bouvier (fn. 28), p. 89. Courtin Report (fn. 33), p. 44.
36. Bloch-Lainé and Bouvier (fn. 28), p. 89.
37. Marjolin (fn. 32), p. 157. Courtin Report (fn. 33), pp. 12, 44–51.
38. Courtin Report (fn. 33), pp. 44–5 (italics above added).
39. Kuisel, (fn. 25), p. 173.
40. Jean Monnet, *Memoirs,* trans. by Richard Mayne (Garden City, NY: Doubleday, 1978), p. 222. André Kaspi, *La Mission de Jean Monnet à Algers: Mars-Octobre 1943* (Paris: Éditions Richelieu, 1971), pp. 216–19.
41. Likewise, Guillaume Guindey viewed a European customs union as "the precondition for the liberalization of trade, itself indispensable for French economic modernization." Michel Margairaz, "Autour des Accords Blum-Byrnes: Jean Monnet entre le Consensus National et le Consensus Atlantique," *Histoire, Économie, et Société*, 37 (1982), pp. 463–66. André Kaspi, "Jean Monnet," *Politique Étrangère* 51 (1986), pp. 70–71. Hervé Alphand, *L'Étonnement de l'Etre: Journal 1939–1973* (Paris: Fayard, 1977), pp. 163–69. Étienne Hirsch, *Ainsi la Vie* (Paris: 1988), pp. 78–79.
42. Frances M. B. Lynch, *France and the International Economy: From Vichy to the Treaty of Rome* (London: Routledge, 1997), p. 13. Georges Bossuat, *La France, l'Aide Américaine, et l'Unité Européene 1944–1954*, Vol. 1 (Paris: Ministère de l'Économie et des Finances, 1992), pp. 68–70.
43. Philippe Mioche, "Aux Origines du Plan Monnet: Les Discours et les Contenus dans les Premiers Plans Francais 1941–1947," *Revue Historique,* 265/2 (April–June 1981), pp. 422–23.
44. Ibid., 425. Kuisel (fn. 25), pp. 191–201.
45. Charles S. Maier, "The Politics of Productivity: Foundations of American International Economic Policy after World War II," in Charles S. Maier, ed., *In Search of Stability: Explorations in Historical Political Economy* (Cambridge: Cambridge University Press, 1987), pp. 121–52. Bloch-Lainé and Bouvier (fn. 28), pp. 94, 123–25. Kuisel (fn. 25), pp. 198–201, 248–49.
46. Zysman (fn. 29), p. 839.

47. Kaspi (fn. 40), pp. 216–17. François Duchêne, *Jean Monnet: The First Statesman of Interdependence* (New York: Norton, 1994), p. 127.
48. Monnet's American friends came to include Harry Dexter White, Harry Hopkins, Felix Frankfurter, Dean Acheson, Walter Lippman, Joseph Alsop, James Reston, John Foster Dulles, Averell Harriman, John McCloy, David Bruce, Robert Bowie, George Ball, William Tomlinson, and Walt Rostow.
49. France received $3.8 billion from 1942–1946. Gerard Bossuat, "L'Aide Américane à la France après la Seconde Guerre Mondiale," *Vingtième Siècle* (January–March 1986), p. 19. Duchêne (fn. 47), pp. 141–42. "Lend-Lease Agreement," *Treaties and Other International Agreements of the United States of America 1776–1949* (Vol. 7: Denmark–France), p. 1078. January 9, 1945, *Foreign Relations of the United States (henceforth FRUS) 1945*, IV, pp. 757–59.
50. James L. Dougherty, *The Politics of Wartime Aid* (Westport, CT: Greenwood Press 1978), pp. 178–99.
51. Ibid., 164–7, Lynch (fn. 42), pp. 8–9, 30.
52. Anton DePorte, *De Gaulle's Foreign Policy 1944–1946* (Cambridge, MA: Harvard University Press, 1986), p. 116. Robert Frank, "The French Dilemma: Modernization with Dependence or Independence and Decline," in Josef Becker and Franz Knipping, eds., *Power in Europe? Great Britain, France, Italy, and Germany in a Postwar World, 1945–1950* (New York: Walter de Gruyter, 1986), p. 264.
53. Monnet (fn. 40), p. 228. Margairaz (fn. 41), pp. 463–66.
54. August 31, 1945, Ministère des Affaires Étrangères [henceforth MAE], B Amérique, p. 245. Kuisel (fn. 25), p. 222.
55. July 30, 1945 and August 1, 1945, *FRUS 1945*, IV, pp. 762–67.
56. Alphand advice of August 26, 1945, in Margairaz (fn. 41), p. 440. August 23, 1945, *FRUS 1945*, IV, p. 717.
57. September 25, 1945, Archives du Fondation Jean Monnet pour l'Europe [AMF] 3/5/6.
58. September 1, 25, 1945, MAE, B Amérique, 245. AMF 3/2/1, 3/5/2, 3/5/10. Mioche, *Le Plan Monnet: Genèse et Élaboration 1941–1947* (Paris: Sorbonne, 1987), pp. 125–26.
59. Byrnes, October 8, 1945, cited in Irwin Wall, *The United States and the Making of Postwar France 1945–1954* (Cambridge: Cambridge University Press, 1992), p. 49. October 6, 1945, AMF 3/5/12.
60. October 10 and 17, 1945, AMF 3/5/15 and 3/5/24.
61. October 17, 19, 1945, AMF 3/3/10, 3/3/11a, 3/3/11b (Italics added). Mioche (fn. 58), pp. 126–27. Bloch-Lainé and Bouvier (fn. 28), p. 130.
62. AMF 3/3/11b, 3/5/10, 3/5/12. October 24, 1945. Archives Nationales (henceforth AN) F60. October 18, 1946, MAE, B Amérique, p. 245. French memo of November 1945. Mioche (fn. 58), pp. 126–27.
63. November 8, 1945, *FRUS 1945*, IV, 770–1. AMF 3/5/35, 3/5/36, 3/5/40. November 12, 1945, MAE, B Amérique, p. 245.

64. November 14, 1945, *FRUS 1945,* IV, pp. 771–73.
65. November 25, 1945, *FRUS 1945,* IV, pp. 773–74. Lynch (fn. 42), 35. Jean–Pierre Rioux, *The Fourth Republic 1944–1958* (Cambridge: Cambridge University Press, 1973), p. 59.
66. State Department Central Files (henceforth *SDCF*), 465–7. Stephen P. Sapp, "The United States, France, and the Cold War: Jefferson Caffery and American–French Relations, 1945–1949" (Ph.D. Dissertation, Kent State University, 1978), pp. 99–100.
67. *Bulletin,* December 9, 1945, pp. 905–09. R. Gardner (fn. 21), pp. 19–20.
68. Lloyd Gardner, *Architects of Illusion: Men and Ideas in Foreign Policy 1941–1949* (Chicago: Quadrangle Books, 1970), p. 125.
69. Duchêne (fn. 47), pp. 159–60.
70. *Bulletin,* December 9, 1945, pp. 918–19. AMF 3/5/44.
71. Pleven, cited in Frank (fn. 52), p. 274. November 16, 1945, MAE, B Amérique, p. 245. Frances M. B. Lynch, "Resolving the Paradox of the Monnet Plan: National and International Planning in French Reconstruction," *Economic History Review,* 37, 2 (May 1984), pp. 231–32.
72. De Gaulle radio address of December 10, 1945, cited in DePorte (fn. 52), p. 237.
73. Kuisel (fn. 25), p. 223. Monnet (fn. 40), pp. 236–40.
74. Duchêne (fn. 47), pp. 150–55.
75. Mioche (fn. 43), p. 427.
76. Marjolin (fn. 32), p. 168.
77. Lynch (fn. 71), pp. 232–33. The Plan would concentrate on six sectors: electricity, coal, steel, agricultural machinery, cement, and railways. Mioche (fn. 43), p. 427. Kuisel (fn. 25), pp. 223–27.
78. Marjolin (fn. 32), p. 167. Bloch-Lainé and Bouvier (fn. 28), p. 123. Kuisel (fn. 25), p. 230.
79. Lynch (fn. 71).
80. Monnet to de Gaulle, January 1946, cited in Margairaz (fn. 41), p. 444. Irwin Wall, "Jean Monnet, the United States and the French Economic Plan," in Douglas Brinkley and Clifford Hackett, eds., *Jean Monnet: The Path to European Unity,* (London: MacMillan, 1991), pp. 89–90. January 15, 1946, *FRUS 1946,* V, pp. 399–400.
81. Marjolin (fn. 32), p. 167. Mioche (fn. 43), p. 435. Peter B. Evans, Harold K. Jacobson, and Robert S. Putnam, eds., *Double-Edged Diplomacy* (Berkeley: University of California Press, 1993).
82. Edward Rice-Maximin, "The United States and the French Left, 1945–1949: The View from the State Department," *Journal of Contemporary History,* 19 (1984).
83. Charles de Gaulle, *Mémoires de Guerre, Vol. 1: L'Appel,* p. 1. Phillip G. Cerny, *The Politics of Grandeur: Ideological Aspects of de Gaulle's Foreign Policy* (Cambridge: Cambridge University Press, 1980).
84. *New York Times,* March 2, 1946. February 4, 1946, *FRUS 1946,* V, pp. 409–10. February 3, 1946, AMF 4/1/3. Lynch (fn. 42), p. 38.

244 • Stewart Patrick

85. February 9, 1946, *FRUS 1946*, V, pp. 412–13.
86. *Wall Street Journal*, February 4, 1946. February 15, 1946, AMF 4/1/4.
87. Bossuat (fn. 42), pp. 88–89. Lynch (fn. 42), pp. 39–40.
88. D. Bruce Marshall, *The French Colonial Myth and Constitution-Making in the Fourth Republic* (New Haven: Yale University Press, 1973), p. 2. John E. Dreifort, *Myopic Grandeur: The Ambivalence of French Foreign Policy Towards the Far East, 1919–1945* (Kent, OH: Kent State University Press, 1991), p. 235. Jean Chauvel, *Commentaire (II): Alger à Berne (1944–1952)* (Paris: Fayard, 1972), p. 175.
89. February 2 and 15, 1946, MAE, Classement Provisoire 'A', pp. 194–95.
90. John Young, *Britain, France, and the Unity of Europe* (Bath: Leicester University Press), p. 7.
91. AMF 4/1/6.
92. Margairaz (fn. 41), p. 447. MAE, Classement Provisoire 'A', 194-5, February 15, 1946. Bossuat (fn. 42), p. 86. Blum Mission Final Report, AN F60 923. 'Negoçiations Franco-Américaines Relatives à La Politique Économique Internationale' (Paris: Imprimerie Nationale, 1946). Wall (fn. 80), p. 110.
93. Monnet (fn. 40), p. 250. *New York Times*, March 2, 1946.
94. Blum assured the NAC that French nationalization would be "limited." Leon Blum, *L'Oeuvre*, Vol. 6 (Paris: A. Michelet, 1954–1972), pp. 188–94.
95. March 22, 25, 28, and April 3, 1946. Alfred Grosser, *La Quatrième République et sa Politique Étrangère* (Paris: Colin, 1967), p. 218.
96. *New York Times*, March 9, April 17, 1946.
97. The alternative of autarky, Acheson continued, "would completely change our constitution, our relations to property, human liberty, our very conceptions of law." William Appleman Williams, *The Tragedy of American Diplomacy* (New York: 1962), pp. 235–36. L. Gardner (fn. 68), pp. 132–34.
98. Lynch (fn. 71), pp. 236–38; April 2, 1946, *SDCF,* frame 463; Grosser (fn. 95), p. 214. *FRUS 1946*, V, pp. 496–511.
99. Pollard (fn. 17), p. 76. May 3–8, 1946, *FRUS 1946*, IV, pp. 435–50.
100. May 6, 1946, *FRUS 1946*, V, pp. 440–46. Wall (fn. 59), pp. 54–55.
101. Dougherty (fn. 50), p. 210.
102. May 28, 1946, *FRUS 1946*, V, pp. 464–65. *Bulletin*, June 9, 1946, pp. 994–97.
103. Wall (fn. 59), p. 53. Margairaz (fn. 41), pp. 455–58. Bossuat (fn. 49), pp. 18–19.
104. France agreed to purchase American imports, return to private commerce, and provide regular data on its monetary policy and balance of payments position.
105. Annie Lacroix-Riz, *La Choix de Marianne: Relations Franco-Américaines* (Paris: Messidor, 1985). Blum Mission Final Report, AN F60 923. Lynch (fn. 42), p. 46.

106. "Report of M. Leon Blum and the French Delegation," AN F60 923. Blum (fn. 94), pp. 201–03.
107. June 12, 1946, AMF 4/6/1. MAE, Classement Provisoire 'A', pp. 194–95. (italics in original). Why France Cannot Live in Autarky," April 20, 1946, AMF 3/5/47.
108. Assembly debate of August 1, 1946, cited in Margairaz (fn. 41), p. 462. Assembly speech, AN F60 923.
109. Norris Chipman, June 28, 1946, cited in Rice-Maximin (fn. 82), p. 733. August 1, 1946 speech, Jacques Duclos, *Batailles pour la République* (Paris: Éditions Sociales, 1947), pp. 336–40.
110. Blum (fn. 94), August 3, 1946, pp. 204–5.
111. Monnet (fn. 40), pp. 253–4.
112. Mioche (fn. 58), p. 93. Marjolin (fn. 32), p. 167.
113. AN F60, p. 923.
114. John Gerard Ruggie, *Constructing the World Polity: Essays on International Institutionalization* (New York: Routledge, 1998), p. 73.
115. Hasenclever, Mayer, and Rittberger (fn. 9), pp. 176–85.
116. G. John Ikenberry and Charles A. Kupchan, "Socialization and Hegemonic Power," *International Organization* 44 (Summer 1990), p. 287. Andrew Fenton Cooper, Richard A. Higgot, and Kim Richard Nossal, "Bound to Follow?", *Political Science Quarterly*, 106 (1991), pp. 391–410.
117. Pollard (fn. 17), p. 4. Maier (fn. 3).
118. *Bulletin,* October 6, 26, 27, 1946, 640–4, 757–60 (Italics added).
119. Margairaz (fn. 41), p. 467. Monnet (fn. 40), p. 268.
120. Jim Hoagland, "France: Slow to Go Global," *Washington Post.* Roger Cohen, "France vs. U.S.: Warring Views of Capitalism," *New York Times*, October 20, 1997.

PART FIVE

The Marshall Plan and Public Opinion

CHAPTER 12

French Public Opinion and the Marshall Plan: The Communists and Others

Roland Cayrol[1]

This chapter deals with the state of French opinion—as measured by the only existing polling company at the time, the IFOP (Institut français d'opinion publique)—regarding the Marshall Plan, and, more broadly, international relations, images of the United States and the USSR, the dangers of "imperialisms" coming from the super-powers, and attachment to French independence. The data show an important discrepancy between the Communist supporters and all the other sectors of the electorate (socialist and gaullist included); the "Marshall Plan" French opinion reveals a "cold war" France, where those who believe in the starred banner (even when they have suspicions about the U.S. "imperialist" visions) strongly oppose those who believe in the red star (even when they have doubts that the USSR will help France's recovery).

In order to study French opinion regarding the Marshall Plan—and its eventual specificities—there is one essential source: the only institute for the study of opinion that existed during that time in France. That organization is called the *Institut française d'opinion publique* (IFOP), or the French Institute for Public Opinion, now part of the Gallup group.

At present, this institute no longer holds the archives of databases, which are missing from this particular period onward. We have thus not been able to carry out specific statistical research using these databases, and instead are dependent on the only "paper" documents from the period. This includes most notably those belonging to collection of the journal *Sondages* (Polls), edited at the time by the IFOP.

The statistics used in this report then will be extracts from reports and articles published by the IFOP, and, for the purposes of some international comparisons, from polls provided by the institutes that make up the Gallup group.

French Opinion from 1945–47

The first preoccupation of the French in the postwar period was clearly shortages and the replenishment of food and jobs. To the question "What is the most important problem which you and your family must currently face?" posed by the IFOP in January of 1946 (from January 17 to 28), the surveyed population responded, significantly (Table 12.1).

Even worries related to money are largely surpassed by the unique desire to survive that "replenishment" represents. The editor of the journal *Sondages* elaborates on this:[2] "Replenishment is expressed generally in one word (replenishment). Some say 'bread' some say 'meat'." And this worry lasted for months, even years.

The France that emerged deathly pale from both the war and the occupation knew that it owed its liberation essentially to the allied war effort. Today, when these lines are written, "the Allies" is really read as the Americans. But it is also necessary to place oneself in the context of the public opinion of the period, during which the Soviet Union weighed in as well, with all of its weight (Figure 12.1). This poll, which includes only the Parisian population in September of 1944 is, for example, incredibly revealing.

Of course, this is just a moment at the end of the war, when the prestige of the USSR is at its highest, but it is an element of opinion that is

Table 12.1

Replenishment	53 percent
Clothing	18 percent
Monetary Worries	16 percent
Heating	9 percent
Housing	4 percent
Agricultural Needs	2 percent
Rebuilding Business	1 percent
Other	4 percent
No Response	2 percent

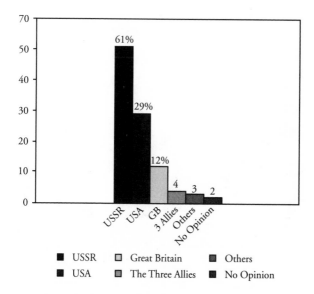

Figure 12.1   Which Nation will have Contributed the Most to the German Defeat? (Parisian Population, 1944)

important to consider: for the French, the Soviets benefit from an image of a strength that played an essential role in the defeat of Nazi Germany.

In this context, if the French are sensitive to the danger of foreign "imperialism," they distinguish themselves from other Western nations by their relatively light consideration of the "Soviet threat," and by their more serious preoccupation over the "American threat." In Spring 1946, the French are, even more than the Americans, Canadians, or Australians, convinced of the hegemonic desires of a world power. But they split almost in half on the identification of the imperialist in power: 26 percent name the USSR, but 25 percent point to the United States, and 12 percent indicate both (which says much for the state of the national spirit in which the pollsters are working; Gallup/ USA, itself, proposes "Great Britain and the USSR", which do not appear in the three other countries!) (Figure 12.2). This specificity in France, this attraction of a portion of French public opinion for the Soviet Union, is clear also if we look at the perceived "democratic" character of different countries (Figure 12.3). Assuredly, three-quarters of the French see in the United States a democratic regime—that is, a smaller portion than in Sweden, or in America itself, but it is as great as in Norway and more than public opinion in Holland registers. France is not exceptional in its estimation of the democratic character of the American system.

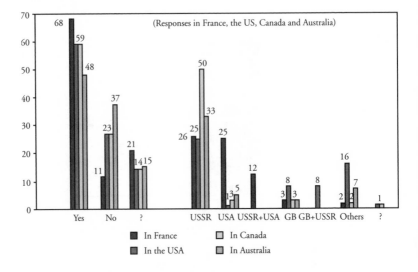

Figure 12.2 Imperialism of the Super Powers (March 1946). Is there, in Your Opinion, one Nation Seeking to Dominate the World? If Yes, which One?

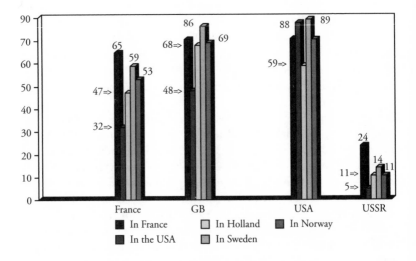

Figure 12.3 Democracy (Countries Considered Democratic, April 1947)

Table 12.2 Sympathies in the case of a USA/USSR conflict

August 2–14 1946	The U.S.	The USSR	Neither/ no opinion
If a conflict erupted between the USSR and the U.S. with which side would your sympathies be aligned?			
Total	40	21	39
Working Class	27	32	41
Merchants and Industrial Workers	47	13	40
Liberal Professions	53	18	29
20–34 yrs old	41	26	33
35–64 yrs old	37	21	42
65 yrs old and over	43	15	42

By contrast, one-fourth of French people recognize certain democratic virtues in the Soviet Union. This is a much larger proportion, not only compared with the 5 percent of the Americans that gave the same response, but the 11–14 percent that did so in Northern European Countries also compared with.

A less "grateful" postwar country with regard to the United States, France is a country where one-quarter of the citizens are wary of the supposed imperialism of the United States, where one-quarter of its inhabitants judge the Soviet regime as democratic: one understands that, asked about their preferences in the case of an open conflict between the Americans and the Soviets, the French of this era certainly choose the American camp by a majority, but with the existence of a significant minority that would opt for the USSR (Table 12.2).

One notes in reading this table that one-fifth of French people—and one-third of those who proclaim themselves in favor of one particular camp—chose the USSR. The percentage was even greater in the youth population, and especially among workers, where it becomes the majority sentiment among those with an opinion. In any case, it is through the lens of these opinion structures that one must judge the French public spirit as it learned of the Marshall Plan in 1947.

The Marshall Plan: Good to Accept!

Suffering, as we noted, from a period dominated by the anguish of replenishment and reconstruction, the French, even if they were tormented by wariness with regard to the Americans and sometimes seduced by the USSR, quickly learned of the Marshall Plan and were strongly in favor of it. As soon as a survey was taken, from June 20–30, 1947, 72 percent of the people questioned in France stated that they "have heard of the Marshall Plan" (compared with only 49 percent of Americans during the same period).

When pressed by an open question to define the Marshall Plan, the French are: 40 percent incapable of answering and 5 percent erroneous in their responses. The other 55 percent (nothing to sneeze at!), from this same month of June, give explanations classed as follows by IFOP:

28 percent:	American aid to Europe (objective responses)
17 percent:	American aid favoring European countries afflicted by the war
6 percent:	American aid to the Europe favoring the economic policy of the United States
4 percent:	American aid to the Europe favoring the politics of the United States: the creation of a western bloc, and an anti-Soviet campaign

Quickly informed of the aid that the Marshall Plan represented, French public opinion soon accepted it. From this same survey done in the second half of June 1947, the French public responded to the question, "Do you believe that France should accept this plan?" as follows:

47 percent:	France should accept it
6 percent:	France should not accept it
47 percent:	No opinion

A great number, it is true, do not have an opinion (but we saw that the majority of the French do not really know at the moment what the plan entails). Those that express an opinion, however, do so spontaneously, and in a very positive manner. Weakened, the country needs help and willingly accepts the outstretched hand of the Americans.

Things become more precise as the weeks pass. IFOP took another poll during the last two weeks in July of this same year (1947)—after the Paris Talks, in which sixteen nations (including France) that have accepted the principle of the Marshall Plan participated. To the question, "Do you believe that France was right or wrong to participate in the talks on the Marshall Plan?" the responses are the following:

64 percent:	France was right
8 percent:	France was wrong
28 percent:	No opinion

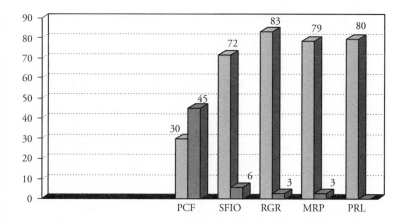

Figure 12.4 Was France Right or Wrong? (July 1947)

Table 12.3

	PCF	SFIO	RGR	MRP	PRL
The Marshall Plan can succeed	24	52	66	57	63
The Marshall Plan cannot succeed	52	19	9	11	18

The French chose between the need for aid and the consideration of the threat of American imperialism, and they chose the Marshall Plan. One no longer finds a quarter of the French opting to combat it, but rather a tiny 8 percent.

The redistribution of these responses by partisan sympathy is enlightening (Figure 12.4). These figures reveal that the sympathizers of the parties of the right, whether the traditional right of the PRL or the Christian Democratic party of the MRP, those of the centrist RGR, or the socialists of the SFIO massively support the French government in its acceptance of the Marshall Plan (Table 12.4).

Only a majority of communist sympathizers (PCF) are opposed to the plan, affirming their specificity within the French political system. Again, it is necessary to underline that their opposition is not as great as the support for the plan manifested by the other parties. 45 percent against and 30 percent for. That means that four voters in ten in the French Communist Party (PCF) favored French participation in the Marshall Plan, despite the Soviet refusal to do so, and despite the resolute opposition demonstrated by their party. This says much about their contradictory pressures. Fidelity to Moscow, and to the orders of the French party, is typical of a majority of Communist sympathizers; that is, an essential given. But it is very far from being unanimous.

The feeling expressed by French public opinion was, thus, very favorable to the announcement of the Marshall Plan, even to the point of overcoming the resistance of four Communist electors in ten, who were strongly conditioned to go against the American government. Transmitting well their mixed feelings, communist sympathizers did not want to believe in the success of the Marshall Plan.

The political opinion debate was not so much going to disappear. However, it would no longer concentrate on France's acceptance of the plan but rather on the true motivations of the United States, on the attitude of the USSR, and on France's acceptance of the eventual political conditions accompanying the plan; in other words, on the theme of the political independence of France in relation to the United States.

The Attitude of the USSR Regarding the Plan

In this second half of July 1947, after the withdrawal of Molotov, the French responded to the question, "Do you believe that the USSR was right or wrong in refusing to participate in the Marshall Plan Talks?" in the following manner:

18 percent   The USSR is right
47 percent   The USSR is wrong
35 percent   No opinion

Youth between the ages of 20–30 (20 percent) and especially workers (29 percent) are the sociodemographic categories that most often attribute correctness to the Soviet Union. The following figure makes the position of the French Communist Party sympathizers, now very divided, especially clear. From the moment it becomes a question of the USSR, there is hardly hesitation nor murmur within the ranks of the Communist Party sympathizers. It no longer has anything to do with the question of balancing the strategic and political choices with the need for aid at the end of the war: The USSR is without a doubt correct. The difference here between the communists and voters for other parties is striking. The electors of all the other parties, the socialists to the traditional right, all believe Moscow is wrong (Figure 12.5).

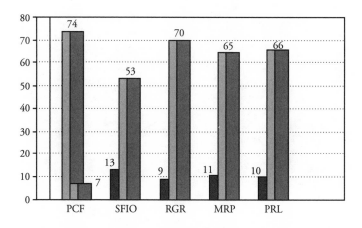

Figure 12.5 Was the USSR Right or Wrong? (July 1947)

The True Motivations of the United States

France is right to accept this American aid, but what is the motivation of the official American side?

In the same period as the preceding surveys, the IFOP asked French people that question formulated in the following manner: "In your opinion, was the proposition of Mr. Marshall a result of America's desire to intervene in the internal affairs of Europe, a result of a sincere desire to help Europe rise up again, or does it reflect a need to find foreign markets in order to avoid an economic crisis in the United States?" The responses were the following (which illustrate the paucity of illusions of French public opinion):

47 percent: The need to find foreign markets
18 percent: The sincere desire to help Europe
15 percent: The desire to intervene in the internal affairs of Europe
3 percent: The first reason, mixed with others
17 percent: No opinion

It is evident that the idea of an American aid proffered only out of generosity does not convince one Frenchman in five. The majority view the Marshall proposition more as an interested strategy, either political (interference in European affairs) or economic (the search for commercial outlets in the European markets) in nature.

(Figure 12.6) The airing of these opinions by partisan sympathy is, yet again, revealing. The responses of communist sympathizers are not

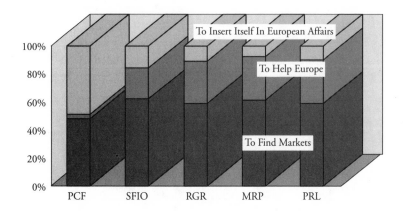

Figure 12.6 The Motivations of the USA

surprising: they leave practically no room for the idea of gratuitous American generosity; instead, they assign the Americans the role of imperialists, sometimes economic, but, more often than not, political.

The surprise comes more from the supporters of the other parties on the political chessboard: The "sincere desire to help Europe" is not the majority opinion anywhere. If the American wish for a political interference in Europe is a relatively marginal view (here the Communists are decidedly exceptional), the strategy of commercial conquest, by contrast, the willingness of the United States to find, thanks to the Marshall Plan, markets in Europe is very much spotlighted throughout, even to the extent of appearing among the voters of the traditionally pro-American parties, where it forms the dominant analysis.

The French, from the right as well as from the left, do not want to be duped by the hand being extended to them—and that they are happy to accept. Perhaps they are even more cynical in their analysis of American motivations because they are reduced to having to accept their help? Perhaps it is, in fact, less humiliating to accept help when one persuades oneself that there is something in it for the other?

French Independence and the Acceptance of the Eventual Political Conditions of the Marshall Plan

Since the American gesture passes for not being devoid of intentions with regard to the beneficiary countries, does France risk losing her independence in this affair?

"In your opinion, does the Marshall Plan risk undermining the independence of France?" Thus questioned in that July of 1947, the French—although many hesitate to give their opinion—provide a nuanced negative response:

23 percent: Yes
38 percent: No
39 percent: No opinion

Mainly, France does not want to believe in any risk of losing independence. Still, choices vary by party commitment.

The Communists are again the only ones to prognosticate the loss of the country's independence. This time, the socialists are not all insensitive to the argument: Many among them, bothered without a doubt, do not declare their views (42 percent), and a less than negligible minority (22 percent) believes in the loss of independence; the relative majority of the socialists, however, does not want to believe this problem. The socialists remain, in spite of their hesitations, closer to the center and the right than the communists.

Among the supporters of parties of the center-right, and *a fortiori* among those of the right, there is a clear rejection of any threat to the independence of the French nation. The plan, such as it is, is generally well accepted—whatever the hidden intentions—political or economic—that one assigns to it.

Except in the communist camp, there is a widespread belief that the sacrosanct independence of France is not at stake. But what if the

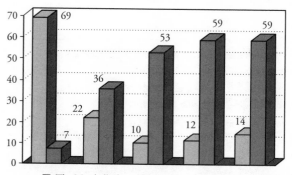

☐ The Marshall Plan will harm French Independence
■ The Marshall Plan will not harm French Independence

Figure 12.7   The Marshall Plan and French Independence

Marshall Plan was laden with conditions? It is here that one finds the limitations of the acceptance of public opinion during the period. Surveyed in October of 1947 by means of the question, "If the United States attached certain political conditions to this aid, should France, in your opinion, accept them?" French opinion responds definitively in the negative:

32 percent Yes
47 percent No
21 percent No opinion

This opinion varies among readers of the primary daily newspapers (Figure 12.8). This selection is very interesting: readers of *L'Humanité,* the communist daily, are certainly most marked in their refusal to accept any eventual American political conditions attached to the Marshall Plan. But they are joined by those readers of the *Franc-Tireur,* the newspaper of the left that emerged from the Resistance, for the most part by those of *Populaire,* the paper of the socialist SFIO party, and by half of the readers of *Combat,* another journal of the Resistance.

By contrast, a narrow majority of readers of the centrist journal, *L'Aurore,* a sizable majority of the readers of the Christian-Democrats, *L'Aube,* and an even larger number of those reading the papers of the right, *Le Figaro* and *L'Epoque,* proclaim themselves without hesitation for the acceptance of possible political compensation demanded by the United States.

Here, the left-right axis becomes—based on a hypothetical question, it is true—more significant than the opposition, registered elsewhere, between the Communists and all the others.

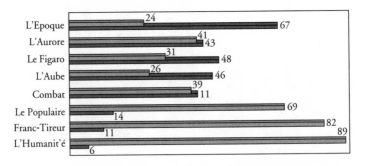

Figure 12.8 Newspaper Readers and the Acceptance or Refusal of the Conditions of the Marshall Plan.

Table 12.4 Utility of the Marshall Plan for France

The Marshall Plan was for France ... November 1947

a good thing	25 percent
more or less good	20 percent
more or less bad	15 percent
a bad thing	8 percent

This French opinion in the second half of 1947 was happy to accept American aid, but riddled with political divisions, first by the effects of the Communist phenomenon, and then by more communally shared reservations regarding American power, its motivations, and its eventual demands. This explains, perhaps, that, consulted on the utility of the Marshall Plan in November 1947, the French were again positive, but to a less impressive degree than that manifested at the time of the acceptance of the aid (Table 12.4).

The Effects of Public Opinion on the Marshall Plan

If one studies the evolution of the polls during 1940s and 1950s, one can confirm that the Marshall Plan on its own transformed the mentality and the point of view of the French. One has the impression that it had an impact on a series of events that marked French public spirit, and that progressively diverted a certain attraction for the USSR, bringing France more naturally into the American orbit.

Let us look at the 1944–48 responses to the question of knowing "On whom should one count to help France rebuild—the United States, the USSR, or Great Britain?"

One notes, in examining the curve below, that the hope placed by the French on the United States was very high in September of 1944; it then experienced a significant slackening at the end of the war, during the strongest period of Franco-Soviet alliance. Then, beginning in April of 1946, the prestige of the Soviet Union declined regularly; at the same time, the United States was confirmed as *the* power from which one hoped to receive aid for reconstruction. The Marshall Plan truly appears as a moment of change. After the implementation of the Plan, the respondents who would say "to wait for aid from the Soviet side" falls below the level of 10 percent (Figure 12.9). We should note in passing that French citizens stating "to count on aid first from the Soviet side"

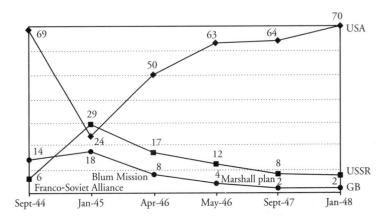

Figure 12.9   Aid Expected from Foreign Sources

Table 12.5

	PCF	SFIO	RGR	MRP	PRL
(April 1946)					
Count on the aid of ...					
USA	21	58	63	67	69
USSR	63	11	4	3	3
(January 1948)					
Count on the aid of ...	L'Humanite	Franc-Tireur	Le Populaire	Combat	L'Aube
USA	7	31	64	76	80
USSR	56	14	4	0	2
	Le Figaro	L'Epoque			
USA	85	91			
USSR	0	0			

are far less numerous than the number of members of the French Communist party. This can be verified in Table 12.5.

Although the criteria are unfortunately not the same for these two surveys from 1946 and 1948, these figures illustrate the territory left to be captured by the USSR among its theoretical supporters in French public opinion: only 63 percent of communist sympathizers in 1946, and—still more serious, because readers of the newspaper are more "militant" than simple sympathizers—56 percent of the readers of *L'Humanité* in 1948 expect, first and foremost, aid from the Soviet Union.

At the beginning of 1948, in any case, the game is over: the quasi-unanimity of the readers of the papers of the right and two-thirds of the readers of the socialist daily identify the United States as the power on which to count.

A Few Years Later

1953: the hour of accounting having arrived—this year, also the year of the death of Stalin—how does France react? See Table 12.6.

In total, 57 percent felt the Plan useful or indispensable for France and 14 percent felt it harmful or very harmful. The retrospective verdict of the opinion is unquestionable.

What about our partisan divisions? Figure 12.10 demonstrates that they have survived. They even survived in a caricaturelike fashion: The Communist sympathizers are completely isolated in regards to all the other parties. They alone, with a three-quarter majority, see the harmful effects of the Plan. In the meantime, the Gaullists establish themselves as a party, the RPF; and the Gaullist sympathizers, at the beginning of 1953, are the most strongly inclined to recognize the benefits of the Marshall Plan.

Table 12.6 The utility of the Marshall Plan for France

The Marshall Plan was for France … January 1953

indispensable	11 percent
very useful	17 percent
useful	29 percent
indifferent	5 percent
harmful	9 percent
very harmful	5 percent

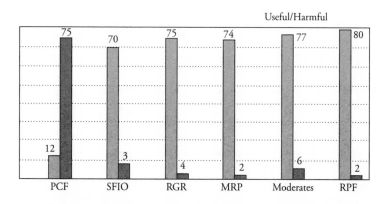

Figure 12.10   Retrospective Evaluation of the Plan (Jan 27–February 7, 1953)

Table 12.7

	Feb–March 1946	July 1947	January 1953
Is there, in your opinion, one nation seeking to dominate the world?			
Yes	68	79	78
No	11	6	2
If yes, which one?			
USSR	26	36	32
USA	25	29	15
USSR and USA	12	13	30

There is little variation, from the Gaullist Right to the socialists, from the Christian Democrats to the center Left. It is really the communists—that is, the hardcore Communists—against everyone else.

The global outlook was set, from this point on. The common view in France was that there were imperialist maneuvers by the super powers, but that those were divergent views on the origin of the threat—the USSR being more and more often designated as the principal source (Table 12.7). In 1946–47, the French were, even more so than in the preceding period, convinced that there was an imperialist risk of great magnitude.

In 1947, the USSR largely surpasses the United States as the principal agent of possible imperialism. It became at this moment, and remained so in 1953, the principal enemy in the eyes of French public opinion. After 1947 (perhaps an effect of the Marshall Plan?), the American "danger" declined dramatically—to the profit of a growing vision (accepted by one in three Frenchmen in 1953) according to which "the two imperialisms," that is, American and Soviet, constituted together the main danger.

But the turning point had occurred: The vast majority of the French refuse from here onward to see in the United States a danger in itself to the future of the world and world peace. This is confirmed in a resounding manner by Table 12.8.

The Communist exceptionalism is striking: In January of 1953, they alone believed in the preparation of a war of aggression by the United States—an idea absolutely rejected by the entirety of the French electorate aside from them.

It is true that socialist sympathizers of the SFIO make up a sizable minority (on the order of about one-quarter), that doubts the American

Table 12.8

January 1953	PCF	SFIO	RGR	MRP	Moderate	RPF
The United States is preparing a war of aggression	58	1	1	1	3	3
The American Government:						
– sincerely desires peace	7	41	51	56	50	57
– does not sincerely desire peace	69	24	14	12	13	11
The Soviet Government:						
– sincerely desires peace	89	27	15	12	13	11
– does not sincerely desire peace	2	31	46	52	47	50

Table 12.9

March 1949	PCF	SFIO	RGR	MRP	PRL	RPF
France should sign the Atlantic Treaty	6	47	69	53	68	61
France should not sign the Atlantic Treaty	71	11	4	2	1	3

desire for peace or that wants to believe in the Soviet desire for peace. Essentially, however, the socialists find themselves with the supporters of all the other parties—the Gaullists included—in seeing the Cold War world through glasses tinted by pro-Americanism and anti-Sovietism. Thus, by 1949, there was overwhelming support for French agreement to the signing of the North Atlantic Treaty.

The Communists were, thus, alone against all, socialists—and Gaullists—included. The France of the Marshall Plan is definitely one of the Cold War. It is a France where those who believe in the stars and stripes—even if they sense a hint of imperialist aims—and those who believe in the red star—even if they hold no illusions about material aid offered by it—are fundamentally opposed to one another.

Notes

1. *Translated from the French by Vanessa Merit Nornberg.*
2. *Sondages,* 1946, p. 47.

References

Sondages, Revue française de l'opinion publique, Paris, IFOP, 1946–49.
Sondages, 1953, Vol 2.
Dupin, E. *Oui, Non, Sans opinion.* (Paris: Interéditions, 1990), 319p.

CHAPTER 13

The Legacy of the Marshall Plan:
American Public Support for Foreign Aid[1]

Robert Shapiro

This article reviews the post-World War II shift of American public opinion away from isolationism. With the high level of public support for the Marshall Plan, and with the perceived success of the Plan and other American policies, the American public has been supportive of foreign aid proposals and policies initiated by its political leaders, despite misperceptions to the contrary. Americans have continued to make clear distinctions between and among different types of foreign assistance and other policies, involving friends and foes alike.

I want to introduce this discussion of the legacy of American public opinion toward the Marshall Plan and postwar American foreign policy in, perhaps, an odd way. While the jury may still be out at this writing (June 1999) regarding American involvement in Kosovo, NATO, and the peace settlement with Serbia, another period of Bill Clinton's presidency has some relevance to this essay. As history will long remember, Clinton successfully weathered a scandal, impeachment, and a Senate trial stemming from improper personal behavior toward a former White House intern. One seemingly puzzling outcome as the scandal unfolded was that Clinton's "presidential approval" rating in the polls increased to its all-time high. At the same time, the public clearly expressed increasing disapproval of the president with respect to his personal life. This was found in many opinion polls, so that this survey finding is real. The puzzle was that no one expected that Clinton's presidential performance rating would rise sharply. For example, based upon some simple assumptions and what I thought was reasonable insight into political and social psychology (cf. Zaller 1992), I predicted the president's approval rating would stay steady after his State of the Union Address, rebounding from a small downturn that might have occurred. The outcome that occurred was praised by some observers who gave the public credit for rejecting the media's "frenzy" over the scandal and for taking revenge on the press and the pundits by supporting Clinton. Others were impressed that the public was capable of distinguishing—let alone being willing to distinguish—Clinton's public behavior and performance as president from what he allegedly did privately (cf. Shapiro 1998; Zaller 1998).

For some of us students of American public opinion, however, the public's ability to make important distinctions is old news. The public has long done this, even in complex areas of policy making such as foreign affairs. We see this very strikingly in the case of its support for the Marshall Plan and other early Cold War–era policies. Further, the kinds of differences that the American public saw between and among postwar policies continued to be pervasive throughout the Cold War. There is no reason to expect that this will not continue in post–Cold War foreign affairs. One particular myth that this disproves is that the American public has opposed spending on foreign aid. This conclusion needs to be appraised in light of a wide range of data.

In this paper, I first review the profound evolution of American public opinion that occurred after World War II. I also explore the influences on public opinion and the ways the public distinguished among different issues. I will then show how the pattern of public support for U.S. foreign policies that emerged with the Marshall Plan and other concurrent policies became the norm thereafter for how Americans viewed their country's involvement abroad.

War and Internationalism

The United States was a reluctant participant in both world wars. In easing itself into war, however, the United States debated and then provided different kinds of assistance to its future allies in ways that the public quite readily distinguished. This was epitomized by the way the public, before the entry of the United States into World War II, distinguished "Lend-Lease" and other related assistance from direct military involvement in the war (see Page and Shapiro 1992: Chap. 5). The profound change brought about by the war's end was that the public had to continue making these hard distinctions after the war in ways it had not done in sustained ways before.

The two profound effects of World War II for Americans were the defeat of fascism and the full-fledged involvement of the United States as a superpower in world affairs after the war. The American public had to continue to think about what large-scale actions the United States should contemplate taking in the postwar world. It was taken as a given that the United States could not retreat back into isolationism.

Figures 13.1 to 13.3 capture the degree of public support for American activism in foreign policy after the war. Support for the Marshall Plan itself stayed in the 61 to 79 percent range throughout the 1949–52 period. Figures 13.2 and 13.3 capture the full-blown end of American isolationism that World War II produced. The Marshall Plan data in Figure 13.1 and most of the trend data in Figures 13.2 and 13.3 were taken from responses to surveys that the National Opinion Research Center conducted for the State Department during this period. It is worth noting that these were part of the only explicitly political polling program that the federal government has ever engaged in *inside* the United States (the United States Information Agency has engaged in opinion polling abroad). While these polls were used to monitor public opinion, the impact that these data had on policy makers, if any, has not been fully determined (cf. Cohen 1973; Foster 1983; Graham 1994;

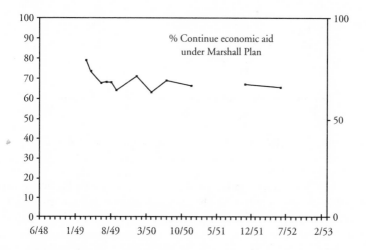

Figure 13.1 Support for the Marshall Plan
Source: NORC/State Department Surveys.

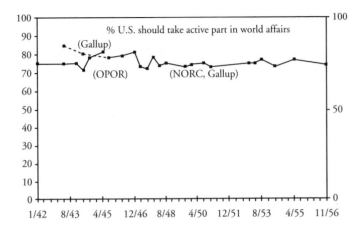

Figure 13.2 Postwar Opinion Foreign Policy Activism, 1942–1956

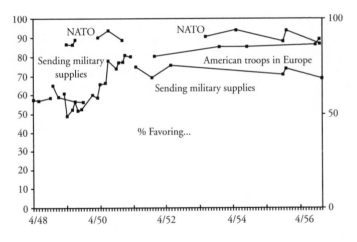

Figure 13.3 Approval of NATO and U.S. Troops in Western Europe 1948–1956 (NORC)

Hinckley 1992; Jacobs 1992; Jacobs and Shapiro 1995; Powlick 1991). What is known, however, is that when Congress learned that federal funds were being used for such polling, it cut off funding for this apparently "secret" survey research program. Among the arguments members of Congress offered in debating the continuation of these surveys was that such polls defied American (republican) democracy; it was argued that Congress conveyed and represented public opinion, not polling by any part of government itself (the lively congressional testimony is described nicely by Robert Eisinger [1994]).

Given these data as well as other data presented below, one important question to ask is what influenced public opinion on these and later foreign policy issues? While some of us might sanguinely wish to think that it was the objective reality of the postwar world that directly affected public opinion, we know better: the public does not react autonomously to events and changes in real-world conditions. The reality is that the public does not always have a lot of information nor know a lot about the most relevant facts concerning public policy and politics (see Delli Carpini and Keeter 1996). Rather, what influences the public is the information, interpretations, and cues that it receives (through the mass media) from political leaders and other elites. Based upon considerable research, we have good reason to believe that what influenced public opinion concerning specific policies such as the initial $400 million aid to Greece and Turkey after the 1947 Truman Doctrine speech, and the Marshall Plan, following Marshall's own speech at Harvard later in 1947, was the perceived *élite consensus* that emerged. Specifically, the public was exposed, *cumulatively*, to information and, especially, arguments and *interpretations* that led it to support specific government actions (see Kernell 1976; Page and Shapiro 1992; Zaller 1992). Not only was the public offered *direction* by Truman and Marshall but also by "experts" (like the anonymous "X," George F. Kennan) who emphasized Cold War "containment" of the Soviets in a way that came to be defined both in economic and military terms (see Foster 1983; Leigh 1976). I say "direction" rather than "leadership," to put aside the question of whether the influences at work represented leadership or "manipulation," which is an important question but one that is beyond the scope of this paper (see Hilderbrand 1981; Page and Shapiro 1992).

Clearly, the consensus among élites that the United States should play an active role in world affairs as a postwar superpower was reflected in public opinion. The public supported American activism in the abstract, and it also supported the Marshall Plan, followed by the NATO defense pact and sending military supplies and American troops to Europe. But along with the impression of substantial overall support for activism, we also see in the data that the public did not support specific policies to the same degree. Figure 13.3, in particular, shows that there was more support for the NATO pact than for "sending military supplies to the countries of Western Europe now, in order to strengthen them against any future attack" (for the full question wordings, the survey organizations, and other information and documentation for the data reported in Figures 13.1–13.9 and elsewhere here, see Page and Shapiro 1992: Chap. 2, 5, 6, and Appendix).

Comparing Figures 13.1 and 13.3, we also see that support for military assistance was initially at a lower level than support for economic assistance through the Marshall Plan, but support for military assistance increased further as tensions increased during the Korean War period. The overall picture, then, was that the public supported foreign policy activism and it clearly distinguished the different types of U.S. involvement that emerged.

The Persistence of the Postwar Pattern: Support for Foreign Aid

From then on during the Cold War, this pattern of public attitudes toward American foreign policy persisted. First, it is well known that support for activism has remained substantial to this day, though there were ups and downs as a result of the Vietnam War, and support dropped off perhaps a bit after the end of the Cold War (for a review of the evidence, see Richman 1996; Rielly 1999; Yankelovich and Destler 1994; Wittkopf 1990, 1996). But the level of public support for the United States taking an active part in world affairs has in general remained not far from the high level shown in Figure 13.2.

Second, the public has continued to draw distinctions among policies, many much sharper than those shown in Figure 13.3. Further, public opinion appears to reflect certain standards of judgment found in public debates led by political leaders and élites. These standards of judgment are revealed in the particular ways the public has distinguished between and among different types of policies. Research has suggested that these standards or principles are derived from the type of problem that a foreign policy issue poses. Specifically, the public has distinguished problems that involve actual or threatened foreign aggression versus problems that stem from the need to consider intervention into another country's internal politics, as in the case of domestic turmoil or civil war. The public also appears to be attuned to situations that exhibit needs for humanitarian aid. Studies have shown that the threat of external aggression evokes more public support for U.S. and international action than does action proposed in response to internal strife within a foreign country; the public also tends to support humanitarian assistance (see Jentleson 1992; Oneal et al. 1996; Sobel 1996). Looking back at public support for military assistance to Western

Europe and for economic aid under the Marshall Plan, we can see that the public began to apply these standards from the beginning. Political leaders succeeded in gaining public support for the Marshall Plan, NATO, and military assistance to Western Europe as a result of the threat of aggression from the East (in this case, the communist threat within European countries could be readily linked—whether correctly or not—to the external communist threat). Humanitarian needs also may have contributed to the public's support for providing economic assistance to countries that had been ravaged by the war.

In light of this discussion, it may seem puzzling to hear it widely acknowledged that the American public opposes "foreign aid" and thinks the country spends "too much" on foreign aid. In one respect there is an element of truth to this: When forced to think in the abstract or ideologically, ordinary citizens will say to pollsters or survey researchers that they think the country spends "too much" on "foreign aid." Figures 13.4 and 13.5, taken together, show this quite clearly. When it comes to getting public support for foreign aid, political leaders would appear to have their work cut out for them. In Figure 13.5 we see strikingly little—less than 10 percent—support for spending more on foreign aid. Not shown in Figure 13.5 is that fully 70 percent of the public persistently say that we are spending "too much" on foreign aid. While support for defense spending, as shown in Figure 13.4 (the three

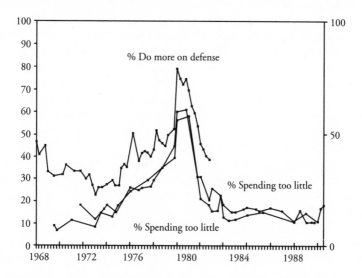

Figure 13.4 Defense, 1968–1996

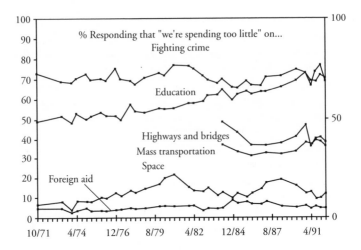

Figure 13.5 Stable and Differentiated Spending Preferences, 1971–1996

trend lines represent the responses to three differently phrased questions asked by different survey organizations) increased noticeably in the 1970s after the Vietnam War and peaked during the Iran hostage crisis and the Soviet invasion of Afghanistan, the trend in support for increasing spending on foreign aid remained very low and very flat throughout this period.

Figure 13.5 does not extend back into the 1950s or 1960s, but there are other data that show limited support for spending on foreign aid. By 1950, even in the case of "our program for European recovery," an increasing percentage of the public began to think we were spending "too much" (Page and Shapiro 1992: p. 201). Thus the public may sour somewhat on aid once it has been given and people are asked in surveys to ponder the dollar amounts spent. In general and in the abstract, support for new foreign assistance initiatives or for increasing current foreign aid programs does not readily spring up into the public's mind.

Policy makers and politicians seem to be well aware of this (e.g., the case of John Kennedy is well documented; see Jacobs and Shapiro 1994). It has clearly, however, not stopped presidents and other policy makers from continuing existing assistance programs and proposing new ones. The reason they can do this is clear and is supported by substantial evidence: the American public does not approach foreign policy issues in the abstract; Americans only do so when forced to in opinion polls. The same has also been said about domestic policy issues, in that the public does not think in broad liberal-conservative ideological terms about specific economic or social issues that come to its attention; for example, the public may say that it opposes "welfare" or the welfare state in the abstract, but it also widely supports high levels of government spending on Social Security, medical care, education, and fighting crime (see Figure 13.5), and other domestic programs (e.g., see Page and Shapiro 1992: Chap. 4).

Thus, to say that Americans oppose foreign aid is too bold a statement—this depends on specific cases and contexts. Public support for the Marshall Plan clearly showed this, and this was a harbinger for things to come as Americans faced and supported active U.S. involvement in international affairs.

The remaining data that I present show how the public has, in fact, distinguished different cases and contexts. Specifically, these cases and contexts have involved American policies toward different countries at different times. Figure 13.6 shows how the American public has drawn distinctions regarding whether the United States should assist and defend different allies, with Western Europe and Japan given high priority during the 1970s and 1980s. The same applied in the case of selling arms, as shown in Figure 13.7. And when it came to trouble spots closer to home, in the cases of El Salvador and Nicaragua in the 1980s, there was much more support for foreign aid to these trouble-spots than was indicated by the general blanket responses about foreign aid in Figure 13.5.

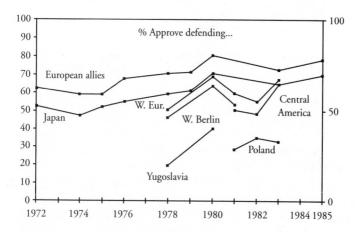

Figure 13.6 Support for Defense of Allies, 1972–1985

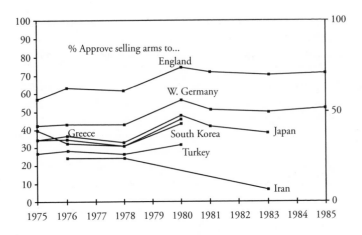

Figure 13.7 Approval of Selling Arms to Allies, 1975–1985

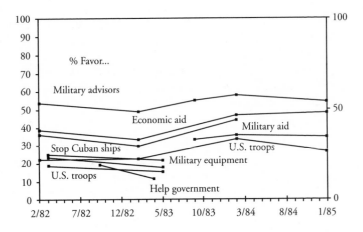

Figure 13.8 Military and Economic Aid to El Salvador, 1982–1985

In Figure 13.8, we see how the public persistently distinguished among different type of assistance to the government of El Salvador as it struggled against leftist rebels. The public was more supportive of economic aid than of military aid or direct U.S. military involvement beyond sending in a small number of advisors. Support for economic aid rose to nearly 50 percent in 1985, hardly a complete lack of public support for foreign aid.

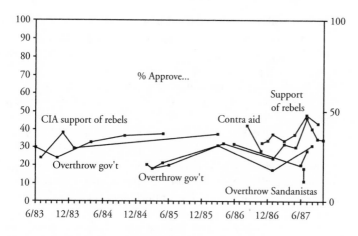

Figure 13.9 Aid to Nicaragua, Contra Rebels, 1983–1987

Figure 13.9 shows the relatively low level of public support for aid to the Contra rebels, whom the Reagan Admistration supported against the popularly elected Sandinista government in Nicaragua. There was clearly less public support here than in the case of El Salvador. But even in this case in which policy was motivated by some ostensible need to intervene in a country's domestic politics, and not in response to a clear threat of external aggression, enough of the public supported the Administration's actions to help sustain aid to the Contras for an extended period before Congress was able to terminate it (see Sobel 1993).

Conclusion

With regard to American public opinion, the legacy of the Marshall Plan and the military the fortification of Western Europe was twofold. First, public opinion toward these policies developed standards of judgment and patterns that came to repeat themselves throughout the Cold War. The public learned to adapt to the new leadership role of the United States in world affairs; specifically, it distinguished what the United States might accomplish through economic aid from what the country could provide through military assistance or direct military involvement. The public also distinguished among different countries and contexts and how that affected particular policy choices. The public had shown that it was capable of behaving this way prior to and during its entry into World War II, but this clearly became the norm after the war, as U.S. foreign policy during the Cold War unfolded. Overall, it can be said (and it has been) that the public responded in explicable and sensible ways to American foreign policy and world affairs during the Cold War, and this has appeared to continue thus far into the post–Cold War world (see Mueller 1994; Page and Shapiro 1988, 1994).

Second, American public opinion toward the country's involvement in foreign affairs in general, and foreign aid in particular, would be different today had the Marshall Plan failed. By "failed," I mean had political leaders and other élites beginning as early as the 1950s, or political analysts, historians, and other élites today, loudly and visibly questioned the justification for the Marshall Plan and its actual impact. Had the Marshall Plan failed, the public's low level of support for foreign aid in the abstract might well be completely mirrored in its opinions toward foreign aid in most, if not all, specific cases and contexts.

Note

1. An earlier version of this chapter was presented at "The Marshall Plan: 50 Years Later," Conference sponsored by the Institute on Western Europe (School of International and Public Affairs, Columbia University), the Center on European Studies (New York University), and The Italian Academy for Advanced Study in America (Columbia University), February 12–14, 1998, New York. I wish to thank the conference organizers. I am also indebted to Benjamin I. Page and Lawrence R. Jacobs for past and current collaborations, and to the Pew Charitable Trusts for support to study presidents, public opinion, and policy making. The responsibility for all analysis and interpretations is the author's.

References

Cohen, Bernard C. (1973), *The Public's Impact on Foreign Policy*, Boston: Little, Brown.

Delli Carpini, Michael, and Scott Keeter (1996), *What Americans Know about Politics and Why It Matters*, New Haven: Yale University Press.

Eisinger, Robert (1994), "Presidential Polling in the 1950s and Beyond," Paper Presented at the Annual Meeting of the American Association of Public Opinion Research.

Foster, H. Schuyler (1983), *Activism Replaces Isolationism: U.S. Public Attitudes, 1940–1975*, Washington, DC: Foxhall.

Graham, Thomas (1994), "Public Opinion and U.S. Foreign Policy Decision Making," in D. Deese, ed., *The New Politics of American Foreign Policy*, New York: St. Martin's Press.

Hilderbrand, Robert (1981), *Power and the People: Executive Management of Public Opinion in Foreign Affairs, 1897–1921*, Chapel Hill: The University of North Carolina Press.

Hinckley, Ronald H. (1992), *People, Polls, and Policymakers: American Public Opinion and National Security*, New York: Lexington Books.

Jacobs, Lawrence R. (1992), "The Recoil Effect: Public Opinion and Policy Making in the United States and Britain." *Comparative Politics*, 24: 199–217.

Jacobs, Lawrence R. and Robert Y. Shapiro (1994), "Issues, Candidate Image, and Priming: The Use of Private Polls in Kennedy's 1960 Presidential Campaign," *American Political Science Review*, 88 (September): 527–40.

Jacobs, Lawrence R. and Robert Y. Shapiro (1995), "The Rise of Presidential Polling: The Nixon White House in Historical Pespective," *Public Opinion Quarterly*, 59: 163–95.

Jentleson, Bruce (1992), "The Pretty Prudent Public: Post Vietnam American Opinion on the Use of Military Force," *International Studies Quarterly*, 36: 49–74.

Kernell, Samuel (1976), "The Truman Doctrine Speech: A Case Study of the Dynamics of Presidential Opinion Leadership," *Social Science History* (Fall): 20–44.

Leigh, Michael (1976), *Mobilizing Consent: Public Opinion and American Foreign Policy, 1937–1947*. Westport, CT: Greenwood.

Mueller, John (1994), *Policy and Opinion in the Gulf War*, Chicago: University of Chicago Press.

Oneal, John R., Brad Lian, and James H. Joyner, Jr. (1996), "Are the American People 'Pretty Prudent'? Public Responses to the U.S. Uses of Force, 1950–1988," *International Studies Quarterly*, 40: 261–80.

Page, Benjamin I., and Robert Y. Shapiro (1992), *The Rational Public: Fifty Years of Trends in Americans' Policy Preferences*, Chicago: University of Chicago Press.

Powlick, Philip J. (1991), "The Attitudinal Bases of Responsiveness to Public Opinion among American Foreign Policy Officials," *Journal of Conflict Resolution*, 35: 611–41.

Richman, Alvin (1996), "The Polls—Trends: American Support for International Involvement: General and Specific Components of Post-Cold War Changes," *Public Opinion Quarterly*, 60 (Summer): 305–21.

Rielly, John E., ed. (1999), *American Public Opinion and U.S. Foreign Policy 1999*, Chicago: The Chicago Council on Foreign Relations.

Shapiro, Robert Y. (1998), "Public Opinion, Elites, and Democracy," *Critical Review*, 12 (Fall): 501–28.

Shapiro, Robert Y., and Benjamin I. Page, 1988. "Foreign Policy and the Rational Public." *Journal of Conflict Resolution*, 32: 212–47.

—— (1994), "Foreign Policy and Public," in Deese, David A., ed., *The New Politics of American Foreign Policy*, New York: St. Martin's Press.

Sobel, Richard, ed. (1993), *Public Opinion in U.S. Foreign Policy: The Controversy Over Contra Aid*, Lanham, MD: Rowman & Littlefield.

—— (1996), "U.S. and European Attitudes toward Intervention in the Former Yugoslavia: Mourir pour la Bosnie," in Richard H. Ullman, ed., *The World and Yugoslavia's Wars*, New York: Council on Foreign Relations.

Wittkopf, Eugene R. (1990), *Faces of International: Public Opinion and American Foreign Policy*, Durham, NC: Duke University Press.

—— (1996), "What Americans Really Think About Foreign Policy," *The Washington Quarterly*, 19(3): 91–106.

Yankelovich, Daniel, and I. M. Destler, eds. (1994), *Beyond the Beltway: Engaging the Public in U.S. Foreign Policy*, New York: Norton.

Zaller, John (1992), *The Nature and Origins of Mass Opinion*, New York: Cambridge University Press.

—— (1998), "Monica Lewinsky's Contribution to Political Science," *PS: Political Science and Politics*, 31 (June): 182–89.

CHAPTER 14

The Marshall Plan and Cold War Political Discourse

James E. Cronin

The Cold War was not only a geopolitical alignment of states, but also a confrontation of rival social systems. Within each bloc it structured economic systems and constrained politics. In closing off certain options, however, the Cold War opened up others and nurtured political cultures and rhetorics that fit within the framework of Cold War politics. This paper examines the way the framework of the Cold War affected political culture in the West by reviewing who and what were excluded and who and what were encouraged. The conclusion, though tentative, is that prior work has focused too narrowly on the exclusions imposed by the Cold War political order and neglected the opportunities opened up, particularly in the center and center/left of the political spectrum, and the creative political work done there. The Marshall Plan thus needs to be understood as a critical moment when the Cold War, its constraints and opportunities, became real to Europeans.

The Marshall Plan is inconceivable without the Cold War. The likelihood of the U.S. Congress agreeing in the late 1940s to a foreign aid package of such magnitude, absent the perceived communist threat, would seem to have been close to zero. And it was not merely the general problem of communism that moved American lawmakers, but the fact that the Red Army was solidly in command in eastern Europe, enjoyed enormous prestige for its role in the defeat of Hitler, and seemed poised to move west upon very short notice and with little prospect of effective resistance. However unrealistic the worries over a possible Soviet invasion of Western Europe, the sense of vulnerability that pervaded the thinking of U.S. policy makers was palpable.

American leaders were also keenly aware of the enormous problems of economic reconstruction and revival facing both former allies and defeated enemies. The notion of a deepening economic crisis in 1947 may in retrospect have been mistaken and the underlying trends more favorable than previously thought, but it would have required a tremendous act of faith in the power of market capitalism for contemporaries to assert at that moment that the European nations stood at the beginning of an era of sustained economic expansion and so did not truly require U.S. aid.[1] Ironically, the only people whose ideological commitments were strong enough to make such an argument possible were the communists. As the French Communist Party leader Jacques Duclos told his comrades at the first meeting of the Cominform in September 1947, "The task of the democratic parties, and, above all, of the Communist Party, was to show the masses of their countries that the countries of Europe were perfectly capable of restoring their economies by themselves, even without help from the U.S.A."[2] That was quite a task the communists set for themselves and it should come as no surprise that they failed utterly.[3] It made sense, then, for the United States to concern itself with the economic health of the Europeans. Even if it was also very much in the economic self-interest of the United States—and of American business in particular—to provide aid to Europe, the policy recommended itself as a genuine response to perceived problems that might, if left untreated, have had considerable negative political consequences.[4]

For U.S. policy makers, the consequence they feared most was a move to the left. Again, it can be argued that the fear was misguided. In retrospect, certainly, the most impressive thing about the European left—both communist and noncommunist—has been its capacity for self-destruction and, hence, its endless ability to squander the opportunities that have presented themselves over the present century.[5] The tendency has been compounded in situations where communists and socialists have joined in coalition and sought to maintain a united front while managing the affairs of state, for such cohabitations have proved especially prone to dissolution. In fact, even before the advent of the Marshall Plan, the postwar coalition governments in France and Italy were coming apart and the moment of maximum communist advance had passed. Still, it would have taken unusual faith, indeed perhaps clairvoyance, to predict in 1947 that Western Europe would soon embark on an era of sustained political stability anchored in the hegemony of the center-right, typically Christian, political parties. Without such a faith, it was quite reasonable to assume that continued economic malaise, combined with the looming Soviet presence in the east and the quite recent successes of indigenous communist or socialist parties and the postwar disarray on the right, might provide yet another opening for the left. On strategic, economic, and political grounds, therefore, it made sense to take the communist threat seriously enough to justify a novel departure in the history of international relations. For all these reasons, the Marshall Plan would not have been possible without the Cold War.

But was the Cold War conceivable without the Marshall Plan? Or, to put the matter more precisely, did the Marshall Plan significantly affect the ways in which the Cold War was fought out?[6] The argument in this paper is that it did: that the Marshall Plan was critical in the creation of what has been called variously neocapitalism, corporate capitalism, or welfare capitalism. This mattered profoundly, because it redefined the choice between capitalism and communism. After the Marshall Plan, the capitalism on offer was not the capitalism of the 1930s, which was not merely marred by depression and unemployment but that also appeared to be the spawning ground of fascism. Capitalism after the Marshall Plan was something different. The Marshall Plan helped Western capitalism to become more prosperous and democratic; it allowed policy makers to avoid severe deflation and austerity whose burden would undoubtedly have fallen disproportionately upon the working class; and it made it possible for governments to implement more generous and progressive social policies. Even if the economic impact of the Plan was less than previously thought and even if recovery was already beginning, the social and political impact of the Marshall Plan was nevertheless significant and perhaps even decisive in shaping the outcome of the contest between capitalism and its critics and opponents on the left.

The Marshall Plan would, thus, be a moment of profound choice, a conscious and informed decision about what it would mean for states, nations, and economies to be part of the "free world," the U.S.-led alliance of advanced capitalist societies. It was a choice that in effect defined capitalism as a social system. Opting for capitalism would no longer mean choosing freedom over equality and market outcomes over just results, but rather choosing a way of life that promised to combine political freedom, consumer freedom, and prosperity. To be sure, it took time for the promise to become real. Truly American-style mass consumption would not come to Europe for at least another decade, in some places for close on two decades. But the promise became plausible with the Marshall Plan, or plausible enough to offer an effective counter to alternative visions of a more collectivist hue and of more left-wing provenance.

The architects of the Marshall Plan did not necessarily see themselves as redefining capitalism, but they surely did understand that they were selling capitalism. And they grasped intuitively that, if the selling job was to work, the product needed to be made as attractive as possible. It was necessary in particular to project a capitalist future that differed fundamentally from the recent past experience of the capitalist states. The specter of the Great Depression haunted those who planned the postwar order and ensured that they would take steps to avoid a relapse into stagnation and unemployment. Just what steps would be required was, of course, the subject of intense and recurring debate. Within the U.S. policy-making elite, for example, there were sharp disagreements about the extent of government intervention and the relative importance of states and markets in guaranteeing the conditions of prosperity.[7] These tensions were reflected in the crafting of the Bretton Woods system and in setting up the institutional framework for the world economy; and, as is well known, John Maynard Keynes's last great battle was to make that system more flexible and less orthodox so as to allow nations more scope for managing their own economies and to lessen the need for painful adjustments to the dictates of the world market. He largely failed to do so, and the loan agreement he negotiated for Great Britain contained within it a commitment to convertibility that was ultimately impossible to meet and, in consequence, impossible to enforce.

Britain's failure to meet the challenge of convertibility was but one indication that the multilateralist optimism embodied in the Bretton Woods system would have to be tempered by reality. But until the announcement and implementation of the Marshall Plan it was unclear in what direction and upon what terms the adjustment would be made. The Marshall Plan was first and foremost a means of dealing with Europeans' inability to pay for imports, and thus a de facto agreement that the requirements of recovery would not be delayed by lack of funds. Marshall himself chose to describe the plan with a very plain and homely metaphor about the temporary breakdown of the mechanisms of exchange that left farmers unable to trade grain for industrial goods, city dwellers without the means to sell or buy and, hence, the factors of production lying idle for no good reason. Marshall dissembled, of course, choosing to focus on relations within rather than between nations, but the focus upon exchange and the notion that contemporary constraints upon economic activity were fundamentally artificial was central to the thinking behind the Marshall Plan. It was in this regard a major posthumous victory for Keynes and probably the most genuinely Keynesian innovation of the early postwar era. Even with Marshall Plan aid, virtually every European nation was forced to go through a program of austerity and fiscal stabilization during the late 1940s, but the process was far less painful than it would have been without U.S. aid. As several scholars have concluded, the Marshall Plan helped to resolve "distributional conflicts" that would likely have resulted from more drastic stabilization policies and that might have had undesirable political consequences.[8] U.S. policy makers and their collaborators in Europe to this extent chose to modify, specifically to relax, the terms on which different nations would be integrated into the world market.

The terms of integration were thereby loosened and greater variation was permitted in the economic policies pursued by various states. It has been argued that Marshall planners sought to export to Europe a version of capitalism modeled on the United States and, more specifically, upon the political economy of the New Deal.[9] Clearly, Marshall Plan administrators regarded the United States as a model that could and should be widely emulated, but what is perhaps most striking about the initial impact of the Marshall Plan was not its success in propagating an American vision of neocapitalism but rather the fact that it provided European nations with the ability to pursue policies that had emerged from bargaining and coalition-building within the domestic political arena. In France, for example, U.S. representatives did not get involved in the details of economic planning but concerned themselves with the problem of fiscal stabilization. Inevitably, the U.S. role was greater in Germany; even so, the Germans took the initiative in setting priorities for economic policy and the "social market economy" was genuinely rooted in a distinctly German tradition of political economy.[10] Likewise in Britain, where fears of U.S. efforts to sabotage British socialism quite quickly evaporated. The Marshall planners made occasional mistakes and offended local sensibilities, but overall they did not impose policy in detail. More important, despite fears that the United States would push the economic and social policies of the Europeans to the right, the overall impact of American influence seems not to have worked out this way. As often as not, the United States edged more conservative European policy makers toward the center. This happened in Italy, Germany, and Belgium, and it happened more than once.[11]

In the aggregate, then, the medium-term effect of the Marshall Plan was to allow the European nations to pursue their own policies of reconstruction while easing the pain of transition. To this extent, the Plan was internationalist, cooperative, and democratic. To this extent, as well, it steered clear of actions that would substantiate the major communist argument against the plan. The Soviets and the parties that followed them massively miscalculated in choosing to oppose the Marshall Plan primarily on the grounds of nationalism. Aside from the irony and hypocrisy of the Soviets, fresh from imposing their will upon the peoples of Eastern Europe, claiming to defend the national sovereignty of West Europeans, the argument that what the Marshall Plan was all about was the furthering of American imperialism lacked any real purchase on the events of the era. Stalin's spokesman Andrei Zhdanov could assert dogmatically that "The economic 'aid' of the United States pursues the broad aim of enslaving Europe to American capital," but local communists would have great difficulty making the argument stick.[12]

The argument did not take for three reasons. The first is that the United States did not dictate policy upon the European states but rather pushed, cajoled, and constrained policy makers to move incrementally toward American goals. The second was that the United States launched its own propaganda effort aimed at countering the communist charge of domination and carried it out much better. And third, to the extent that the Marshall Plan did envision the creation of economies and social systems modeled on the United States, the vision was largely utopian and thus not something to be implemented right away. It was an aspiration, a project, a program and a rhetoric, but not a set of policy prescriptions for immediate application.

Both the U.S. propaganda campaign and the vision of a transformed Europe have been discussed before, but their interaction has not been fully appreciated. Right from the beginning, Marshall planners understood the need for "publicity" and "information" and the agreements reached for each participating nation acknowledged "that wide dissemination of information on the progress of the program is desirable in order to develop the sense of common effort and mutual aid which is essential to the accomplishment of the objectives of the program."[13] To accomplish this end, the Plan's administrators employed both American and local journalists and academics and undertook the production of documentaries and the staging of exhibits, as well as the planting of news stories in the press. The effort was overseen by the American journalist, Al Friendly, and he was assisted by similarly experienced professionals stationed in the capitols of Europe. Andrew Berding, for example, had worked for Associated Press in Rome and was tapped to run the campaign in Italy. As Berding explained his mission, it was to "[C]arry the message of the Marshall Plan to the people. Carry it to them directly—it won't permeate down." To that end, another official argued, the Americans would use "every method possible ... to reach Giuseppe in the factory and Giovanni in the fields."[14]

How to reach Giuseppe and Giovanni was not a simple problem, however, because however attractive the message of American-style prosperity, it remained a fairly distant prospect. What made it more real to ordinary people was the medium through which the message was delivered. A critical component of the Marshall Plan was the participation of labor leaders and even some rank-and-file workers. The United States was vitally interested in countering the influence of the communists among workers and in trade unions and as part of that worked to create "non-political" trade unions. The effort had mixed results in terms of the shape of the union movement in various countries, but the involvement of workers and their leaders did have an important effect in selling the Marshall Plan.[15] The participation of the unions reinforced the sense that in the reformed capitalism of postwar, or post-Marshall Plan, unions would play a key role. If any single feature distinguished the welfare capitalism of postwar from the harsher capitalism of the interwar era, it was the integration of the unions into the routine workings of the system. Unions were better organized in some nations than others and would have more clout over policy-making in some nations than in others, but everywhere they would be accorded a legitimacy and respect that had been lacking, or in doubt, before 1939. The involvement of American and European trade unionists in the discussion of, and propaganda for, the Marshall Plan thus sent an important message about inclusion, about who might expect to benefit from the plan and the prosperity it promised. Even in nations like France and Italy, where communists dominated the major union federations and so resisted the lure of the American model and refused to take part in exchanges sponsored by the Marshall Plan, the effort to project a message about labor, enhanced productivity and growth had positive results.

In this regard, it was not the message or the medium that mattered, but the messenger. But the message would matter as well, and here, too, the architects of the Marshall Plan succeeded brilliantly. The vision communicated in and through the Marshall Plan was a vision of sustained growth and material progress.[16] The key to growth was productivity, which would come through the application of new technology and new techniques of management.[17] Under Marshall Plan auspices businessmen, politicians, and trade unionists would be brought to the United States to get a glimpse of the secrets of American economic success.[18] They would visit factories, farms, and shops, they would talk to businessmen and workers, and they would hear about the virtues of American styles of mass production and consumption. These visits and exchanges would be formally organized by groups like the Anglo-American Council on Productivity or analogous groups in other countries.[19] Roughly a quarter of the total visitors were Frenchmen: over the course of the Marshall Plan, three hundred missions had brought more than twenty-seven hundred French visitors—including business-men, engineers, government officials, and trade unionists—to see and testify to the glories of the American system of production.[20]

The propagation of an essentially Fordist future combined elements of reality, flights of fancy, and a deliberate effort to reshape the percep-tions and understanding of capitalism. What was real enough and most visibly on display was the impressive system of mass production left in place by war mobilization and procurement in the United States. Also genuinely concrete and meaningful was the American system of indus-trial relations that, although marked by frequent, and occasionally bitter, battles over wages and over control of the shop floor, nonetheless afforded workers in the United States solid job protections and a share in the fruits of rising productivity.[21]

More fanciful was the vision of unlimited prosperity that could supposedly be achieved by continued improvements in productivity generated by new investment in the latest technology. American busi-nessmen were far less innovative and risk-taking, less committed to industrial harmony—or at least to its distributional prerequisites—and less technologically savvy than the propaganda of the Marshall Plan implied. Still, they were on average well in advance of their European counterparts in their use of newer technologies and newer approaches to management, and it is clear that the adoption of American "best prac-tice" across Europe would, and thus did, constitute a significant step forward in technological sophistication and in productivity. The rapid catching-up that occurred as European economies revived was proof enough of this, and the evidence would be evident soon enough in their growing ability to compete internationally.[22]

Even more interesting than the partly real and partly fantastic vision of technical progress and soaring productivity was the new understand-ing of capitalism spread by the Marshall Plan. The capitalism put on display in the late 1940s was a system in which the power of owners, of capitalists, had been displaced and their role in the firm taken over by professional managers. Postwar capitalism was thus depicted not merely as a humanized, Keynesian neocapitalism or welfare capitalism but as "managerial capitalism." The idea that management was in control, or should be in control, proved extremely attractive and elicited support across Europe. It captured in particular the imagination of social theorists who elaborated the argument about the transition to a new stage of capitalism and marketed it as the latest in sociological wisdom. The concept was also very attractive to a generation of politicians who grabbed hold of the idea because it seemed to offer a means of transcending the debates over capitalism versus socialism, over the role of the market, the firm, and the state. The theory was also functionally useful for policymakers, for it appeared to license the intervention of the bureaucrat, or of the expert working either for the state or for the large corporation.[23]

An especially important convert was Sir Stafford Cripps who, first as president of the Board of Trade, then as Minister for Economic Affairs and finally as Chancellor of the Exchequer in Britain's postwar Labor government, sought to transform the practices of industrial management.[24] For Cripps, the focus upon management was part of a very effective and telling critique of the failures of established élites in Britain. In this narrative, the same people who had failed Britain in the 1930s, the "Guilty Men" who had presided over the depths of the Depression with no sense of urgency and who had failed also to provide leadership against Hitler, still controlled industry. To Cripps and his colleagues, then, the effort to reform management practice and culture and to replace "old boys" and amateurs with professional and technically competent managers was integral to Labor's effort to create a new Britain. Cripps is thus widely credited with introducing the very concept of productivity into the discourse of economic policy making in Britain and he was without question the driving force behind the setting up, with Treasury funding, of the British Institute of Management.

The zeal displayed by Cripps was exceptional, but across Europe the attention to management and to the possibility of modernizing industry furthered decisively the process by which the understanding of capitalism was reconceptualized under the influence of both the Marshall Plan itself and the rhetoric surrounding it. At the level of reality and in the realm of the imagination, then, the Marshall Plan served to signal that the competition between capitalism and socialism had changed because it could now plausibly be claimed that capitalism itself had changed and was continuing to evolve in a more humane and egalitarian direction and with the promise of sustained growth. The Marshall Plan made the politics of growth possible, and it made capitalism more populist and democratic.[25] It was a major achievement to the extent that the transformation was real; it was even more impressive in that so much of it was a vision of the future.

The Marshall Plan thus helped to equip capitalism and the Western powers with a program of reform, a plan for growth and prosperity, and the promise of inclusion and representation, the combination of which would constitute an invaluable weapon in the ideological battle that was at the heart of the Cold War. It was a weapon, moreover, that would not soon be matched.[26] The Soviet Union managed to explode an atom bomb as early as 1949 and seemed capable of meeting the military challenge of the West in the 1950s. But they would never catch up ideologically, for they were unable for decades to craft a credible critique of the reformed capitalism of postwar. Indeed, the sterility of Marxist thought among those still influenced or inspired by the Soviet model after the war was the essential precondition for the rise of the so-called New Left of the 1960s. Among non-Marxist democratic socialists, by contrast, there were serious efforts to assess the novelty of neocapitalism and to update the appeal of social democracy. The earliest manifestation was probably the publication of *New Fabian Essays* in 1952; the most successful the adoption by the SPD of the Bad Godesberg program in 1959.[27] But revisionism was a hard sell everywhere: it was received with ambivalence within the social-democratic left; and it made even less progress among communists both within and outside the Soviet bloc. There was a brief fascination with reforms emanating from Eastern Europe in the late 1950s and 1960s, but revisionism in the east was so weak, so constrained, and so quickly and easily suppressed that it remained more a vague aspiration than a genuine alternative.[28]

By the time the Marshall Plan has been implemented, then, the rhetorical structure of the Cold War was largely set: and it was set in a frame that gave a tremendous edge to the supporters of capitalism, or neocapitalism. Its advocates could claim to be proposing a novel vision of economic progress linked with democratic rights and personal freedoms. And by looking forward, or overseas, they were spared the necessity of defending the indefensible connections between capitalism and depression and, still worse, between capitalism and fascism that had seemed so plausible during the antifascist mobilization that accompanied World War II. It is difficult in retrospect to grasp just how critical it was in the 1940s and 1950s to escape the legacy of depression and fascism and to find political formulae and, even more difficult, parties and politicians who could do so. The processes through which this would be accomplished would differ from one nation to another. It was most challenging in those defeated nations like Germany, Japan, and Italy, where the prewar parties and leaders had either been crushed or joined with the regime and were thereby either absent or utterly discredited. It was hard, too, in places like France and other nations that had suffered wartime occupation, for collaboration was typically pervasive. Success would require in the first place the identification of politicians who were not tainted by past sins and the reestablishment of viable parties, like the Church-oriented parties in Italy and Germany, whose sins could be forgiven or overlooked. Beyond that, however, it was essential that these new or rehabilitated political forces should also offer to voters a new vision of the future. Without the Marshall Plan and its program for building a reformed capitalism, it is difficult to see quite how that would have happened. Whether this advantage was critical to the long-term outcome of the Cold War is more difficult to say, but at the very least it prefigured the final result.

Notes

1. Alan Milward, *The Reconstruction of Western Europe, 1945–51* (London: Methuen, 1984), Chap. 1.

2. *The Cominform: Minutes of the Three Conferences, 1947/1948–1949,* ed. Giuliano Procacci (Milan: Feltrinelli Foundation, *Annali,* 1994), p. 123.

3. For the country by country details, see the essays in Francesca Gori and Silvio Pons, eds., *The Soviet Union and Europe in the Cold War, 1943–53* (New York: St. Martin's, 1996).

4. As Jacqueline McGlade has argued, however, the attitudes of American businessmen were actually more varied and complex and moved rather sharply against the Marshall Plan over time. See McGlade, "A Single Path for European Recovery? American Business Debates and Conflicts over the Marshall Plan," this volume.

5. See Donald Sassoon, *One Hundred Years of Socialism: The West European Left in the Twentieth Century* (New York: The New Press, 1996).

6. For a review of recent literature on the Cold War, see Melvyn P. Leffler, "The Cold War: What Do 'We Now Know'," *American Historical Review,* CIV, 2 (April, 1999), pp. 501–24. From that essay, it would appear that the historiography of the Cold War has advanced a great deal, but remains more focused on diplomacy, military rivalry, and blame than on the internal politics to which it gave rise.

7. Fred Block, *The Origins of International Economic Disorder* (Berkeley: University of California Press, 1977), Chap. 3; Harold James, "The IMF and the Creation of the Bretton Woods System, 1944–58," in Barry Eichengreen, ed., *Europe's Post-War Recovery* (Cambridge: Cambridge University Press, 1995), pp. 93–126.

8. Lucrezia Reichlin, "The Marshall Plan Reconsidered," in Eichengreen ed., *Europe's Post-war Recovery,* pp. 49–50.

9. Michael Hogan, *The Marshall Plan: America, Britain and the Reconstruction of Western Europe, 1947–1952* (Cambridge: Cambridge University Press, 1987).

10. See Charles Maier and G. Bischof, eds., *The Marshall Plan and Germany* (Oxford: Berg, 1991); and Anthony Nicholls, *Freedom with Responsibility: The Social Market Economy in Germany, 1918–1963* (Oxford: Clarendon, 1994).

11. The most comprehensive review of the impact of the Marshall Plan is contained in Hogan, *The Marshall Plan.* For the darker side, see Sallie Pisani, *The CIA and the Marshall Plan* (Lawrence: University of Kansas Press, 1991).

12. Zhdanov, in *The Cominform,* p. 235.

13. *Test of agreement reproduced in Documents in American Foreign Relations* (1948) (Princeton: Princeton University Press, 1950), p. 235, and quoted in David Ellwood, "The Marshall Plan and the Politics of Growth," in Peter Stirk & David Willis, *Shaping Postwar Europe: European Unity and Disunity, 1945–1957* (New York: St. Martin's, 1991), pp. 18–19.

14. Cited in David Ellwood, "The Marshall Plan and the Politics of Growth," in Peter Stirk and David Willis, *Shaping Postwar Europe: European Unity and Disunity, 1945–1957* (New York: St. Martin's, 1991), pp. 18–19 and Alan Berding, note of 16 January 1950, and Lt. F. R. Shea to Berding, February 24, 1949, cite in Ellwood, p. 19.

15. See, in general, Lutz Niethammer, "Structural Reform and a Compact for Growth: Conditions for a United Labor Union Movement in Western Europe after the Collapse of Fascism," in Charles Maier, ed., *The Cold War in Europe* (New York: Markus Wiener, 1991), pp. 273–311.

16. See Richard Pells, *Not Like Us: How Europeans Have Loved, Hated, and Transformed American Culture since World War II* (New York: Basic Books, 1997), pp. 52–58.

17. Charles S. Maier, "The Politics of Productivity: Foundations of American International Economic Policy after World War II," in Maier, *The Cold War in Europe,* pp. 169–201. (Maier's article was originally published in 1977 and has been much reprinted.)

18. Anthony Carew, *Labour under the Marshall Plan* (Detroit: Wayne State University Press, 1987).

19. Nick Tiratsoo and Jim Tomlinson, *Industrial Efficiency and State Intervention: Labour, 1939–51* (London: Routledge, 1993), Chap. 7.

20. Richard Kuisel, *Seducing the French: The Dilemma of Americanization* (Berkeley: University of California Press, 1993), p. 80; Pells, *Not Like Us,* p. 55.

21. On the trade-offs, see Nelson Lichtenstein, "From Corporatism to Collective Bargaining: Organized Labor and the Eclipse of Social

Democracy in the Postwar Era," in Steve Fraser and Gary Gerstle, eds., *The Rise and Fall of the New Deal Order* (Princeton, NJ: Princeton University Press, 1989).

22. Despite the subtitle, this is the basic argument of Charles Kindleberger, *Europe's Postwar Growth: The Role of Labor Supply* (Cambridge, MA: Harvard University Press, 1967). For a discussion of growing competition and its consequences, see Robert Brenner, "The Economic of Global Turbulence," *New Left Review*, 229 (May–June, 1998).

23. See Harold Perkin's *The Third Revolution* (London: Routledge, 1996), for an analysis and an argument about the virtues of professional society.

24. See Tiratsoo and Tomlinson, *Industrial Efficiency and State Intervention.*

25. See Alan Wolfe, *America's Impasse: The Rise and Fall of the Politics of Growth* (New York: Pantheon, 1981).

26. Charles Maier has suggested that while "the Communist project of legitimizing a dictatorial party authority on the supposed basis of the working class had never attracted more than a minority of West European workers and intellectuals before World War II," "it could emerge as a plausible principle for an international coalition after the Soviet Union played so key a role in defeating Nazi Germany." If so, the moment of its plausibility was nonetheless very short-lived. See Maier, "After the Cold War," in *The Cold War in Europe*, p. 16.

27. See Sassoon, *One Hundred Years of Socialism*, Chap. 10.

28. The hope of reform nevertheless remained essential to intellectual and political life within the Soviet bloc. See James Cronin, *The World the Cold War Made: Order, Chaos and the Return of History* (New York: Routledge, 1996), pp. 9–11.

INDEX